The Princeton Review

Cracking the COOP/HSPT

JEFF RUBENSTEIN

FIRST EDITION

RANDOM HOUSE, INC.
NEW YORK

www.PrincetonReview.com

The Independent Education Consultants Association recognizes The Princeton Review as a valuable resource for high school and college students applying to college and graduate school.

Princeton Review Publishing, L. L. C.
2315 Broadway
New York, NY 10024
E-mail: booksupport@review.com

Published in the United States by Random House., Inc. New York, and simultaneously in Canada by Random House of Canada Limited, Toronto.

ISBN 0-375-76143-8

Editor: Gretchen Feder
Designer: Stephanie Martin
Production Editor: Kristen Azzara
Production Coordinator: Jennifer Arias

Manufactured in the United States of America on partially recycled paper.

9 8 7 6 5 4 3

First Edition

Acknowledgments

Thanks to my friends and colleagues at The Princeton Review, a group of people who are thoroughly dedicated to the well-being of students. Special thanks to Gretchen Feder, Laurie Barnett, and Evan Schnittman for editorial advice and general frivolity, and to Kristen Azzara, Stephanie Martin, and Jennifer Arias for making it all look good.

Contents

AN INTRODUCTION FOR PARENTS

Congratulations on taking the first step in helping your child prepare for the COOP or the HSPT! There are ways besides using this book in which you can increase your child's performance on these tests and improve his or her chances of admission to a given private secondary school. We've compiled a few suggestions that you can follow to help your child have a healthy and productive educational experience during the application and admission process.

THE RIGHT PERSPECTIVE

Many parents and students have the false impression that doing poorly on a standardized test means that the student has not learned mathematics or English. It's important for you and your child to know that standardized tests such as the COOP and the HSPT are *not* intelligence tests. Nor are they really tests of what your child has learned in primary school. While many of the problems involve mathematics or English language mechanics, what the tests really measure are *extremely narrow* skills, which bear only a passing resemblance to the skills taught in school. Certainly, knowing the basics of mathematics and English language mechanics is important and will be covered in this book, but what is just as important is for students to learn how these basic skills are tested on the COOP and the HSPT. Learning how to do well on standardized tests is a skill unto itself that many students have never learned. This explains why many students who are perfectly capable in math and English still score poorly on these tests.

It's important that your child understand what these tests truly measure. Placing too much emphasis on standardized tests can lead to one stressed-out kid! The prospect of doing poorly puts an incredible burden on students. While a little anxiety can be motivational, too much anxiety can be hurtful to the learning experience.

HOW YOU CAN HELP YOUR CHILD

First and foremost, be supportive and involved. Preparing for these tests and applying to private school can be intimidating. The more you can accompany your child through the process, the more comfortable she will feel. Help your child learn vocabulary. Review the practice tests together and help reinforce the basic skills outlined in this book. You'll probably find it an interesting experience, and it will help you to get to know your child better as well as make the educational process fun.

Second, understand that standardized tests are very different than tests that are taken in school. The expected rules that apply to school tests may not apply here. Many students, for instance, actually hurt their scores by trying to answer every question. On these kind of timed tests, accuracy is much more important than speed. Students should adopt a strategy that will get them the greatest number of points, which usually means slowing down and doing fewer problems.

Finally, be understanding. Your child may not yet have learned how to take standardized tests or how to perform well on them. This is especially intimidating. Imagine how a good student must feel who scores poorly on a standardized test despite the fact that he knew the material tested. Remember that test-taking is a skill that can be learned. It simply takes expert instruction, practice, and time (the first two of which we will provide in this book!).

Of course, a little cajoling is also in order. Make sure that your child is committed to spending the time necessary to work through this book thoroughly and accurately.

Encourage your child to read something every day and to look up the difficult vocabulary words. With a bit of concentrated time and effort—and a lot of support—almost all students can learn to perform well on these tests.

WHAT COUNTS AS A GOOD SCORE? WHAT ABOUT THE ADMISSIONS PROCESS?

The writers of the COOP and the HSPT do not publicly release data on the performance of everyone who takes the test, so there is no way to know how students do in relation to one another. Moreover, each school has its own policies regarding the significance of these tests. Most consider a number of factors in addition to test scores when making admissions decisions. There is, therefore, no way to know exactly what score will qualify a student for admission at a particular school. You should simply try to help your child perform her best by giving her all the support and attention you can. You should, however, contact the schools to which your child is interested in applying to find out more information about their admissions criteria.

WHAT ARE THE SSAT AND THE ISEE?

The SSAT and the ISEE are two other common tests used by private high schools for admissions purposes. Although this book will provide some overlap in preparation for these tests, we highly recommend that you purchase *The Princeton Review Cracking the SSAT/ISEE*, which is specifically designed to prepare students for these tests.

We hope that you find this book to be a useful, accessible, and helpful tool in your preparations, and we wish you the very best of luck in your child's future success.

AN INTRODUCTION FOR STUDENTS

HOW DO I USE THIS BOOK?

This book will review the basic concepts, question types, and problem-solving techniques you'll need to improve your score on either the COOP or the HSPT. The practice tests will help you get used to the timing and pace of the tests. The more quality time you put into studying this book, the better you'll do. Learning to take standardized tests is like learning to play any sport: The first time you try you may feel clumsy, but with practice you can always improve.

STUDY RULES

Set aside a time when you can concentrate with no distractions. It's a good idea to have a place (such as your room or a library) where you always study. Have a few sharpened pencils and a dictionary handy.

As you read each chapter, try the techniques and do all the exercises. Check your answers against the answer keys, and note any problems you get wrong. Review your errors carefully, and work through them. Remember: Now is the chance to make all the errors you want (and learn from them) so that you won't make them on the actual test!

WHEN SHOULD I START TO STUDY?

We suggest that you start studying for the test about a month before it's given. If you're starting earlier than that, we suggest that you do two things from now until the test to help improve your score: Read as much as you can and learn new vocabulary words.

Reading

Both the COOP and the HSPT—as well as almost every other standardized test you're ever going to take—place a lot of weight on reading comprehension. How do you get better at reading? By reading. The more you read, the better you'll be at it. Follow these tips to get started:

- Try to find a short article or story every day to read. After you read it, try to explain it to a friend or parent. By trying to explain it to someone else, you'll see how much of it you really understood.

- Pick something to read that is just a bit above your current reading level. It can be an adventure book, a weekly magazine, or a column in a newspaper.

- Mark any words you don't know. Try to figure out what a word means from the context (the sentence and paragraph it's in); if you can't, look up the word. Write down these words and definitions on index cards to help you remember them.

Vocabulary

Having a good vocabulary will not only help you better understand what you read, but it will also help you do well on vocabulary-heavy tests such as the HSPT and, later, the SAT. A good place to start learning vocabulary words is the Hit Parade in this book (see page 188). You should also learn the meaning of words that you come across in school or in your reading that you don't know. Here are some pointers for using vocabulary.

- Every time you find an unfamiliar word, write it on the front of an index card and write its definition and a sample sentence on the back. Then quiz yourself to practice memorizing the meanings of your words. Remember to include a sample sentence—it's easier to learn words in context.

- Pick five words each day and use them every chance you get. Your friends may think you are a little strange when you walk around saying things like, "*Dawson's Creek* was an unusually *mediocre* episode last night." But you'll certainly learn those words. (By the way, *mediocre* means "of moderate or low quality.")

WHEN YOU TAKE A PRACTICE TEST

You'll see in the study plan below when to take the practice tests. Here are some tips for getting the most out of them:

- Time yourself correctly. Use a timer, watch, or stopwatch that will make a noise, or have someone else time you. You want to get a feel for exactly how much time you'll have for each section.

- Take the practice test at one sitting, just like the real thing. It's important to build up your endurance for the actual test.

- Take the practice tests using the answer sheet with bubbles to fill in (you can find this in the back of this book), just like on the real test. You should practice filling in your bubbles thoroughly and checking to make sure that you're filling in the correct bubble for a given question.

A STUDY PLAN

COOP STUDY PLAN

If you are taking the COOP, follow this nine-session study plan.

Session 1

Before you do anything else, besides reading this introduction, take the first practice COOP in this book. Correct it and pay particularly close attention to your mistakes.

Write down anything you notice that you had difficulty with, such as "triangle problems." This will help you remember to pay extra attention to those concepts when you study those chapters.

If you got more than 25 percent incorrect in any section, tell yourself to *slow down* and do fewer problems. You are much better off doing only 75 percent of the questions and getting more of them correct than doing all of the problems and getting many of them wrong.

Session 2

Read chapter 1: General Test-Taking Skills

Session 3

Read chapter 2: What is the COOP?
Read chapter 3: Memory

Session 4

Read chapter 4: Sequences
Read chapter 5: Analogies

Session 5

Read chapter 6: Verbal Reasoning

Session 6

Read chapter 7: Reading Comprehension

Session 7

Read chapter 8: Mathematics (You may find that you need to spread this chapter over two sessions. That's okay.)

Session 8

Read chapter 9: Language Expression

Session 9

Take the second practice COOP test in this book. Correct the test, ooh and ahh over how much your score improved, and review the concepts in the book for the questions you answered incorrectly.

Use any additional days before the test to continue to review the concepts and test-taking techniques covered in the book.

HSPT STUDY PLAN

If you are taking the HSPT, follow this nine-session study plan.

Session 1

Before you do anything else, besides reading this introduction, take the first practice HSPT in this book. Correct it and pay particularly close attention to your mistakes.

Write down anything you notice that you had difficulty with, such as "triangle problems." This will help you remember to pay extra attention to those concepts when you study those chapters.

If you got more than 25 percent incorrect in any section, tell yourself to *slow down* and do fewer problems. You are much better off doing only 75 percent of the questions and getting more of them correct than doing all of the problems and getting many of them wrong.

Session 2

Read chapter 1: General Test-Taking Skills

Session 3

Read chapter 10: What is the HSPT?
Read chapter 11: Vocabulary

Session 4

Read chapter 12: Verbal Skills

Session 5

Read chapter 13: Quantitative Skills

Session 6

Read chapter 14: Reading Comprehension and Vocabulary

Session 7

Read chapter 15: Mathematics

Session 8

Read chapter 16: Language

Session 9

Take the second practice HSPT test in this book. Correct the test, ooh and ahh over how much your score improved, and review the concepts in the book for the questions you answered incorrectly.

Use any additional days before the test to continue to review the concepts and test-taking techniques covered in the book.

THE DAY OF THE EXAM

No matter how much you prepare for the test, if you don't do all of these things the day of the exam, you are likely to run out of steam and do poorly.

- Wake up refreshed from a good night's sleep.

- Eat a good breakfast.

- Arrive early to the testing session.

- Remind yourself that you do not need to solve every problem to get a good score. Pace yourself!

And one more thing: Good luck!

General Test-Taking Skills

1

Whether you are taking the COOP or the HSPT, there are certain test-taking skills that you should learn and follow. These alone, without other review, will already improve your score on any standardized test.

PACING

One of the most important test-taking skills is pacing, or how you spend your time. Of course, you want to do as many problems as you can so that you can get as high a score as possible. But on standardized tests, accuracy is more important than speed.

This may sound a little confusing: Although you should fill in every single bubble on the answer sheet, you shouldn't feel that you have to work every single problem on the test. You're better off if you slow down and work at a steady pace to make sure that you get as many problems correct as you can. Most "dumb mistakes" are caused by working too quickly, so make sure that you aren't rushing and doing sloppy work. When you have only a few minutes left, quickly fill in the remaining bubbles randomly. Why? Read on and we'll explain.

Most students think that they need to get every problem on the test to get a great score, and most students hurt their score because they try to do too many problems. There are two reasons why you shouldn't try to do every single problem.

First, it's very hard to find time to answer every question correctly. So, naturally, people rush, then make careless errors and lose points. Almost everyone is better off *slowing down*, using the whole time to work on fewer problems and answering more of those problems correctly. Think about it this way: You'll get a higher score if you do *only 75 percent* of the problems on this test and answer them correctly than if you do all of the problems and answer about half correctly. Weird, huh?

Second, some questions are easier than others, but they're all worth the same number of points. So why waste time working on hard problems when there are easier ones you can do?

In short, if you follow this advice, your score will improve:

- **Slow down.** Make sure you work slowly and carefully enough to make sure that you get most of the problems correct. If you find that you are making lots of mistakes, slow down even more. It may feel funny, but it will help your score.

- Guess at any problems that you don't have time to try. This means that you should **absolutely fill in every bubble on your answer sheet.** You are not penalized for wrong choices, and you will probably get a few extra points by random chance.

- If you find that a problem is too hard or isn't making sense, **skip it and go on to an easier one.** You can always go back if you have time. If you don't, you're better off taking your best guess.

PROCESS OF ELIMINATION

Another very important test-taking skill is Process of Elimination. This is a strategy in which you don't have to know the answer to the question to get the correct answer. Have a look at the following problem.

1. What is the capital of Malawi?

   (A) Washington
   (B) Paris
   (C) Tokyo
   (D) London
   (E) Lilongwe

(Don't worry—you won't see any questions like this on your test. It's just an example.)

How did you know the answer was E? Because you knew that it couldn't be A, B, C, or D. That's Process of Elimination. When you are solving a problem, always cross off the choices you know are wrong, for whatever reason. Especially on the English and reading comprehension sections of the test, you'll often find that you can cross off every answer except one—the right one! Even if you can't always narrow the choices down to only one, you will certainly cross off a few choices and improve your chances of guessing correctly. **Using Process of Elimination whenever you need to will improve your score.**

BALLPARKING

In mathematics sections, another great tool is Ballparking. This means "take a guess and see which answers are in the ballpark." This can help you save time and make a good guess when you don't know or don't have time to figure out the correct answer. Have a look at the following problem:

2. What is $\frac{1}{2}$ of 1022?

   (A) 51
   (B) 52
   (C) 511
   (D) 512

Before you try to solve this, look at the answer choices. Which ones are in the ballpark? Certainly not A and B. These can be eliminated. If you're out of time or have a hard time solving the problem, you can now guess between C and D.

If you can eliminate choices for any reason, you improve your odds of making a correct guess, and you will improve your score.

PART I

Cracking the COOP

2

What is the COOP?

The COOP (Cooperative Admission Exam) is given to students in October or November; check with your local diocese during the summer before the year you plan to test for more precise information.

The COOP begins with a 12-minute period in which you have to memorize the definitions of imaginary words, followed by seven test sections. Here is the format of the COOP at the time this book was published; the test may undergo slight changes from one year to the next, so your test may vary slightly from the model you see here.

- Memory definitions (12 minutes)
- Sequences (15 minutes)
- Analogies (7 minutes)
- Memory (5 minutes)
- Verbal reasoning (15 minutes)
- Reading comprehension (40 minutes)
- Mathematics (35 minutes)
- Language expression (30 minutes)

The following chapters will take you through each of these sections in detail and will review all of the types of problems you'll see.

3

Memory

MEMORIZING WORDS

At the beginning of the COOP, you will be given 12 minutes to memorize the definitions of twenty made-up words. They'll look like this:

> A palooka is a spoon
> A klawo is a cat
> Modolo means to draw
> A yimpax is a belt
> Skevi means to call

HOW CAN YOU MEMORIZE THESE WORDS?

The best way to memorize words is to come up with a funny image or story (called a mnemoic device) that will help you remember them. It's very hard to memorize words without any context. It's always easier to remember something that fits into a story or makes you laugh.

Look at each word and try to make it into a quick story based on how it sounds and what it means. For instance, how does *klawo* relate to *cat*? You might think of claws. You could then make up the story "Ouch! Sharp cat's klaws!" to help you remember that *klawo* means *cat*.

The story you create doesn't have to be great, and it doesn't have to fit the word exactly. Be silly for a few minutes—that's okay. Whatever kind of story you can come up with will probably help you remember the word.

Here are some sample stories for the words above. Notice that we've boldfaced the letters in the stories that you can use as triggers to remember the made-up words.

> I need my **pal**'s soup sp**oo**n (palooka)
> sharp cat's **claw**s (klawo)
> an artist draws a **mod**el (modolo)
> **y**our **pa**nts require a belt (yimpax)
> I need to a**sk Eve** to call me (skevi)

Remember that you have 12 minutes to memorize twenty words. This means that you have a little more than 30 seconds per word. This is actually a lot of time. You obviously can't spend *too* long on any one word, but you should try an idea or two for each word and try to make a funny story for yourself.

CRACKING THE MEMORY QUESTIONS

Part 3 of the COOP asks you to remember the definitions of the words you memorized at the beginning of the test. Of course, it's hard to remember all twenty words after having worked hard on the previous two sections of the test. However, if you've done a good job making up little stories or word associations, you should be able to get a lot of points on this section.

The best news, of course, is that with some intelligent techniques, *you can get all the answers right even if you don't remember the definitions of all the words.* Here's how:

Step 1: Go through the whole list of twenty questions and answer all the questions you are sure of. There will probably be seven or eight you'll remember right away. Answer these first.

Step 2: Go back to the first question you were sure of. The answer you picked as the correct answer on this question *can't* be the correct answer on any other question. So go through all the other questions and *cross off that answer choice.* Repeat this step for each of the questions you were sure of.

Step 3:   Look at the remaining questions and see which choices you have left. You should probably be able to answer a few more now that you have narrowed down the choices.

Step 4:   For any questions that are left, take your best guess.

Let's see how to crack the memory questions above using this method.

1. Which word means <u>a belt</u>?

   (A) klawo
   (B) yimpax
   (C) carmit
   (D) veex
   (E) palooka

2. Which word means <u>to call</u>?

   (A) yimpax
   (B) deebla
   (C) modolo
   (D) skevi
   (E) buzat

3. Which word means <u>a spoon</u>?

   (A) modolo
   (B) figer
   (C) klawo
   (D) palooka
   (E) yerksm

4. Which word means <u>a cat</u>?

   (A) klawo
   (B) buzat
   (C) skevi
   (D) modolo
   (E) ostimpe

5. Which word means <u>to draw</u>?

   (A) yimpax
   (B) ostimpe
   (C) modolo
   (D) klawo
   (E) palooka

Let's say that you are sure of three words: You remember "your pants need a belt," so *belt* is *yimpax*; you remember "sharp cat's claws," so you know that a *cat* is a *klawo*; and you remember "draw a model," so you know that to *draw* is *modolo*.

Step 1:   Go ahead and answer question 1 as B, question 4 as A, and question 5 as C.

Step 2:   Since we know that a *klawo* is a *cat*, it can't be the answer to any other questions. So go ahead and cross off *klawo* anywhere you see it on questions 2 and 3. Also, since we know that a *yimpax* is a *belt*, we can cross off *yimpax* anywhere on questions 2 and 3. Likewise, we can also cross off *modolo*.

Step 3: Notice that we have crossed off several of the choices for questions 2 and 3. Look back to them now and see if you can answer them from the choices that are left.

Step 4: If you still can't answer questions 2 and 3, you have a good chance at a correct guess. Take a guess and move on.

YOUR TURN

Here are twenty words. Take 12 minutes to memorize them, and then try the problems on the next page.

A pessci is a shark

A nettep is a building

Erindo is mother

Lauhen means to dig

A wureca is a bicycle

A tareg is a door

A rinranfa is an airplane

A kulati is a window

A xanthu is a telephone

A hacmil is a guitar

Atnanus means to sing

An idgalo is a fork

A yulun is a piece of cake

A verice is a bird

Maxpati means angry

A fiditac is a plant

A piytha is a loud noise

An oolulu is a book

Zinflut is oil

A goulti is a snake

COOP MEMORY EXERCISE (ANSWERS ARE ON PAGE 80)

1. Which word means <u>a bicycle</u>?

   (A) verice
   (B) hacmil
   (C) rinranfa
   (D) wureca
   (E) zinflut

2. Which word means <u>a building</u>?

   (A) hacmil
   (B) wureca
   (C) verice
   (D) nettep
   (E) zinflut

3. Which word means <u>mother</u>?

   (A) maxpati
   (B) oolulu
   (C) xanthu
   (D) tareg
   (E) erindo

4. Which word means <u>a door</u>?

   (A) yulun
   (B) pessci
   (C) fiditac
   (D) goulti
   (E) tareg

5. Which word means <u>a shark</u>?

   (A) oolulu
   (B) erindo
   (C) idgalo
   (D) pessci
   (E) yulun

6. Which word means <u>to dig</u>?

   (A) kulati
   (B) piytha
   (C) atnanus
   (D) nettep
   (E) lauhen

7. Which word means <u>an airplane</u>?

   (A) atnanus
   (B) erindo
   (C) rinranfa
   (D) fiditac
   (E) wureca

8. Which word means a book?

   (A) tareg
   (B) yulun
   (C) goulti
   (D) oolulu
   (E) xanthu

9. Which word means a telephone?

   (A) goulti
   (B) rinranfa
   (C) wureca
   (D) xanthu
   (E) maxpati

10. Which word means a fork?

   (A) lauhen
   (B) atnanus
   (C) verice
   (D) zinflut
   (E) idgalo

11. Which word means to sing?

   (A) atnanus
   (B) wureca
   (C) xanthu
   (D) piytha
   (E) fiditac

12. Which word means a snake?

   (A) nettep
   (B) goulti
   (C) lauhen
   (D) kulati
   (E) atnanus

13. Which word means a piece of cake?

   (A) erindo
   (B) yulun
   (C) idgalo
   (D) kulati
   (E) goulti

14. Which word means a bird?

   (A) verice
   (B) pessci
   (C) erindo
   (D) rinranfa
   (E) fiditac

15. Which word means <u>angry</u>?

   (A) maxpati
   (B) lauhen
   (C) idgalo
   (D) piytha
   (E) xanthu

16. Which word means <u>a plant</u>?

   (A) rinranfa
   (B) zinflut
   (C) fiditac
   (D) kulati
   (E) pessci

17. Which word means <u>a loud noise</u>?

   (A) nettep
   (B) piytha
   (C) tareg
   (D) hacmil
   (E) maxpati

18. Which word means <u>a window</u>?

   (A) kulati
   (B) pessci
   (C) yulun
   (D) verice
   (E) piytha

19. Which word means <u>oil</u>?

   (A) hacmil
   (B) idgalo
   (C) zinflut
   (D) oolulu
   (E) lauhen

20. Which word means <u>a guitar</u>?

   (A) nettep
   (B) tareg
   (C) maxpati
   (D) hacmil
   (E) oolulu

4

Sequences

WHAT IS A SEQUENCE?

A sequence is a list of items that follows a pattern. In this section of the COOP, the questions will show you a sequence made up of pictures, numbers, or letters. You will be asked to figure out what picture(s) or number(s) should fill the blank in the sequence. Your job is to figure out the pattern in the sequence. For instance, the numbers 2, 4, 6, 8 make a sequence because each number is 2 more than the number before it.

First, let's look at the sequences made of pictures:

□■ | △▲ | ◇◆ | ___   (a) ○■   (b) ○○   (c) ○●   (d) ●○

⊃ | ε | Ʒ | ___   (a) Ɛ   (b) Ɛ   (c) Ʒ   (d) Ʒ

To answer these questions, look at what is similar and what changes from one picture to the next.

The first sequence is made up of pairs of similar shapes, where the first shape is white and the second shape is black: A white square with a black square, a white triangle with a black triangle, and a white diamond with a black diamond. Since all three pairs have two similar shapes, the correct answer will also be made up of similar shapes. Therefore we can eliminate choice A. Since all three pairs have the white shape before the black shape, the answer must be C.

The second sequence is made up of numbers of half-circles. You can see that the first picture has one, the second picture has two, and the third picture has three half-circles. Therefore the missing picture should continue the series and contain four half-circles. So we know that A and D can be eliminated. How can we decide between B and C? In the first picture, the half-circles are open on the left, in the second picture they are open on the right, and in the third picture they are open on the left. Since they change direction from one picture to the next, the missing picture will have half-circles that are open to the right. Therefore the answer is B.

Other sequences will be made up entirely of numbers. In these examples there are three numbers in each grouping. All three groupings follow a pattern. You have to figure out what the pattern is in order to choose the correct number.

1.   1 5 9 | 3 7 11 | 8 12 ___
   (A) 10
   (B) 14
   (C) 16
   (D) 17

Here's how to crack it

Between the first and second and second and third numbers in each group, write the number that—by performing an operation like adding, subtracting, multiplying, or dividing—takes you from the first number to the next.

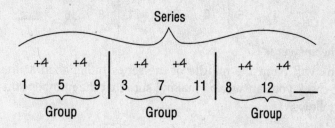

Because in the three groups each number is 4 more (+ 4) than the previous number, the next number in the series must be 16: **8** (+ 4) = **12** (+ 4) = **16**. The answer is C.

On more complicated problems, you'll need to use more than one kind of operation (multiplication, addition, division, subtraction) between each pair of numbers to figure out how the pattern works. You might have to subtract the first and second numbers in each group and then multiply to get the third. Here's an example.

2. 7 5 12 | 19 17 24 | 12 10 __

   (A) 8
   (B) 14
   (C) 17
   (D) 18

$$\begin{array}{ccc|ccc|ccc}
& {\scriptstyle -2} & {\scriptstyle +7} & & {\scriptstyle -2} & {\scriptstyle +7} & & {\scriptstyle -2} & {\scriptstyle +7} \\
7 & 5 & 12 & 19 & 17 & 24 & 12 & 10 & \_\_
\end{array}$$

In this sequence problem, you have to *subtract* 2 from the first number to get the second number and then *add* 7 to the second number to get the third number. Look at the last group to see how easy it can be: **12 – 2 = 10** and **10 + 7 = 17.** The pattern is 12 10 17, so C is correct.

What if I can't figure out the whole pattern?

Even if you can get only *part* of the pattern, you can still find the correct answer. Take a look at this example.

3. 2 4 5 | 10 20 21 | 8 16 __

   (A) 8
   (B) 14
   (C) 17
   (D) 18

Suppose you have a hard time figuring out what operation you need to use to get from the first to the second number. In this problem, as long as you can figure out that you add 1 to the second number to get the third number, you can get the answer. (By the way, the first operation in this sequence was to multiply by 2.)

```
              +1          |          +1          |          +1
    2     4     5   |   10     20     21   |    8     16     ___
```

Since 16 + 1 = 17, the answer is C.

Sometimes the blank will be in the middle of the series rather than at the end. Follow the same technique, and double-check your answer by making sure that the number you put in the blank works with the number that follows.

4. 3 5 10 | 9 11 22 | 12 ___ 28

    (A) 14
    (B) 16
    (C) 18
    (D) 24

```
        +2    ×2    |      +2     ×2    |     +2     ×2
    3     5     10   |   9     11     22   |  12     ___     28
```

In this example, the first operation is to add 2, and the second operation is to multiply by 2: 12 + 2 = 14 and 14 × 2 = 28. The answer is A.

SUBSTITUTE NUMBERS FOR LETTERS TO CRACK LETTER SEQUENCES

The sequence problems toward the end of the section will probably combine letters and numbers or use all letters. These tend to be the most difficult problems on the test. If one of them stumps you, move on to the next one and go back. Try to do as many as you can. Don't forget that you can often solve the problem (or eliminate a few choices) by figuring out just one part of each group in the sequence. You don't always have to figure out the entire sequence. If you're completely stumped, don't forget to guess so that you haven't left anything blank.

One way to make the sequences that use letters easier to solve is to substitute the letters with numbers according to the location of each letter in the alphabet. This often helps you see the pattern of the sequences more easily. The first step is to write the following on your test booklet.

A	B	C	D	E	F	G	H	I	J	K	L	M	N	O	P	Q	R	S	T	U	V	W	X	Y	Z
1	2	3	4	5	6	7	8	9	10	11	12	13	14	15	16	17	18	19	20	21	22	23	24	25	26

This will help you change letters into numbers easily. Now look at the following problem.

5. B D F I H J L I N P R I _____

    (A) S U W
    (B) T V X
    (C) R S T
    (D) U W Y

Look at the chart of numbers and letters above. B is 2, D is 4, F is 6, H is 8, and so on. By using numbers instead of letters, you should be able to figure out the pattern much more easily.

2 4 6 I 8 10 12 I 14 16 18 I _____

Now we can see the pattern. The numbers are all even and increase by 2: **2 + 2 = 4** and **4 + 2 = 6**. The original question, before we made the substitution, would look like this:

$$\overset{+2\quad\times2}{}\quad\overset{+2\quad\times2}{}\quad\overset{+2\quad\times2}{}$$
B   D   F | H   J   L | N   P   R

The correct answer will also have even numbers that increase by 2. Substitute numbers for letters in the answer choices.

(A) S U W	**(A)**	19 21 23
(B) T V X	**(B)**	20 22 24
(C) R S T	**(C)**	18 19 20
(D) U W Y	**(D)**	21 23 25

Only B follows the pattern: **20 + 2 = 22** and **22 + 2 = 24**. On our number and alphabet chart, 20 is T, 22 is V, and 24 is X, so you know the answer has to be T V X.

COOP SEQUENCE EXERCISE (ANSWERS ARE ON PAGE 80)

1. (A) OOOO | OO●● | O●●● | ____   (A) O●O● (B) ●●●● (C) OOOO (D) ●OOO

2. (B) □ – □ | □ + □ | O – O | ____   (A) □ + O (B) O + □ (C) O + O (D) □ – □

3. (C) F | ⊐ | ⊣ | ____   (A) ⌐ (B) ⊢ (C) ⌐ (D) ⊣

4. 4 8 12 | 11 15 19 | 21 25 __

   (A) 22
   (B) 23
   (C) 27
   (D) 29

5. 38 32 26 | 17 11 5 | 42 __ 30

   (A) 36
   (B) 34
   (C) 32
   (D) 24

6. 6 12 16 | 4 8 12 | 5 10 __

   (A) 8
   (B) 14
   (C) 15
   (D) 20

7. 10 5 15 | 13 8 18 | 22 __ 27

   (A) 15
   (B) 17
   (C) 22
   (D) 25

8. 8 16 20 | 4 8 12 | 20 __ 44

   (A) 24
   (B) 28
   (C) 35
   (D) 40

9. 20 18 25 | 23 21 28 | 30 28 __

   (A) 25
   (B) 26
   (C) 35
   (D) 38

10. HFD | LJH | PNL | TRP | ___

   (A) RQP
   (B) XVT
   (C) VUT
   (D) YWV

11. A1FK | D2IN | G3LQ | J4OT | ____

   (A) M5RW
   (B) N5QS
   (C) N6ST
   (D) U6VW

5
Analogies

WHAT IS AN ANALOGY?

An analogy is just a fancy word that means two pairs of objects have the same relationship. For instance, kittens/cat and puppies/dog are analogies. Each pair of words has the same relationship: Kittens are baby cats, just as puppies are baby dogs. On the COOP, instead of making analogies with words, you will be asked to make them with pictures.

HOW TO APPROACH ANALOGIES

Here is what an analogy question will look like on the COOP:

1.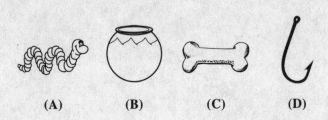

Here's how to crack it

Even though the COOP asks you to make analogies with pictures, the best way to solve them is to turn those pictures into words. To figure out the relationship between two words, *make a sentence* using the words. Finally, use that *same sentence* for each of the answer choices, and see which one fits best.

The top two pictures show a dog and a doghouse. What sentence could we make with these two words?

A dog **lives in** a doghouse.

Now let's use that same sentence with the remaining picture and each of the answer choices.

A fish **lives in** a _____.

Does a fish live in a worm? No. Cross off A. Does a fish live in a fish tank? Yes. Let's leave B in. Does a fish live in a dog bone? No. Cross off C. Does a fish live in a hook? No. Cross off D. Since we have crossed off A, C, and D, the best answer must be B.

Let's try one more:

2.

(A)   (B)   (C)   (D)

What kind of sentence could we make using the words boy and man?

A boy is a small man.

Now let's try that same sentence with the answer choices. Is a cat a small dog? No. Cross off A. Is a cat a small bowl of milk? No. Cross off B. Is a cat a small lion? Maybe. Let's leave C in. Is a cat a small bird? No. Cross off D. This makes C the best choice.

As you can see, you should expect to use Process of Elimination on these questions. The one that fits *best* is the one you should pick.

MAKING GOOD SENTENCES

Of course, some sentences you can make are more helpful than others. If we had said, "Dog and doghouse both begin with the letters D-O-G," that wouldn't have been very useful in solving the analogy. When you think of a sentence for the first two pictures, try to use one word to *define* the other. For example, the sentence "A dog lives in a doghouse" defines for us what a doghouse is.

COOP ANALOGY EXERCISE 1 (ANSWERS ARE ON PAGE 81)

Try making sentences from the following words.

mansion / house   _____

leaf / tree   _____

desert / sand   _____

engine / automobile   _____

bread / baker   _____

brush / painter   _____

Now let's put it all together.

COOP ANALOGY EXERCISE 2 (ANSWERS ARE ON PAGE 81)

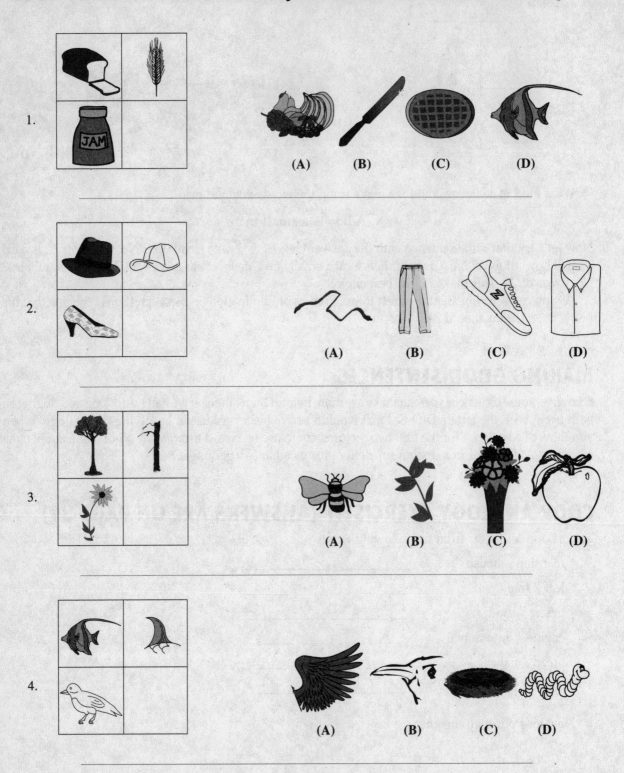

1. (A)   (B)   (C)   (D)

2. (A)   (B)   (C)   (D)

3. (A)   (B)   (C)   (D)

4. (A)   (B)   (C)   (D)

5.

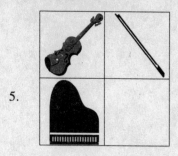

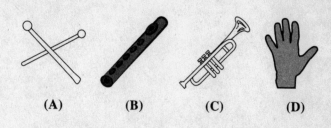

(A)   (B)   (C)   (D)

TIMING

On the COOP, you have 7 minutes to complete twenty analogies. This means that you have to move along fairly quickly. If you get stuck on one problem, move on to the next. There are probably easier ones later in the section, and you can always come back to a difficult problem if you have time left at the end. Now that you understand how to crack these questions, go back to the first practice test and rework any of the analogy problems that you found difficult.

6

Verbal Reasoning

The verbal reasoning section of the COOP has several different kinds of questions:

- Necessary part
- Two-story analogies
- Must be true
- Mystery language

NECESSARY PART QUESTIONS

The first of the questions in the verbal reasoning section will ask you to think carefully about the meaning of a word and to find the answer choice that is a necessary part of the meaning of that word.

What does *necessary* mean? It means that you're looking for a choice that describes something that the word *cannot do without*. For instance, could you have an apple that was not red? Yes. Could you have an apple that did not have a stem? Yes. Could you have an apple that was not a piece of fruit? No. This means that the word *fruit* is something that is necessary to the idea of the word *apple*. You can't do without the word *fruit*.

Here is what a necessary part question will look like:

1. <u>apple</u>

   (A) red
   (B) fruit
   (C) store
   (D) stem

Here's how to crack it

The best way to approach this is to look at the answer choices one at a time, and ask yourself, "Could you do without it?" If the answer is "No," you've found the correct choice. You could have an apple that wasn't red, that wasn't in a store, or that didn't have a stem. Therefore you can eliminate these choices. But you can't have an apple that is not a piece of fruit. You can't do without B. Therefore B is the best answer.

Let's try another example:

2. <u>shirt</u>

   (A) button
   (B) blue
   (C) chest
   (D) sleeve

Here's how to crack it

Does a shirt have to have a button? No. Cross off A. Does a shirt have to be blue? No. Cross off B. Does it have to cover your chest? Probably. Let's leave choice C. Does it have to have sleeves? Well, most shirts do, but they don't have to. Therefore we can cross off D. The best answer is C.

Whenever you find a choice that you're sure is incorrect, cross it off. On more difficult problems, you may find that there are two choices, both of which seem necessary. If you're stuck, take your best guess and move on.

TWO-STORY ANALOGY QUESTIONS

Remember the analogy questions from the last chapter? The next questions you will see are a bit more complicated. We'll call them two-story analogies.

These problems are trickier because the analogies may go in two directions. The words may relate to each other left to right (horizontally) or up and down (vertically). Let's look at an example of an analogy that relates left to right:

> 3. <u>inch   foot   yard</u>
>   ounce   pound
>
> **(A)** gallon
> **(B)** ton
> **(C)** ruler
> **(D)** mile

Here's how to crack it

As with the ordinary analogies, the best way to solve this type of problem is to make a sentence. In this case, we can make sentences with the words on top of the line.

> An **inch** is a smaller distance than a **foot**, and a **foot** is a smaller distance than a **yard**.

In this case, the words on top of the line represent sizes that go from smaller to larger. Now let's use that same idea with the words below the line.

> An **ounce** is a smaller amount than a **pound**, and a **pound** is a smaller amount than a _____?

Is a pound a smaller amount than a gallon? Not really. A pound measures solid things, and a gallon measures liquids. Cross off A. Is a pound smaller than a ton? Yes. Is a pound smaller than a ruler? This doesn't make any sense. Cross off C. Is a pound smaller than a mile? This doesn't make sense, either. It's talking about distance, not weight. Cross off D. The best answer is B.

Here's an example of a two-story analogy that goes up and down:

> 4. <u>dog   pig   horse</u>
>   kennel   sty
>
> **(A)** saddle
> **(B)** hoof
> **(C)** gallop
> **(D)** stable

Here's how to crack it

You can tell this analogy goes up and down, because there's no relation among the words above the line. We can make a sentence only between a word above the line and a word below the line.

> A group of **dogs** lives in a **kennel**.

> A group of **pigs** lives in a **sty**.

Now let's use that same sentence with the last pair. Does a group of horses live in a saddle? No. Does a group of horses live in a hoof? Definitely not. Does a group of horses live in a gallop? No. Does a group of horses live in a stable? Yes. This makes D the best answer. Neat, huh?

MUST BE TRUE QUESTIONS

For a must be true question, you will be asked to read a few sentences that describe people, places, or things. These sentences will be followed by four short statements. Your job is to find the choice that *must be true* based on the sentences you read.

WHAT DOES "MUST BE TRUE" MEAN?

Look at these two statements.

> Jason scored a 92 on his math test.
> Lisa scored a 96 on her math test.

There are many things you might assume to be true, given these two statements. Here are some of them.

> Lisa is a better student than Jason.
> Lisa knows math better than Jason.
> Lisa and Jason are in the same math class.

However, none of these choices *must* be true. Sure, they might be true, but we don't really know. Lisa might not be a better student than Jason—maybe she just got lucky on this test, or maybe in most other subjects she scores much worse than Jason. Lisa might not be better at math—maybe she's just taking an easier math class than Jason is taking. We don't whether they're in the same math class. We don't even know whether they're in the same grade or the same school! Don't make any assumptions on must be true questions.

What is something that *must* be true given the information above? Only this:

> Lisa scored higher on her math test than Jason scored on his math test.

That's the only statement that really *must* be true. It's something that we *know* for certain is true given the facts.

MUST BE TRUE QUESTIONS ON THE COOP

Here is an example of the way the COOP will give you a must be true problem.

> Jason goes to math class for exactly two hours per day, English class for
> exactly one hour per day, and science class for exactly three hours per day.
> Jason never takes math and science at the same time. If all of the information
> above is true, which of the following must also be true?

- **(A)** Jason likes science class better than he likes math class.
- **(B)** Jason never goes to history class.
- **(C)** Jason spends more time in science class per day than in math class.
- **(D)** For exactly two hours per day, Jason does not take math or science.

Here's how to crack it

Take each choice one at a time, and ask yourself, "Does this *really* have to be true based on the information in the passage?"

Do we know anything about what Jason likes or does not like? The passage says nothing about this. Therefore we can cross off A. Do we know that Jason never goes to history class? The passage doesn't say this. Cross off B. Do we know that he spends more time each day in science class than in math class? Yes, since he spends three hours in science class and two hours in math class. Leave C in. Do we know Jason does not take math or science for exactly two hours per day? If we knew how many total hours were in Jason's school day, we might be able to figure it out. But as it stands, we can't know whether this is true or not, so we can cross off D. The best answer is C.

MYSTERY LANGUAGE QUESTIONS

Finally, you will see a couple questions that we call mystery language questions. These questions ask you to figure out the way to say something in an imaginary foreign language.

The following is an example of a mystery language question.

> maxelipoti means science book
>
> yipipoti means history book
>
> maxeligolub means science teacher
>
> Which of the following could mean history teacher?
>
> (A) yipigolub
> (B) maxeliyipi
> (C) maxeligolub
> (D) yipipoti

Here's how to crack it

Step 1: Find two mystery words that have one set of letters that is the same, and then see what English word they have in common. This is what that set of letters must mean.

In this case, we can see that the first two mystery words both have "poti" in them. These two words share the English word "book," so "poti" must mean "book."

We can also see that the first and third mystery words have the letters "maxeli" in them. These two words share the English word "science," so "maxeli" must mean "science."

Step 2: Use Process of Elimination to eliminate those parts of the mystery words that do not correspond with the English word you are asked for.

In this case, we are asked for the word that means "history teacher." We know that "poti" means "book" and that "maxseli" means "science." There fore we can cross off any choice with "poti" or "maxeli" in it. This will allow us to cross off B, C, and D. A is the correct answer: "Yipi" means history and "golub" means teacher.

COOP VERBAL REASONING EXERCISE (ANSWERS ARE ON PAGE 82)

1. pen
   - (A) letter
   - (B) ink
   - (C) hand
   - (D) black

2. book
   - (A) picture
   - (B) history
   - (C) page
   - (D) introduction

3. walk   skip   rug
   tug   pull
   - (A) yank
   - (B) draw
   - (C) lift
   - (D) push

4. tie   bracelet   belt
   neck   wrist
   - (A) watch
   - (B) waist
   - (C) joint
   - (D) jewelry

5. At a track meet, Irene ran in 8 races. She won one gold medal, two silver medals, and three bronze medals. After the track meet she saw a movie and had dinner with her parents.

   According to the information above, which of the following must be true?
   - (A) Irene's family watched her win her medals at the track meet.
   - (B) Irene's favorite activity is running races.
   - (C) Irene set a record in one of the events.
   - (D) Irene won a greater number of silver medals than gold medals.

6. Paul can jump farther than David and Jeff. Jeff and Edwin can both jump farther than Larry.

Based on the information above, which of the following must be true?

(A) Larry cannot jump as far as Paul can.
(B) Paul can jump farther than anyone else at school.
(C) Larry does not practice jumping very often.
(D) Jeff jumps farther than David.

7. uticitho means pear tree

oopicitho means pear juice

utilanno means orange tree

Which of the following could mean orange juice?

(A) utioopi
(B) oopilanno
(C) oopicitho
(D) uticitho

8. tolomaguni means front window

tolokala means back window

werimaguni means front door

Which of the following could mean back door?

(A) werikala
(B) weritolo
(C) tolomaguni
(D) kalamaguni

7

Reading Comprehension

HOW TO THINK ABOUT READING COMPREHENSION

Reading the passages on the COOP is different from most other kinds of reading that you will do in school. You might think that you have to read slowly enough to learn all the information in the passage. But there is much more information in the passage than you can learn in a short time, and you will be asked about only a few facts from the passage. So trying to understand all of the facts in the passage is not the best use of your time.

Most importantly, you don't get points for understanding everything in the passage. You only get points for answering questions correctly. Therefore, we're going to teach you the best strategy to get you the most correct answers.

There is one more important thing to know, which works to your advantage: *The answer to every question can be found somewhere in the passage.* All you've got to do is find it. This means that you should think of reading comprehension like a treasure hunt: You need to use clues in the questions to find the answers in the passage and earn your points.

STRATEGY FOR ATTACKING READING COMPREHENSION

Step 1: Read the passage and label each paragraph. Don't try to learn every single fact in the passage; you can always go back later. It is important only to get a general idea of what each paragraph talks about.

Step 2: Answer the general questions based on your paragraph labels.

Step 3: Answer the specific questions by looking back at the passage and finding the answer.

Important! In steps 2 and 3, answer your questions by using Process of Elimination. The test-writers will often try to disguise the correct answer by using different words that mean basically the same thing as the words used in the passage. You might not recognize these words right away as the ones used in the passage. Why do the test-writers do this? If they gave you the exact same words straight out of the passage, that would be too easy. So your best bet is to cross off the choices that you know are wrong and pick from the choices that are left.

Now let's look at each step in more detail.

STEP 1: LABEL YOUR PARAGRAPHS

Every good treasure hunt needs a map, which will help you locate the answers in the passage. The best way to make a map is to label your paragraphs as you read. This will help you understand the main idea of the pa4sage and at the same time make it easier to locate facts in the passage while you're reading.

After you finish each paragraph, stop for a moment and ask yourself, "What is this paragraph about?" Try to summarize the idea of this paragraph in seven or eight words, and quickly write this summary in the margin. This way you'll have a guide to important parts of the passage when you have to answer a question.

After you have read the entire passage, take a moment and ask yourself, "What is this whole passage about?" Write a one-sentence summary at the bottom of the page. This will help you answer any main-idea questions you may see. Try doing step 1 for the following passage:

Contrary to popular belief, the first European known to lay eyes on America was not Christopher Columbus or Amerigo Vespucci, but a little-known Viking named Bjarni Herjolfsson. In the summer of 986, Bjarni sailed from Norway to Iceland, heading for the Viking settlement where his father Heriulf resided.

When he arrived in Iceland, Bjarni discovered that his father had already sold his land and estates and set out for the latest Viking settlement on the subarctic island called Greenland. Discovered by an <u>infamous</u> murderer and criminal named Eric the Red, Greenland lay at the limit of the known world. Dismayed, Bjarni set out for this new colony.

Since the Vikings traveled without a chart or compass, it was not uncommon for them to lose their way in the unpredictable northern seas. Beset by fog, the crew lost their bearings. When the fog finally cleared, they found themselves before a land that was level and covered with woods. They traveled farther up the coast, finding more flat, wooded country. Farther north, the landscape revealed glaciers and rocky mountains. Without knowing it, Bjarni had arrived in North America.

Though Bjarni realized this was an unknown land, he was no intrepid explorer. Rather, he was a practical man who had simply set out to find his father. Refusing his crew's request to go ashore, he promptly turned his bow back to sea. After four days' sailing, Bjarni landed at Herjolfsnes on the southwestern tip of Greenland, the exact place he had been seeking all along.

What is this whole passage about?

Your labels and passage summary should look something like this:

Paragraph 1: America was first visited by Bjarni Herjolfsson.
Paragraph 2: Herjolfsson wanted to follow his father to Greenland.
Paragraph 3: He got lost and ended up at America.
Paragraph 4: He turned around and finally reached Greenland.

Summary: How Bjarni Herjolfsson got lost and saw America before anyone else.

Now we have a good picture of the overall point of the passage, and we should be able to look back and find any details we need. So let's turn to the questions.

STEP 2: ANSWER THE GENERAL QUESTIONS

It's usually best to answer the general questions first. These questions ask you about the passage as a whole. There are several types of general questions, and they look like this.

Main Idea/Purpose

The passage is mostly about

The main idea of this passage is

The best title for this passage would be

The purpose of this passage is to

The author wrote this passage in order to

Tone/Attitude

The author's tone is best described as

The attitude of the author is one of

General Interpretation

The author would most likely agree that

It can be inferred from the passage that

The passage implies that

You would probably find this passage in a

This passage is best described as

To answer a main idea/purpose question, ask yourself, "What did the passage talk about most?" Look at the choices and cross off anything that was not discussed or that was only a detail of the passage.

To answer a tone/attitude question, ask yourself, "How does the author feel about the subject?" Cross off anything that doesn't agree with the author's view.

To answer a general interpretation question, ask yourself, "Which answer sounds most like what the author said?" Cross off anything that was not discussed in the paragraph or that does not agree with the author's view.

Let's take a look at some general questions for this passage:

1. The passage is mostly about

    (A) the Vikings and their civilization
    (B) the waves of Viking immigration
    (C) sailing techniques of Bjarni Herjolfsson
    (D) one Viking's glimpse of America

To answer this question, let's look back at our labels and our summary of the passage. We said that the main idea of the passage was how Bjarni Herjolfsson got lost and saw America before anyone else. A and B are about the Vikings in general and not about Herjolfsson, so they can be eliminated. C is about Herjolfsson, but his sailing techniques are not really discussed. This makes D the best choice.

2. Which of the following can be inferred from the passage?

    (A) The word *America* was first used by Herjolfsson.
    (B) Herjolfsson's discovery of America was an accident.
    (C) Herjolfsson was helped by Native Americans.
    (D) Greenland and Iceland were the Vikings' most important discoveries.

You should make quick work of this problem using Process of Elimination. The passage never says anything about Native Americans, so C can be eliminated. Also, it doesn't say that Herjolfsson ever used the word *America*, so you can cross off A. (If you're not positive whether this is true or not, quickly skim back and double-check this in the passage.) We're already down to two choices. D is an extreme choice—meaning it uses strong language that makes something absolutely true or false—due to the word *most*, so it probably is not the answer. If you check the passage, you can see that D is never stated. Therefore B is the best choice.

STEP 3: ANSWER THE SPECIFIC QUESTIONS

Specific questions ask you about a fact or detail mentioned in the passage. For these questions, look back at the passage to find your answer. These are the different kinds of specific questions.

Fact

> According to the passage
>
> According to the author
>
> Which of these questions is answered by the passage?

Vocabulary in Context

> The word <u>pilfer</u> probably means
>
> What does the passage mean by <u>pilfer</u>?

Specific Interpretation/Purpose

> The author mentions Mother Goose in order to
>
> From the information in the passage, Mother Goose would probably

To answer a **Fact** question, look back at the passage and find the lines that mention the thing you are asked about. Use your passage labels to find the information quickly, or simply skim until you find it. Reread those lines to see exactly what the passage says. Then look for a choice that best restates what the passage says. Cross off anything that is never stated or that says the opposite of the information in the passage.

To answer a **Vocabulary in Context** question, look back at the passage and find the underlined word. It will probably be a word that you don't know. Cover the word with your finger. Reread the lines around that word, and think of the word that you would put there. Then look at the answer choices and see which comes closest to the word that you think should go there. If you can't think of the exact word, it's okay to simply note that the word should be a "positive word" or a "negative word."

To answer a **Specific Interpretation/purpose** question, look back at the passage and find the lines that discuss the thing you are asked about. Use your passage labels or skim the passage. Reread those lines to see exactly what the passage says. The correct answer will always be very closely based on the information in the passage. For instance, if a passage tells us that John likes to play tennis, we can infer that he will probably play tennis if he is given the chance. Cross off any choices that are not stated in the passage or sound very far off from what the passage says.

3. According to the passage, Greenland was discovered by

   (A) Amerigo Vespucci
   (B) Bjarni Herjolfsson's father
   (C) Bjarni Herjolfsson
   (D) Eric the Red

To answer this question, we should look back at the passage and find the line that talks about the discovery of Greenland. If you skim for the word *Greenland*, you'll find it in the second paragraph: "Discovered by an <u>infamous</u> murderer and criminal named Eric the Red, Greenland lay at the limit of the known world." Therefore the answer is D.

4. The word <u>infamous</u> probably means

   (A) lazy
   (B) strong
   (C) wicked
   (D) intelligent

Let's reread the line that mentions the word *infamous*: "Discovered by an <u>infamous</u> murderer and criminal named Eric the Red . . . ." Since the word *infamous* describes a *murderer and criminal*, it must be a word that describes someone who is bad. B and D are positive words, so you can eliminate them. C sounds much more like a description of a bad person than A, so the best choice is C.

5. According to the passage, Bjarni Herjolfsson left Norway to

   (A) start a new colony
   (B) open a trade route to America
   (C) visit his relatives
   (D) map the North Sea

The end of the first paragraph discusses Herjolfsson's departure. There it states, "Bjarni sailed from Norway to Iceland, heading for the Viking settlement where his father Heriulf resided." The correct answer will use different words, but it should restate this same idea. Can we find anything here about starting a colony? No, so A can be eliminated. Does it mention opening a trade route to America? No, so B can also be eliminated. (It's true that he does eventually reach America, but that isn't the reason why he left.) Does it mention visiting his relatives? Well, it does say that he wanted to find his father. So let's leave C. Does this sentence mention mapping the North Sea? No. C is the answer.

6. Bjarni's reaction upon landing in Iceland can best be described as

   (A) disappointed
   (B) satisfied
   (C) amused
   (D) fascinated

Where can we find a description of Bjarni Herjolfsson's arrival in Iceland? At the beginning of the second paragraph. There it states, "When he arrived in Iceland, Bjarni discovered that his father had already sold his land and estates and set out for the latest Viking settlement on the subarctic island called Greenland." Since he had missed his father, he was probably unhappy. Which word best states this idea? A.

7. When the author says, "The crew lost their bearings," this probably means that

   (A) the ship was damaged beyond repair
   (B) the sailors did not know which way they were going
   (C) the sailors were very angry
   (D) the sailors misplaced their clothes

Let's reread the lines around "the crew lost their bearings": "Since the Vikings traveled without a chart or compass, it was not uncommon for them to lose their way in the unpredictable northern seas. Beset by fog, the crew lost their bearings." Since the story says that the crew would often "lose their way," the best answer is B.

PROCESS OF ELIMINATION

If you're stuck on which answer is correct, remember to use Process of Elimination to cross off answers you know are wrong. On *general* questions, you'll usually want to cross off answers that:

- Are not mentioned in the passage.

- Are too detailed. If the passage mentions something in only one line, it is a detail, not a main idea.

- Go against, or say the opposite of, information in the passage.

- Are too big. You can't say much in four or five paragraphs; any answer that says something like, "The passage proves that the theory Einstein spent his entire life creating was right" is probably a wrong answer.

- Are too extreme. If a choice uses absolute terms such as "all," "every," "never," or "always," it's probably a wrong answer.

- Go against common sense.

On *specific* questions, you should probably cross off answers that:

- Are extreme.

- Go against information in the passage.

- Are not mentioned in the passage.

- Go against common sense.

If you look back at the questions in the sample reading comp passage above, you'll see that following these guidelines eliminates many of the wrong answer choices. Use these guidelines when you take the COOP!

WHAT KIND OF ANSWERS DO I KEEP?

Correct answers tend to be:

- Restatements or paraphrases of what is said in the passage.
- Traditional and conservative.
- Moderate, using words such as "may," "can," and "often."

COOP READING COMPREHENSION EXERCISE (ANSWERS ARE ON PAGE 82)

Try the following reading comprehension passage. Don't forget to label your paragraphs!

Although many people associate indoor lighting with modern electrical wiring, practical indoor lighting existed thousands of years before Thomas Edison invented the light bulb. <u>Rudimentary</u> oil lamps, a primitive ancestor of the gaslight, were used in the caves in which prehistoric humans lived.

_____

Approximately 50,000 years ago, cave-dwelling humanoids fashioned a basic oil-based lamp out of animal fat that was kept inside a stone base as well as a wick made out of a cloth-like material. Due to the fact that animal fat smells awful when burned, the lamp gave off a terrible odor.

_____

Thousands of years later, during the Egyptian era (around 1300 B.C.) the structure and design of the lamp changed. Instead of using only stone, the Egyptians used a form of decorated pottery with a papyrus-based wick and vegetable oil instead of the <u>foul</u>-smelling animal fat.

_____

In times of need people burned whatever oil was plentiful. Because vegetable oil and animal fat are both edible, in times of hunger people did not burn lamps; they used the oil for food. But oil lamps brought with them other problems. Wicks for the lamps did not always burn away and had to be changed periodically. Soon the oil lamp gave way to the candle, which became a popular source of light in Rome during the first century B.C.

_____

1. What is this passage mostly about?

    (A) how Egyptians lit their homes
    (B) why the candle is better than the oil lamp
    (C) the history of indoor lighting
    (D) why vegetable fat replaced animal fat in oil lamps

2. It can be inferred that the author views the change from oil lamps to candles as

    (A) the most important discovery of human history
    (B) a mistake made by the Romans
    (C) important to the discovery of electricity
    (D) a step in the development of indoor lighting

3. The word <u>rudimentary</u> most likely means

    (A) expensive
    (B) basic
    (C) colorful
    (D) handy

4. The author mentions Thomas Edison in the passage in order to

    (A) explain his discoveries
    (B) compare him with other modern inventors
    (C) introduce someone that the author will discuss later
    (D) show that Edison was not the first to discover indoor lighting

5. The word <u>foul</u> probably means

    (A) awful
    (B) sweet
    (C) fruity
    (D) clean

6. People probably stopped burning animal fat in lamps because

    (A) vegetable oil was more plentiful
    (B) they needed the animal fat for cooking
    (C) animal fat smelled bad
    (D) burning animal fat was against the law

7. The author's tone can best be described as

    (A) angry
    (B) unconcerned
    (C) instructive
    (D) critical

8

Mathematics

Most of the questions in this section require you to do some amount of arithmetic. Let's take a moment to review the basics.

MATH VOCABULARY

Term	Definition	Examples
integer	any number that does not contain either a fraction or a decimal	−4, −1, 0, 9, 15
positive number	any number greater than zero	$\frac{1}{2}$, 1, 4, 101
negative number	any number less than zero	$-\frac{1}{2}$, −1, −4, −101
even number	any number that is evenly divisible by two	−2, 0, 2, 8, 24 (note: 0 *is* even)
odd number	any number that is not evenly divisible by two	−1, 1, 5, 35
prime number	any number that is evenly divisible only by one and itself	2, 3, 5, 7, 11, 13 (note: 1 is *not* a prime number)
sum	the result of addition	The sum of 6 and 2 is 8.
difference	the result of subtraction	The difference between 6 and 4 is 2.
product	the result of multiplication	The product of 3 and 4 is 12.

COOP MATH VOCABULARY EXERCISE (ANSWERS ARE ON PAGE 83)

1. How many integers are there between −4 and 5?
2. How many positive integers are there between −4 and 5?
3. What is the sum of 6, 7, and 8?
4. What is the product of 2, 4, and 8?

ORDER OF OPERATIONS

How would you do the following problem?

$$4 + 5 \times 3 - (2 + 1)$$

Whenever you have a problem such as this, remember the rule.

Please Excuse My Dear Aunt Sally

Believe it or not, this sentence tells you the order in which you should solve the above problem. This stands for:

Parentheses
Exponents
Multiplication and Division (from left to right)
Addition and Subtraction (from left to right)

Therefore we need to solve the parentheses first.

$$4 + 5 \times 3 - (2 + .1)$$

becomes

$$4 + 5 \times 3 - 3$$

Next, we do multiplication and division to get

$$4 + 15 - 3$$

Finally, we add and subtract to get our final answer of 16.

COOP ORDER OF OPERATIONS EXERCISE (ANSWERS ARE ON PAGE 84)

1. $15 - 5 + 3 = $ __
2. $15 - 2 \times 3 = $ __
3. $2 \times (2 + 3) - 5 = $ __
4. $20 + 3 \times 5 + 10 = $ __
5. $(3 + 6) \times 3 \times 4 = $ __

FRACTIONS

A fraction is just another way of representing division. For instance, $\frac{2}{5}$ actually means two divided by five (which is 0.4 as a decimal). Another way to think of this is to imagine a pie cut into five pieces: $\frac{2}{5}$ means two out of the five pieces. The parts of the fraction are called the numerator and the denominator. The numerator is the number on top; the denominator is the number on the bottom.

$$\frac{\text{numerator}}{\text{denominator}}$$

REDUCING FRACTIONS

Often you'll need to reduce your fractions after you have made a calculation. This means that you want to make the numbers as small as possible. To reduce a fraction, simply divide top and bottom by the same number. Don't spend too long trying to figure out the best number to divide by; use 2, 3, or 5, and keep dividing until you can't divide anymore.

For example, if you have the fraction $\frac{42}{18}$, we can divide the top and bottom each by 3 to get $\frac{14}{6}$. Then we can divide top and bottom by 2 and get $\frac{7}{3}$. It can't be reduced any further than this, so this is your final answer.

ADDING AND SUBTRACTING FRACTIONS

To add or subtract fractions, the fractions have to have a common denominator. This means that they have to have the same number on the bottom (the denominators need to be the same). If the fractions already have a common denominator, you can add or subtract them by adding or subtracting the numbers on top.

$$\frac{4}{7}+\frac{2}{7}=\frac{6}{7}$$

If the fractions do not have a common denominator, the easiest way to add or subtract them is to use the Bowtie.

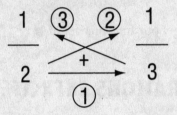

Step 1: Multiply the two bottom numbers together. Their product goes on the bottom of your two new fractions.

Step 2: Multiply diagonally from the bottom left to the top right. Write this product on the top right.

Step 3: Multiply diagonally from the bottom right to the top left. Write this product on the top left.

See—it looks like a bowtie! Now you have two fractions with a common denominator, and you can add or subtract them.

For example:

① $\frac{1}{2}$ ⟶ $\frac{1}{3}$ $\frac{}{6}$ + $\frac{}{6}$

② $\frac{1}{2}$ ⟋ $\frac{1}{3}$ $\frac{}{6}$ + $\frac{2}{6}$

③ $\frac{1}{2}$ ⟍ $\frac{1}{3}$ $\frac{3}{6}$ + $\frac{2}{6}$ = $\frac{5}{6}$

MULTIPLYING AND DIVIDING FRACTIONS

To multiply fractions, multiply straight across the top and bottom.

$$\frac{3}{5} \times \frac{1}{3} = \frac{3 \times 1}{5 \times 3} = \frac{3}{15}$$

To divide fractions, flip the second fraction and multiply.

$$\frac{3}{5} \div \frac{1}{3} = \frac{3 \times 3}{5 \times 1} = \frac{9}{5}$$

COOP FRACTIONS EXERCISE (ANSWERS ARE ON PAGE 83)

1. Reduce $\frac{12}{60} = $ ___

2. $\frac{3}{8} + \frac{2}{3} = $ ___

3. $\frac{3}{4} - \frac{2}{3} = $ ___

4. $\frac{3}{5} \times \frac{3}{2} = $ ___

5. $\frac{1}{3} \div \frac{1}{2} = $ ___

DECIMALS

Remember that decimals are just another way of writing fractions. Be sure to know the names of all the decimal places.

$$3 \; 4 \cdot 8 \; 5 \; 7$$

tens
units
tenths
hundredths
thousandths

ADDING DECIMALS

To add decimals, just line up the decimal places and add.

$$\begin{array}{r} 24.05 \\ +\ 12.23 \\ \hline 36.28 \end{array}$$

SUBTRACTING DECIMALS

To subtract decimals, just line up the decimal places and subtract.

$$\begin{array}{r} 24.05 \\ -\ 12.23 \\ \hline 11.82 \end{array}$$

MULTIPLYING DECIMALS

To multiply decimals, count the total number of digits to the right of the decimal point in the numbers you are multiplying. Then multiply the numbers without the decimal points. Once you have your answer, add back into the new number all of the decimal places you removed from the first two numbers.

To solve 0.2 × 3.4, remove two decimal places and multiply.

$$\begin{array}{r} 34 \\ \times\ 2 \\ \hline 68 \end{array}$$

Now put back the two decimal places we removed to get 0.68.

DIVIDING DECIMALS

To divide decimals, move the decimal places in both numbers the same number of places to the right until you are working with only integers. But unlike when you're multiplying decimals, you don't have to put the decimals back in when you're dividing.

$$3.4 \div 0.2 = 34 \div 2 = 17$$

CONVERTING DECIMALS TO FRACTIONS

Remember that multiplying by 10 means the same thing as moving the decimal point one place to the right, and dividing by 10 means the same thing as moving the decimal points one place to the left.

$$9 \div 10 = \frac{9}{10} = 0.9$$

$$5 \div 100 = \frac{5}{100} = 0.05$$

This is why the first place to the right of the decimal is called "tenths" and the second place to the right is called "hundredths." Nine tenths = 0.9 = $\frac{9}{10}$. Five hundredths = 0.05 = $\frac{5}{100}$. So to convert a decimal to a fraction, all you need to do is change the numbers after the decimal to their fraction form.

$$5.24 = 5 + \frac{2}{10} + \frac{4}{100}$$

COOP DECIMALS EXERCISE (ANSWERS ARE ON PAGE 83)

1. $2.43 + 5.25 = \underline{\quad}$

2. $5.75 - 3.12 = \underline{\quad}$

3. $1.5 \times 3 = \underline{\quad}$

4. $2.5 \times 0.5 = \underline{\quad}$

5. $2.5 \div 0.5 = \underline{\quad}$

6. What is 6.32 in fraction form? $\underline{\quad}$

EXPONENTS, SCIENTIFIC NOTATION, AND SQUARE ROOTS

Exponents are just a short way of writing multiplication. 3^2 means to multiply two 3s together: 3×3. Likewise, 3^4 means to multiply four 3s together: $3 \times 3 \times 3 \times 3$. On the COOP you will not see very complex exponents, so the best way to solve them is to write them out longhand and multiply.

Scientific notation is also a short way of writing big numbers. Whenever you see a number such as 3.44×10^2, this means that you should move the decimal point to the right the same number of places as the exponent to the 10. In this case, you move the decimal two places to the right (10^2), and you get 344. Likewise, 4.355×10^2 is just another way of writing 435.5.

Square root is just the opposite of raising a number to the second power. $\sqrt{4} = 2$, since $2^2 = 4$. On the COOP you will not have very big square roots. Your best bet is simply to memorize these common ones.

$$\text{Since } 2^2 = 4, \quad \sqrt{4} = 2.$$
$$\text{Since } 3^2 = 9, \quad \sqrt{9} = 3.$$
$$\text{Since } 4^2 = 16, \quad \sqrt{16} = 4.$$
$$\text{Since } 5^2 = 25, \quad \sqrt{25} = 5.$$

COOP EXPONENTS, SCIENTIFIC NOTATION, AND SQUARE ROOTS EXERCISE (ANSWERS ARE ON PAGE 84)

1. $4^3 = \underline{}$

2. $2^4 = \underline{}$

3. $3.4 \times 10^2 = \underline{}$

4. $5.23 \times 10^4 = \underline{}$

5. $\sqrt{4} + \sqrt{16} = \underline{}$

SOLVE FOR X

To solve an equation, you want to get the variable (the x) on one side of the equation and put everything else on the other side.

To get only the variable on one side, follow these two steps.

Step 1: Move elements around using addition and subtraction. Put the variables on one side of the equation and numbers on the other. As long as you do the same operation on both sides of the equal sign, you aren't changing the value of the variable.

Step 2: Divide both sides of the equation by the coefficient, which is the number in front of the variable. If that number is a fraction, multiply everything by the denominator.

For example:

$$3x + 5 = 17$$
$$3x + 5 = 17$$

Subtract 5 from each side.

$$\underline{-5 = -5}$$
$$3x = 12$$

Divide 3 from each side.

$$\underline{\div 3 = \div 3}$$
$$x = 4$$

Always remember the rule of equations: *Whatever you do to one side of the equation, you must also do to the other side.*

COOP SOLVE FOR *X* EXERCISE (ANSWERS ARE ON PAGE 84)

1. If $4x = 20$ then $x =$ __

2. If $4x + 3 = 31$ then $x =$ __

3. If $6 = 8x + 4$ then $x =$ __

4. If $4x - 3 = 3x$ then $x =$ __

PERCENT TRANSLATION

Everyone knows how easy it is to make a simple mistake on a percent problem. Should you write "5% of 100" as $\dfrac{5}{100}$ or as $\dfrac{100}{5}$ or as something else? To make sure to avoid silly mistakes, here's a foolproof method for solving percent questions. Any percent problem can be translated word for word into an equation if you know the mathematical equivalent of the English words. For instance, "percent" means the same thing as "divide by 100," and "of" means the same thing as "multiply." Therefore, "5% of 100" can be written as $\dfrac{5}{100} \times 100$, which equals 5.

The chart below shows you the mathematical translation of the English words you will probably see. To solve any percent question, read the problem back to yourself and replace the words on the left side of the chart with the math symbols on the right. Then you can easily solve.

Percent	÷ 100
Of	×
What	x (or any variable)
Is, Are, Equals	=

Here are two examples:
20% of 50 is?

$$\begin{array}{ccc} 20\% & \text{of} & 50 \\ \downarrow & \downarrow & \downarrow \\ \dfrac{20}{100} & \times & 50 \end{array}$$

5 is what percent of 80?

$$\begin{array}{cccc} 5 & \text{is} & \text{what percent} & \text{of } 80 \\ \downarrow & \downarrow & \downarrow & \\ 5 & = & \dfrac{x}{100} & \times \quad 80 \end{array}$$

$$5 = \dfrac{x}{100} \times 80$$

COOP PERCENT TRANSLATION EXERCISE (ANSWERS ARE ON PAGE 84)

1. 30% of 60 = __

2. 40% of 200 = __

3. 15 is what percent of 60? __

4. What is 25% of 10% of 200? __

RATIOS AND PROPORTIONS

WHAT IS A RATIO?

A ratio is a way of stating the relationship of two numbers in a reduced form. For instance, if there are 50 boys and 25 girls in a room, we can say that the ratio of boys to girls is 50 to 25. But we can also reduce this ratio just like a fraction: $\frac{50}{25} = \frac{2}{1}$. So we can also say that the ratio of boys to girls is 2 to 1. This is sometimes written as "The ratio of boys to girls is 2:1."

Of course, if we say that the ratio of boys to girls is 2 to 1, this doesn't tell us exactly how many boys and girls there are. The actual number could be 8 boys and 4 girls, or 10 boys and 5 girls, or 200 boys and 100 girls. Each of these can be reduced to the ratio 2 to 1.

But if we know one of the actual values, we can always solve for the other one. For instance, if we know that the ratio of boys to girls is 2 to 1, and there are 200 boys, we know that there must be 100 girls. Most of you can probably do that in your heads. But how do you calculate it?

SOLVING RATIO AND PROPORTION PROBLEMS

The way you solve almost all ratio and proportion questions is by setting up two fractions and cross multiplying.

$$\frac{A}{B} = \frac{C}{D}$$

Whenever you set up two equal fractions, you know that A × B is equal to C × D. The only thing you have to make sure to do is keep the same thing on top and bottom of each fraction.

In this case, if we know that the ratio of boys to girls is 2 to 1 and that there are 200 boys, we can figure out the number of girls by setting up these fractions.

$$\frac{\text{boys}}{\text{girls}} \frac{2}{1} = \frac{200}{x}$$

Now we can cross multiply: We know that $2x = 1 \times 200$. This means that $x = 100$.

Take a look at the following problem.

10. John has a bowl of red and blue marbles. The ratio of red to blue marbles is 5 to 4. If there are 35 red marbles in the bowl, how many blue marbles are in the bowl?

   (A) 16
   (B) 20
   (C) 28
   (D) 39

Here's how to crack it

Let's set up our fractions, with red marbles on top and blue marbles on the bottom. It will look like this.

$$\frac{red}{blue}\frac{5}{4} = \frac{35}{x}$$

Now we can cross multiply. We know that $5x = 4 \times 35$. After we multiply, $5x = 140$. We can solve for x by dividing both sides by 5 to get $x = 28$. Therefore there are 28 blue marbles in the bowl, which is C.

AVERAGES

The formula we use to figure out the average is

$$average = \frac{sum\ total}{\#\ of\ things}$$

For instance, if you take 3 tests on which you score 50, 55, and 57, the sum total of your scores is $50 + 55 + 57$, or 162. Since the number of tests was 3, the average on these tests must be $\frac{162}{3} = 54$.

Try the following problem.

11. During a certain month, David counted the number of apples he ate each week. He ate 2 apples during the first week, 4 apples during the second week, and 2 apples during the third week. The fourth week he ate no apples. On average, how many apples did David eat each week of the month?

   (A) 2
   (B) $2\frac{1}{2}$
   (C) $3\frac{1}{3}$
   (D) 7

The total number of apples David ate was $2 + 4 + 2$, or 8. This sum total, over the number of weeks, will give us the average: $\frac{8}{4} = 2$.

PLUGGING IN THE ANSWER CHOICES

Very often you may think that you need to do a lot of complicated math work to set up a problem. This is especially true on those long, wordy problems that give everyone headaches.

You know, however, that one of the answer choices given has to be the correct answer. All you've got to do is figure out which one. Therefore, the easiest way to solve many problems is by simply plugging in each answer choice until you find the one that works. Plugging In just means substituting numbers to figure out the answer quickly.

Take a look at the following problem.

12. If $x(x + 4) = 12$, which of the following could be the value of x?
    - **(A)** −1
    - **(B)** 0
    - **(C)** 1
    - **(D)** 2

You might think that you have to do some complicated algebra to solve this problem, but you really don't. Let's just try plugging in each answer choice for the value of x and see which one makes the equation work.

If we plug in −1 for x, does $-1(-1 + 4) = 12$? No. Cross off A. If we plug in 0 for x, does $0(0 + 4) = 12$? No. Cross off B. If we plug in 1 for x, does $1(1 + 4) = 12$? No. Cross off C. If we plug in 2 for x, does $2(2 + 4) = 12$? Yes, so D is the answer.

Let's try one more:

13. David is five years older than his brother Jim, and Jim is twice as old as Ann. If David is 12 years older than Ann, how old is Jim?
    - **(A)** 20
    - **(B)** 15
    - **(C)** 10
    - **(D)** 8

The question asks how old Jim is, so this is what we'll be plugging in for. Let's start with A. Could Jim be 20? We know that David is five years older than Jim, so if Jim is 20, then David is 25. We also know that Jim is twice as old as Ann, so Ann must be 10. But the last sentence says that David should be 10 years older than Ann, which he's not. Therefore A can't be the answer.

How about B? Could Jim be 15? We know that David is five years older than Jim, so if Jim is 15, then David must be 20. We also know that Jim is twice as old as Ann, so Ann must be $7\frac{1}{2}$. But the last sentence says that David should be 10 years older than Ann, which he's not. Therefore B can't be the answer.

Let's try C. Could Jim be 10? We know that David is five years older than Jim, so if Jim is 10, then David is 15. We also know that Jim is twice as old as Ann, so Ann must be 5. Does this make David 10 years older than Ann? Yes. So C is the answer.

Here's a slightly harder problem. Trying to solve it using algebra is difficult, but by plugging in the answer choices, it becomes very easy.

14. If the average of 4 and x is equal to the average of 5, 4, and x, what is the value of x?

    (A) 1
    (B) 2
    (C) 6
    (D) 8

Let's start with A, and plug 1 in for x. Does the average of 4 and 1 (which is 2.5) equal the average of 5, 4, and 1 (which is $\frac{10}{3}$)? No, so A can be eliminated. Let's try B. Does the average of 4 and 2 (which is 3) equal the average of 5, 4, and 3 (which is 4)? No. B can also be eliminated. How about C? Does the average of 4 and 6 (which is 5) equal the average of 5, 4, and 6 (which is 5)? Yes. C is the answer.

PLUGGING IN YOUR OWN NUMBERS

The problem with doing algebra is that it's just too easy to make a mistake. Whenever you see a problem with variables (x's) in the answer choices, PLUG IN. Start by picking a number for the variable in the problem (or for more than one variable, if necessary); solve the problem using that real number; then see which answer choice gives you the correct answer.

Have a look at the following problem:

15. If x is a positive integer, then 20 percent of $5x$ equals

    (A) x
    (B) $2x$
    (C) $5x$
    (D) $15x$

Let's start by picking a number for x. Let's plug in the nice round number 10. When we plug in 10 for x, we change every x in the whole problem into a 10. Now the problem reads:

15. If 10 is a positive integer, then 20 percent of 5(10) equals

    (A) 10
    (B) 2(10)
    (C) 5(10)
    (D) 15(10)

Look how easy the problem becomes! Now we can solve: 20 percent of 50 is 10. Which answer says 10? A does.

Let's try it again.

16. If $0 < x < 1$, then which of the following is true?
    (A) $x > 0$
    (B) $x > 1$
    (C) $x > 2$
    (D) $2x > 2$

This time when we pick a number for x, we have to make sure that it is between 0 and 1, because that's what the problem states. So let's try $\frac{1}{2}$. If we make every x in the problem into $\frac{1}{2}$, the answer choices now read:

(A) $\frac{1}{2} > 0$

(B) $\frac{1}{2} > 1$

(C) $\frac{1}{2} > 2$

(D) $1 > 2$

Which one of these is true? A. Plugging In is such a great technique that it makes even the hardest algebra problems easy. *Anytime you can, plug in!*

GEOMETRY

LINES AND ANGLES

On every line, all the angles must add up to a total of 180 degrees.

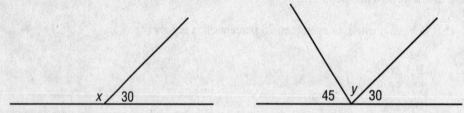

Since x and 30 must add up to 180, we know that x must measure $180 - 30$, or 150 degrees. Since 45, y, and 30 must add up to 180, we know that y must measure $180 - 45 - 30$, or 105 degrees.

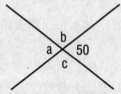

In this case, b and the angle measuring 50 are on a line together. This means that b must measure 130 ($180 - 50 = 130$). Also, c and the angle measuring 50 are on a line together. This means that c must also measure 130 ($180 - 50 = 130$). Finally, a must measure 50, because $a + b$ (and we already know that $b = 130$) must measure 180 ($50 + 130 = 180$).

This explains why vertical angles (the angles opposite each other when two lines cross) are always equal. Angles b and c are both 130, and angle a (which is opposite the angle 50) is 50.

In a triangle, all the angles must add up to 180 degrees. In a four-sided figure, all the angles must add up to 360 degrees.

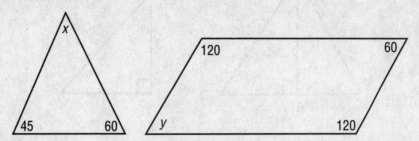

In this triangle, two of the angles are 45 and 60. They make a total of 105 degrees. The sum of the angles needs to equal 180. Therefore angle x must be 180 – 105, or 75 degrees.

In the figure on the right, three of the angles have a total of 300 degrees. Therefore y must be equal to 360 – 300, or 60 degrees.

A triangle is *isosceles* if it has two equal sides. This means that the two opposite angles are also equal. A triangle is *equilateral* if it has three equal sides. This means that all three angles are equal. Since these angles must equally divide 180 degrees, they must each be 60.

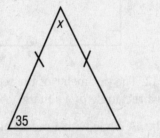

The triangle on the left is isosceles, so the two bottom angles must each be 35 degrees. This makes a total of 70 degrees for the two bottom angles. Since all of the angles must add up to 180, we know that x is equal to 180 – 70, or 110 degrees.

AREA, PERIMETER, AND CIRCUMFERENCE

The area of a square or rectangle is length × width.

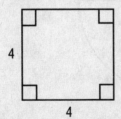
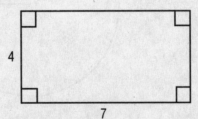

The area of this square is 4 × 4, or 16. The area of the rectangle is 4 × 7, or 28.

The area of a triangle is $\frac{1}{2}$ base × height.

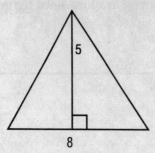
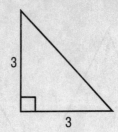

The area of the triangle on the left is $\frac{1}{2} \times 5 \times 8$, or 20.

The area of the triangle on the right is $\frac{1}{2} \times 3 \times 3$, or $4\frac{1}{2}$.

The perimeter of any object is the sum of the lengths of its sides.

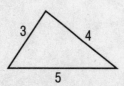
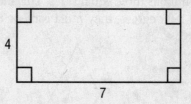

The perimeter of the triangle is 3 + 4 + 5, or 12. The perimeter of the rectangle is 4 + 7 + 4 + 7, or 22 (opposite sides are always equal to each other in a rectangle or a square).

The circumference of a circle with radius *r* is $2\pi r$. A circle with a radius of 5 has a circumference of 10π. The area of a circle with radius *r* is πr^2. A circle with a radius of 5 has an area of 25π.

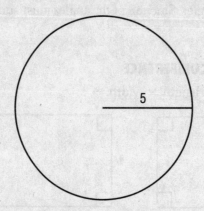

COOP GEOMETRY EXERCISE (ANSWERS ARE ON PAGE 84)

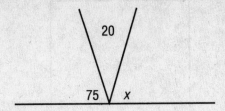

1. In the figure above, what is the value of x?

2. In the figure above, what is the value of $y + z$?

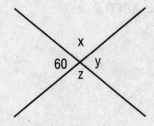

3. In the figure above, what is the value of x?

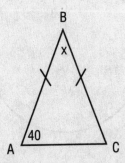

4. If triangle ABC is isosceles, what is the value of x?

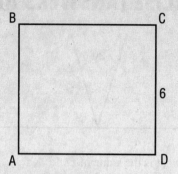

5. What is the area of square *ABCD* above?

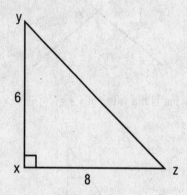

6. What is the area of triangle *XYZ* above?

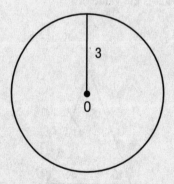

7a. What is the area of the circle above with center *O*?

7b. What is its circumference?

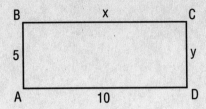

8a. If *ABCD* is a rectangle, *x* = __ and *y* = __

8b. What is the perimeter of rectangle *ABCD*?

9
Language Expression

USAGE QUESTIONS

Most of the questions in the language expressions section of the COOP will ask you to look at five sentences and figure out which one is correctly written. Some of the sentences can be eliminated because they violate the rule of English grammar. Others are wrong because they are awkward or hard to understand.

> **Follow this procedure for attacking usage questions.**

> Step 1: Read all five sentences, and eliminate any choice that breaks a rule of grammar.

> Step 2: Reread the choices that are left, and cross off any that are awkward or don't make sense.

The sentence you are left with may not sound great, but you should always pick the one that is the best of the bunch—the one that makes the *most* sense. If you can't narrow it down to only one sentence, that's okay. Cross off what you can, and guess from among the remaining choices.

ERRORS

What kind of errors should you look for? The COOP tests only a few kinds of errors. Learn them, and you'll know what to look for and can greatly increase your score.

SUBJECT/VERB AGREEMENT

What is wrong with the following sentences?

1. The cats in the house watches the bird.

2. A wild dingo from Sydney were caught last year.

To spot subject/verb agreement errors, always find the subject and the verb in the given sentence. To find the subject, ask yourself, "Who or what is acting or being described?" To find the verb, find the action word by asking yourself, "What is the subject doing?" Then make sure that the subject and the verb agree. Subjects and verbs have to agree in both number (singular or plural) and person (I, she, we, you). You may have to read around other parts of the sentence to make it clear to yourself.

What is the subject in sentence 1? It's the cats who are watching the bird. Can you say, "The cats **watches** the bird"? No. *Cats*, in this case, is plural—more than one cat—so the verb has to agree. It should be "The cats **watch** the bird."

What is the subject in sentence 2? A wild dingo is the thing being described. Can you say, "A wild dingo **were** caught last year"? No; in this case *dingo* is singular, and the verb has to agree with a singular subject. It should be "A wild dingo **was** caught last year."

VERB FORM AND TENSE

What is wrong with the following sentences?

3. Yesterday, John is going to the playground.

4. Patricia has took her hamster to the vet.

Verb Tense

The word yesterday in sentence 3 tells us that the verb should be in the past tense. You can see that this sentence has an error because it clearly says that the action happened yesterday, but the verb "is going" is in the present tense. The sentence should read "Yesterday, John **went** to the playground." *Went* is the past tense of the infinitive verb *to go*. To spot tense problems, look for words and phrases that indicate present or past, such as:

- today (present)
- now (present)
- yesterday (past)
- last week (past)
- in 1956 (past)
- once (past)
- a long time ago (past)
- during the Second World War (past)

Verb Form

Sometimes the error will be in the verb form, such as in sentence 4. Recognizing correct verb form is as simple as knowing the proper present, past, and future forms of verbs. The COOP will ask you not to identify and name verb forms, just to choose the correct version of the sentence. Usually, it should be obvious to you when a verb form is wrong because the sentence just won't make sense. The past tense form of the verb *to take* would be either *took* or *has taken*. You could say, "Patricia **took** her hamster to the vet" or "Patricia **has taken** her hamster to the vet." But *has took* is not a possible form. Make sure that you review proper verb forms as part of your preparation for the COOP.

ADJECTIVE/ADVERB

What is wrong with the following sentence?

5. Kim ran quick around the track.

What is the word *quick* describing? The way that Kim ran around the track. If a word describes a person or a thing, it should be an adjective like *quick*. But if a word describes an action (verb), it should be an adverb like *quickly*. Don't forget: Most adverbs end in *-ly*.

Remember this rule: Adjectives modify nouns; adverbs modify everything else.

COMPARISON WORDS

What is wrong with the following sentences?

6. He was one of the most greatest authors of his time.

7. She is intelligenter than he is.

Some questions on the COOP will ask you to determine the right form of a comparison word. In the sentences above, *greatest* and *more intelligent* are the correct forms of the comparison words. For most adjectives that have only one syllable, we make them into comparison words by adding *-er* and *-est* to the end of the word, such as big, bigger, biggest and great, greater, greatest.

For most adjectives with more than one syllable, we make the comparison using the words *more* and *most*, as with intelligent, more intelligent, most intelligent and interesting, more interesting, most interesting.

PRONOUN AGREEMENT AND CASE

What is wrong with the following sentences?

8. The dog ran away, but they came back soon.

9. Murray is a man which loves to play the piano.

10. Olivia gave the assignment to Peter and I.

Pronouns are words such as *I*, *it*, *they*, *me*, and *she* that take the place of nouns. Whenever you see pronouns in a sentence, check to make sure that they agree with the nouns they stand for and that they are in the proper case. Pronoun *agreement* means that singular pronouns stand in for singular nouns, and plural pronouns stand in for plural nouns. In sentence 8, the subject is "the dog," which is singular, but the pronoun "they" is plural. The sentence should read "The dog ran away, but **it** came back soon."

Another important rule to remember is to use the pronoun *who* for people and *which* or *that* for things. Therefore sentence 9 should read "Murray is a man **who** loves to play the piano."

Pronoun *case* means that the subject of the sentence (the thing doing the acting) needs a subject pronoun, and the object of a sentence (the thing receiving the action) needs an object pronoun. In the sentence "Mary threw the ball to John," Mary is the subject and John is the object. Below is a chart that tells you how to use a pronoun whether it is the subject or the object.

Subject	Example		Object	Example
I	I left the office.		me	My boss told me to go home.
you	You should get some rest.		you	A good night's sleep would do you some good.
he/she/it	He knew the best route to take.		him/her/it	Jenny refused to tell him the best route to take.
we	We love to visit our grandparents.		us	Our grandparents love us.
they	They live in California.		them	We visited them in California.

In sentence 10, does the word *I* describe someone who is giving the book (a subject) or someone to whom the book was given (an object)? Think about it this way: We say *I* gave it to *him*, but *he* gave it to *me*. In the example sentence, the word *I* describes someone who received the action, not someone who was doing the action. So the pronoun used should be the object pronoun, and the sentence should read "Olivia gave the assignment to Peter and **me**." If you are confused about the correct answer, try this trick: Take away the word *Peter* and see what is left. You wouldn't say, "Olivia gave the assignment to I," but you would say, "Olivia gave the assignment to me."

Important note: Whenever a pronoun follows a preposition (such as *to, of, in, at, around, between*, and *from*) the pronouns are *always* in the object case.

Here are some common pronoun mix-ups. Don't forget them because recognizing them is a simple way to rack up points on the COOP.

it's = it is	It's raining outside.
its = belongs to it	The dog eats its bone.
you're = you are	You're a great friend.
your = belongs to you	I love your shoes.
who's = who is	Who's at the door?
whose = belongs to who	Whose car is this?

SENTENCE FRAGMENTS

What is wrong with the following sentences?

11. Told me that I would have to see the dentist.

12. The elephant, after eating dinner, walking around the zoo.

Every sentence has to express a complete thought and have both a subject and a verb. What is the subject in sentence 11? Who or what told me to go to the dentist? There is no subject in this sentence, and therefore it is only a sentence fragment. Sentence fragments are not complete sentences and are never the correct answer on the COOP.

Sentence 12 has a subject—the elephant—but it has no true verb. It is also a fragment so we know it's an error!

PARALLELISM

What is wrong with the following sentences?

13. Lawrence left the house and going to school.

14. Erica wanted to eat lunch, visit her friend, and to play soccer.

Whenever you read a sentence that contains a list of actions or objects, check to make sure that the items in the list are all in the same form. For instance, in sentence 13 there are two actions. The first action is that Lawrence left the house. So the second action must be in the same form; however, *left* and *going* aren't in the same form. The second part of the sentence should read "Lawrence **went** to school" to make this a parallel sentence.

In sentence 14, there are three items that Erica wanted: *to eat* lunch, *visit* her friend, and *to play* soccer. Are these three items in the same form? No. The first and third items in the list use the infinitive verb forms—*to eat* and *to play*—but the second does not. To be parallel and correct, the sentence should read "Erica wanted to eat lunch, **to visit** her friend, and to play soccer."

DOUBLE NEGATIVE

What is wrong with the following sentence?

Paul has hardly seen no birds today.

In English, you should have only one negative word in the same phrase. When a sentence has two, it is called a double negative. All of the following are double negatives, and are always considered incorrect.

- can't hardly
- can't never
- barely none
- barely never
- won't never
- won't hardly
- hardly never
- hardly none
- hasn't got none

COOP ERRORS EXERCISE (ANSWERS ARE ON PAGE 85)

1. There is already many people in the auditorium.
2. Since my father's company has so much business, they are very busy.
3. My uncle often help my parents to make dinner.
4. Henry going to school, runs into his friend.
5. The giant mouse ran through the house and escaping from the cat.
6. Last year, Ines won the first prize and receives a beautiful trophy.
7. Roger finished his most biggest assignment.
8. Colin cleaned the bowl and gives it to his mother.

SENTENCE COMPLETIONS

A few questions in the language expression section will ask you to complete a sentence by filling in a blank.

Some of the questions in this section of the COOP will test how well you can pick the correct word based on the "direction" of the sentence.

How would you fill in the blanks in the following sentences?

1. I really like you _____ you are very friendly.
2. I really like you _____ you are a very nasty person.

In sentence 1, you probably picked a word like "because." How did you know that this word was the right one to choose? Because the idea after the blank ("are very friendly") kept going in the *same direction* as the idea before the blank ("I really like you"). The sentence started out with a positive idea and continued with a positive idea.

In sentence 2, you probably picked something like "but," "although," or "even though." Why? Because the idea after the blank ("you are a very nasty person") went in the *opposite direction* from the idea before the blank ("I really like you"). The sentence started out with a positive idea and then changed to a negative idea.

Here are lists of same-direction and opposite-direction words:

Same-Direction

- and
- moreover
- in fact
- for instance
- for example
- so
- therefore
- because
- since

Opposite-Direction

- however
- but
- yet
- although
- though
- nevertheless
- nonetheless
- despite
- rather
- instead
- in contrast

Try the following example:

3. Susie's mother wanted her to be a dancer; _____ Susie felt like becoming a doctor.

   (A) because,
   (B) however,
   (C) in fact,
   (D) rather,
   (E) in general,

Here's how to crack it

In this case, the idea after the blank ("becoming a doctor") goes in the opposite direction from the idea before the blank ("be a dancer"). Therefore we can eliminate A, C, and E. If you get no further, you have a great guess. The best choice is B.

Other questions will test the same rules of grammar you have already learned earlier in this chapter—especially the rules of comparison words and double negatives.

Here is a sample problem.

4. John is the _____ player on our soccer team.

   (A) more important
   (B) most important
   (C) much important
   (D) importanter
   (E) importantest

Here's how to crack it

We've already learned that with comparison words that have more than one syllable, we can only use *more* or *most*. C, D, and E are not grammatically correct and can be eliminated. Since we are comparing John with all the other players on the team, we want to use *most important*, B.

FIND THE SUBJECT/PREDICATE

You'll also see a set of questions that asks you for the simple subject of the sentence, while some questions will ask you for the simple predicate (verb) of the sentence.

What is a simple subject? The simple subject is always the noun that is performing the action or being described in a sentence. This means that the simple subject:

1. must be a noun (person, place, or thing) and

2. is not describing something else

The tricky part is usually #2. Nouns can be used to describe things when they are used after words such as *in, on, at, around, under, after, when*, and *that*.

Look at the following sentences:

5. The cat is on the mat.

6. The cat that belongs to John is on the mat.

7. After eating lunch in the kitchen, the cat took a bath.

8. When John came home, the cat began to run around the house.

In sentence 5, the word *mat* is a noun, but it is part of the phrase "on the mat," which describes where the cat is sitting. Therefore *mat* cannot be the simple subject. In sentence 6, the word *John* is a noun, but it is part of the phrase "that belongs to John," which describes the cat. Therefore *John* cannot be the simple subject. In sentence 7, the words *lunch* and *kitchen* are nouns, but they are part of the phrase "After eating lunch in the kitchen," which describe what the cat did earlier in the day. In sentence 8, the words *John, home*, and *house* are nouns, but they are part of phrases that describe the cat.

In all four sentences, "the cat" is the simple subject.

Follow these steps to answer questions that ask you for the simple subject.

Step 1: Cross off any words that you know are not nouns—verbs, adjectives, and adverbs.

Step 2: Cross off any words that are not the simple subject—any noun that follows a preposition such as *in, at, of,* or *to* and any noun that appears in a phrase that begins with *if, when, since, after,* or *that.*

What is a simple predicate (verb)? The simple predicate is always the main verb in a sentence. This means that the simple predicate:

1. must be a verb (an action word) and

2. is not describing something else

Again, the tricky part is #2. Just like nouns, verbs can be used to describe other things when they appear in phrases that begin with words such as *if, when, after,* and *that.*

9. The cat slept on the mat that John made in school.

10. Since she was tired from running in the park, the cat slept on the mat.

11. While John cooked dinner, the cat slept on the mat.

In sentence 9, the word *made* is a verb, but it is part of the phrase "that John made," which describes who made the mat. Therefore *made* cannot be the simple verb. In sentence 10, the word *was* is a verb, but it is part of the phrase "Since she was tired," which describes the cat. Therefore *was* cannot be the simple verb. In sentence 11, the word *cooked* is a verb, but it is part of the phrase "While John cooked dinner," which describes what John did while the cat was asleep.

In all three sentences, "slept" is the simple predicate.

Follow these steps to answer questions that ask you for the simple predicate.

Step 1: Cross off any words that you know are not verbs—nouns, adjectives, and adverbs.

Step 2: Cross off any words that are not the simple verb—any verb that follows a word such as *if, when, since, after,* or *that.*

COOP SIMPLE SUBJECT EXERCISE (ANSWERS ARE ON PAGE 86)

1. After many years, Jonathan finally found his favorite cat.

2. The most important part was probably the discovery of the Northwest Passage.

3. When she figured out the answer, her teacher was very pleased with her.

4. If he had known about his neighbor's collie, he never would have said that his dog was the fastest.

COOP SIMPLE PREDICATE EXERCISE (ANSWERS ARE ON PAGE 86)

1. Since his sister had already washed the dishes, Jonas volunteered to dry them.

2. In order to finish the race without falling down, Alexandra drank a great deal of water.

3. Adrienne never imagined that she would be chosen to play the leading role in the production.

4. Because Laurie ate too much, she felt too sick to play soccer.

STRUCTURE QUESTIONS

A few questions in this section will ask you to choose which sentences fit best with other sentences in a paragraph. You may be asked to find:

- The best topic sentence
- The sentences that best follow a topic sentence
- Which sentence belongs in the paragraph
- Which sentence does not belong in the paragraph

To answer all of these questions, make sure that the ideas are in a logical order from one sentence to the next.

What is a topic sentence? A topic sentence is the first sentence in a paragraph, and it is supposed to introduce the idea that will follow. The sentences that follow the topic sentence should talk more about the subject that is mentioned in the topic sentence. To answer a question that asks you to find the best topic sentence, you should read the sentences in the paragraph and ask yourself, "What are these sentences talking about?" Then look at the choices and find the choice that talks about this idea.

To answer a question that asks you to find the sentences that should follow a topic sentence, read the topic sentence and ask yourself, "What is the main idea in this topic sentence?" Then find the sentences that describe this idea in more detail.

To answer a question that asks you which sentence belongs in the paragraph, read the sentences before and after the blank. You should find a sentence that discusses the same ideas as the sentences before and after it, while watching out for same-direction or opposite-direction words.

To answer a question that asks you which sentence does not belong, read the paragraph and ask yourself what the paragraph is about. Then reread it, and find the sentence that does not discuss this same idea or suddenly changes the topic.

Take a look at the following examples.

20. Which of the following is the best topic sentence for this paragraph?

_____. It was first made in China around 100 B.C. from bits of plants and tree bark. At first it was rough, and not very suitable for official documents. Soon, however, people found ways to make it flat and even. Over the next few hundred years, paper was introduced to the rest of Asia, where it was used to keep government documents and religious inscriptions.

(A) Today, many documents are stored electronically instead of on paper.
(B) The ancient Chinese discovered many useful things.
(C) Paper has a long and interesting history.
(D) Modern governments would not be able to survive without paper.
(E) One interesting kind of art is the making of beautiful paper.

If we read the paragraph, we see that it is mostly about the history of paper. Therefore, the topic sentence should introduce this idea. B is not specifically about paper at all, and A, D, and E are not about the history of paper. Therefore, C is the best choice.

21. Which of the following sentences does not belong in the paragraph?

[1]One of the most loved musical styles today is blues. [2]Blues originated in the early 1900s in America. [3]It was born from a combination of African-American work chants and gospel songs. [4]The blues got its name from the introduction of special "blue notes," which are created by "bending" normal notes up or down. [5]These blue notes give the song a certain sad sound that people recognize as part of the blues. [6]While some people like sad music, other people prefer happier songs. [7]In the 1920s, blues began to incorporate elements from jazz, dance music, and show tunes. [8]Today, blues has spread to many different countries and is one of the most popular types of music in the world.

(A) sentence 2
(B) sentence 3
(C) sentence 4
(D) sentence 5
(E) sentence 6

If we read the paragraph, we see that it is about the musical style called blues. Each sentence talks about this idea except for sentence 6, which talks about whether people like happy or sad music. This makes E the best choice.

10

Answers to
COOP Exercises

CHAPTER 3

COOP MEMORY EXERCISE

1. D
2. D
3. E
4. E
5. D
6. E
7. C
8. D
9. D
10. E
11. A
12. B
13. B
14. A
15. A
16. C
17. B
18. A
19. C
20. D

CHAPTER 4

COOP SEQUENCE EXERCISE

1. B   The first element has 1 black dot, the second has 2, and the third has 3, so the fourth should have 4 black dots.

2. C   The middle of each element should follow the pattern – + – + , so D can be eliminated. The first two groups have all squares, so the final two elements should have all circles.

3. A   In each element, the letter "F" makes a quarter-turn. Therefore the missing element should be a quarter-turn more.

4. **D**   4 (+ 4) 8 (+ 4) 12 | 11 (+ 4) 15 (+ 4) 19 | 21 (+ 4) 25 (+ 4) **29**

5. **A**   38 (– 6) 32 (– 6) 26 | 17 (– 6) 11 (– 6) 5 | 42 (– 6) **36** (– 6) 30

6. **B**   6 (× 2) 12 (+ 4) 16 | 4 (× 2) 8 (+ 4) 12 | 5 (× 2) 10 (+ 4) **14**

7. **B**   10 (– 5) 5 (+ 10) 15 | 13 (– 5) 8 (+ 10) 18 | 22 (– 5) **17** (+ 10) 27

8. **D**   8 (× 2) 16 (+ 4) 20 | 4 (× 2) 8 (+ 4) 12 | 20(× 2) **40** (+ 4) 44

9. **C**   20 (– 2) 18 (+ 7) 25 | 23 (– 2) 21 (+ 7) 28 | 30 (– 2) 28 (+ 7) **35**

10. **B**   If you transform the letters into numbers, you see that they decrease by 2. For instance, HFD is the same as 8 6 4; 8 (– 2) 6 (– 2) 4. The only choice that also does this is XVT: 24 22 20; 24 (– 2) 22 (– 2) 20.

11. **A**   Since the number in each group increases by 1 from each group to the next, the missing group should contain the number 5. This will allow us to eliminate C and D because the only number in those groups is 6. If you change the letters into numbers, you see that they increase by 5. For instance, AFK is the same as 1 6 11; 1 (+ 5) 6 (+ 5) 11. The only choice whose letters are each separated by 5 is MRW: 13 18 23; 13 (+ 5) 18 (+ 5) 23.

CHAPTER 5

COOP ANALOGY EXERCISE 1

A mansion is a very large house.

A leaf is part of a tree.

A desert is full of sand.

An engine allows an automobile to run.

Bread is made by a baker.

A brush is used by a painter.

COOP ANALOGY EXERCISE 2

1. **A**   Bread is made from grain; jam is made from fruit.

2. **C**   A dress hat is a more formal kind of baseball cap; a dress shoe is a more formal kind of sneaker.

3. **B**   A tree grows from its trunk (or the bottom part of a tree is a trunk); a flower grows from its stem (or the bottom part of a flower is a stem).

4. **A**   A fish moves with its fins; a bird moves with its wings.

5. **D**   A violin is played with a bow; a piano is played with a hand.

CHAPTER 6

COOP VERBAL REASONING EXERCISE

1. B
2. C
3. A
4. B
5. D
6. A
7. B
8. A

CHAPTER 7

COOP READING COMPREHENSION EXERCISE

1. **C** If you summarized the passage well, you probably wrote something like "People have had lights for a long time in different ways." A is too precise, since the Egyptians are discussed in only one paragraph. B and D are just details that are discussed in only one or two lines.

2. **D** In the final paragraph, the author says that "oil lamps brought with them other problems." Therefore the Romans began to use candles. B and C are not stated in the paragraph, so they can be eliminated. A is extreme because of *most important*.

3. **B** If we reread the line that mentions the word *rudimentary*, it states, "Rudimentary oil lamps, a primitive ancestor of the gaslight . . ." Therefore the word *rudimentary* must be something like *primitive*. This will eliminate A, C, and D.

4. **D** If we skim the passage looking for Edison, we can find him mentioned in the first paragraph. There it states that "practical indoor lighting existed thousands of years before Thomas Edison invented the light bulb." Now we need to find the choice that best restates this idea. Does this sentence explain his discoveries or mention other inventors? No, so we can eliminate A and B. Does the author later discuss Edison? No, so C can also be eliminated.

5. **A** The passage says that "the lamp gave off a terrible odor," and "foul-smelling" is used to describe the odor of the lamp.

6. **C** There is no evidence in the passage to support A, B, or D. The passage does say that the "animal fat smells awful when burned," so C is the best answer.

7. **C** Nothing in the passage sounds angry, so we can eliminate A. B probably isn't right, since someone who was unconcerned wouldn't have written the passage. If that's as far as you get, take a guess between C and D. Critical means that the author disagrees with something, but there's nothing in the passage that shows disagreement.

CHAPTER 8

COOP Math Vocabulary Exercise

1. –3, –2, –1, 0, 1, 2, 3, 4 are all integers. That makes a total of 8.
2. 0, 1, 2, 3, 4 are all positive integers. That makes a total of 5.
3. $6 + 7 + 8 = 21$
4. $2 \times 4 \times 8 = 64$

COOP Order of Operations Exercise

1. 13
2. 9 (Do multiplication first!)
3. 5 (Do parentheses, then multiplication.)
4. 45 (Do multiplication first!)
5. 108 (Do parentheses first!)

COOP Fractions Exercise

1. $\frac{1}{5}$ (Divide the top and bottom by 12.)

2. $\frac{3}{8} \times \frac{2}{3} = \frac{9}{24} + \frac{16}{24} = \frac{25}{24}$

3. $\frac{3}{4} \times \frac{2}{3} = \frac{9}{12} - \frac{8}{12} = \frac{1}{12}$

4. $\frac{3}{5} \cdot \frac{3}{2} = \frac{9}{10}$

5. $\frac{1}{3} \div \frac{1}{2} = \frac{1}{3} \div \frac{2}{1} = \frac{2}{3}$

COOP Decimals Exercise

1. 7.68
2. 2.63
3. 4.5
4. 1.25
5. 5
6. $\frac{632}{100}$

COOP Exponents, Scientific Notation, and Square Roots Exercise

1. $4 \times 4 \times 4 = 64$

2. $2 \times 2 \times 2 \times 2 = 16$

3. 340

4. 52,300

5. This becomes $2 + 4 = 6$.

COOP Solve for x Exercise

1. $x = 5$

2. $x = 7$

3. $x = \dfrac{1}{4}$

4. $x = 3$

COOP Percent Translation Exercise

1. $\dfrac{30}{100} \times 60 = 18$

2. $\dfrac{40}{100} \times 200 = 80$

3. $15 = \dfrac{x}{100} \times 60 = 25$

4. $x = \dfrac{25}{100} \times \dfrac{10}{100} \times 200 = 5$

COOP Geometry Exercise

1. Since these angles must add up to 180 degrees, $x = 85$.

2. x and z must be 120 and y must be 60, so $y + z = 180$.

3. The angles in a triangle must add up to 180. Since we already have angles 90 and 30, the remaining angle must be 60.

4. Since this triangle is isosceles, the two bottom angles measure 40 degrees each. To make a total of 180 degrees, $x = 100$.

5. The area of this square is 6×6, or 36.

6. The area of a triangle is $\frac{1}{2}$base × height, or $\frac{1}{2} \times 8 \times 6 = 24$.

7a. The area of this circle is $3^2\pi$, or 9π.

7b. The circumference of this circle is $2(3)\pi$, or 6π.

8a. Since this figure is a rectangle, $x = 10$ and $y = 5$.

8b. The perimeter is $10 + 5 + 10 + 5 = 30$.

CHAPTER 9

COOP ERRORS EXERCISE

1. Since "many people" is plural, it needs the plural verb form *are*: "There **are** already many people in the auditorium."

2. Since "my father's company" is singular, the pronoun and verb should be the singular *it is* instead of the plural *they are*: "Since my father's company has so much business, **it is** very busy."

3. "My uncle" is singular, so it needs the singular verb form *helps*: "My uncle often **helps** my parents to make dinner."

4. This is a sentence fragment. A complete sentence would read "On his way to school, Henry ran into his friend."

5. The first verb, "ran," is in the past tense; to maintain parallel form, the second verb, "escaping," should also be in the past tense: "The giant mouse ran through the house and **escaped** from the cat."

6. The first verb, "won" is in the past tense, and the second verb, "receives," is in the present tense. You know the sentence should be in the past tense because of the clue words *Last year*. To maintain parallel form, the verbs should both be in the same tense: "Last year, Ines won the first prize and **received** a beautiful trophy."

7. "Most biggest" is not a valid comparative form. The sentence should simply read "Roger finished his **biggest** assignment."

8. The first verb, "cleaned," is in the past tense, but the second verb, "gives," is in the present tense. To maintain parallel form, these verbs should both be in the same tense: "Colin cleaned the bowl and **gave** it to his mother."

COOP SIMPLE SUBJECT EXERCISE

1. Jonathan
2. part
3. her teacher
4. he

COOP SIMPLE PREDICATE EXERCISE

1. volunteered
2. drank
3. imagined
4. felt

II

COOP Practice Tests

11

The Princeton Review
COOP Practice Test 1

COOP Practice Test 1

Memory
(12 Minutes)

You have 12 minutes to memorize the following definitions for these imaginary words.

A flagatan is a book

A calno is a fruit

A symproag is a bag

A gummilac is a wheelbarrow

A stitryic is a room

An anstig is a waterfall

A plafoun is a hand

A lymenori is a scarf

Milgoum means to buy

An ognath is a building

Erierdi means young

A gouperi is a planet

An imunmo is a door

A plathpe is a flower

An unblatri is a baby

A browian is a painting

A linabe is a bird

A wetowh is a school

Omheps means angry

A melsof is a stone

GO ON TO THE NEXT PAGE.

Part 1
Sequences
20 Questions, 15 Minutes

Choose the letter that shows what should fill the blank in the sequence.

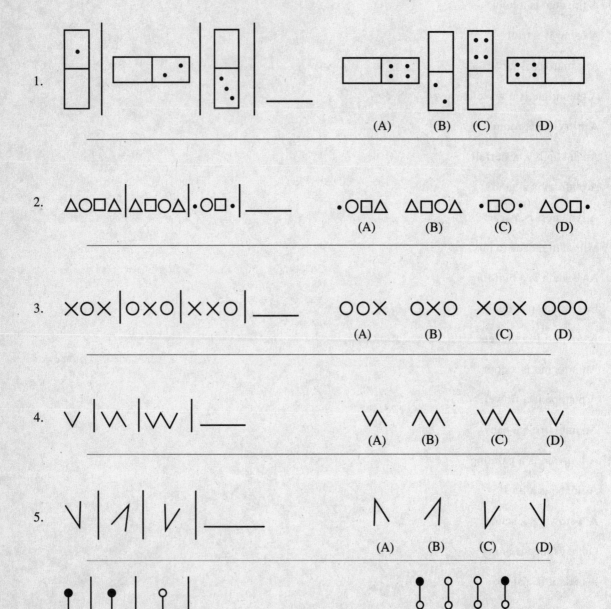

GO ON TO THE NEXT PAGE.

7. 21 32 38 | 56 67 73 | 16 ___ 33   (A) 22   (B) 27   (C) 31   (D) 32

8. 63 65 63 | 18 20 18 | 52 54 ___   (A) 5   (B) 8   (C) 2   (D) 52

9. 32 16 8 | 52 26 13 | 24 ___ 6   (A) 16   (B) 12   (C) 10   (D) 8

10. 2 8 32 | 3 12 48 | 1 ___ 16   (A) 3   (B) 4   (C) 8   (D) 12

11. 5 6 18 | 2 3 9 | 8 ___ 27   (A) 9   (B) 12   (C) 24   (D) 26

12. 15 15 5 | 24 24 8 | 9 9 ___   (A) 3   (B) 6   (C) 9   (D) 12

13. 6 12 24 | 8 16 32 | 2 ___ 8   (A) 2   (B) 4   (C) 6   (D) 8

14. ABC | ACE | ADG | ___ | AFK   (A) ABD   (B) ACF   (C) ADF   (D) AEI

15. EGI | IKM | MOQ | ___ | UWY   (A) QSU   (B) RTU   (C) MPT   (D) LMO

16. J1L | M2O | P3R | ___ | V5X   (A) S4U   (B) A1C   (C) L3M   (D) T4V

GO ON TO THE NEXT PAGE.

17. CB2 | ED4 | GF8 | ___ | KJ32   **(A)** JK10 **(B)** IH16 **(C)** MN16 **(D)** PQ32

18. VWXY | RSTU | NOPQ | ____ | FGHI **(A)** CDEF **(B)** GHIK **(C)** KMNO **(D)** JKLM

19. AZBY | CXDW | EVFU | ____ | IRJQ **(A)** GTHS **(B)** XATB **(C)** GSHT **(D)** KTLS

20. CEHL | EGJN | GILP | ___ | KMPT **(A)** MOPQ **(B)** JLOP **(C)** IKNR **(D)** SUVY

GO ON TO THE NEXT PAGE.

Part 2
Analogies
20 Questions, 7 Minutes

For the following questions, look at the pictures in the top two boxes. Then choose the picture that should go in the empty box so that the bottom two pictures have the same relation as the top two pictures.

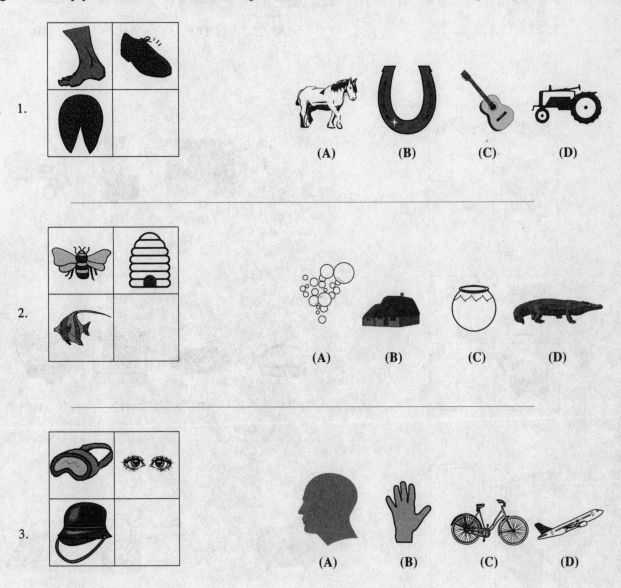

1.

(A)   (B)   (C)   (D)

2.

(A)   (B)   (C)   (D)

3.

(A)   (B)   (C)   (D)

GO ON TO THE NEXT PAGE.

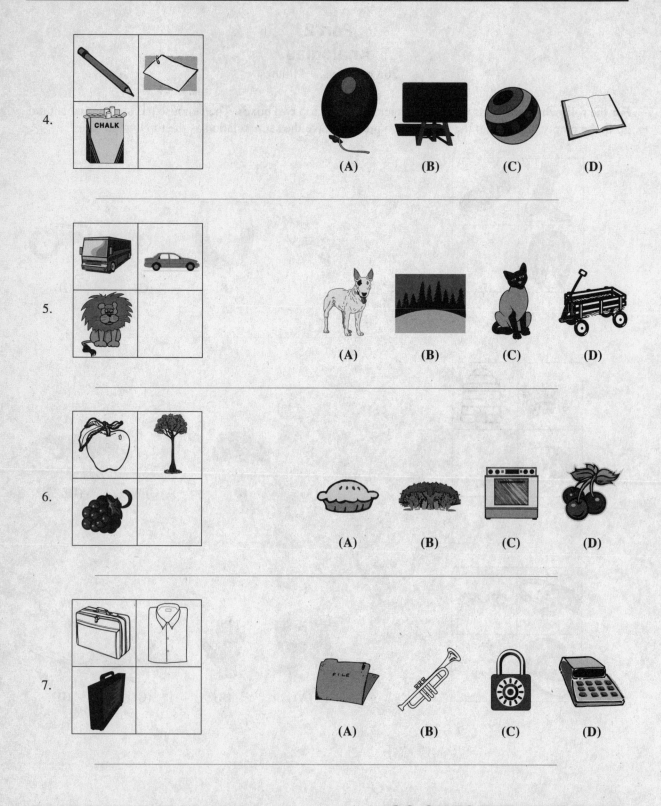

4.

(A)   (B)   (C)   (D)

5.

(A)   (B)   (C)   (D)

6.

(A)   (B)   (C)   (D)

7.

(A)   (B)   (C)   (D)

GO ON TO THE NEXT PAGE.

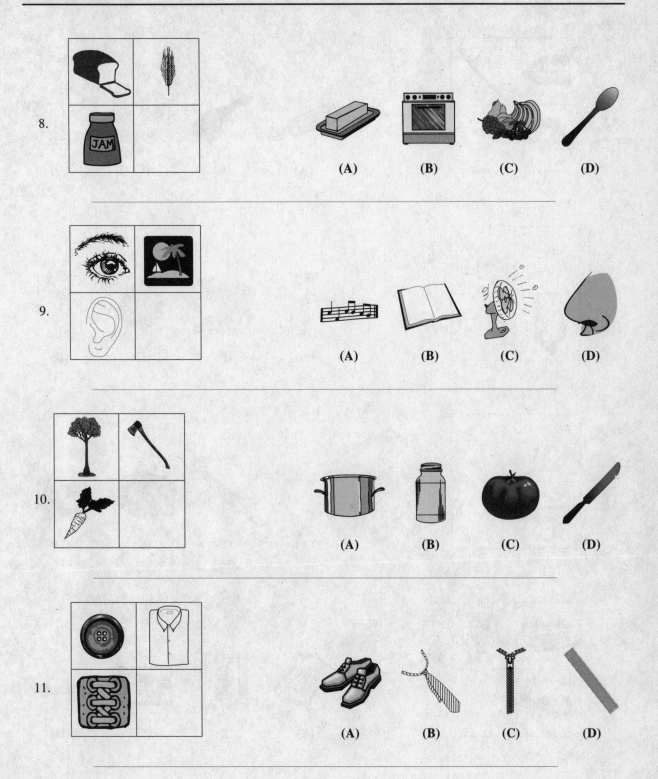

8.

(A)   (B)   (C)   (D)

9.

(A)   (B)   (C)   (D)

10.

(A)   (B)   (C)   (D)

11.

(A)   (B)   (C)   (D)

GO ON TO THE NEXT PAGE.

12.

(A)   (B)   (C)   (D)

13.

(A)   (B)   (C)   (D)

14.

(A)   (B)   (C)   (D)

15.

(A)   (B)   (C)   (D)

GO ON TO THE NEXT PAGE.

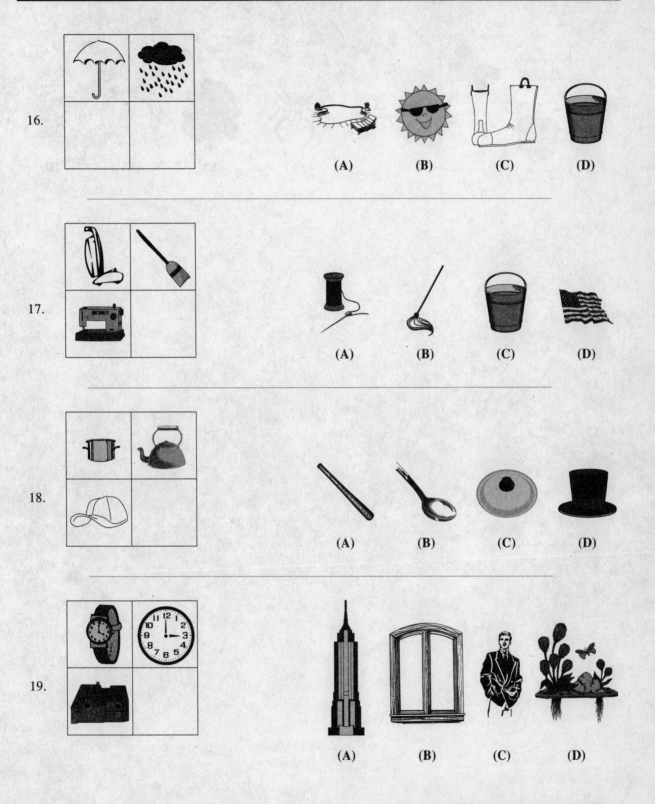

16.

(A)   (B)   (C)   (D)

17.

(A)   (B)   (C)   (D)

18.

(A)   (B)   (C)   (D)

19.

(A)   (B)   (C)   (D)

GO ON TO THE NEXT PAGE.

20.

(A)   (B)   (C)   (D)

GO ON TO THE NEXT PAGE.

Part 3
Memory
20 Questions, 5 Minutes

The following questions ask you about the words you memorized at the beginning of this test. Choose the word that means the same as the underlined word or phrase.

1. Which word means *a bag*?
   - (A) erierdi
   - (B) flagatan
   - (C) melsof
   - (D) symproag
   - (E) unblatri

2. Which word means *a planet*?
   - (A) lymenori
   - (B) symproag
   - (C) browian
   - (D) linabe
   - (E) gouperi

3. Which word means *a book*?
   - (A) browian
   - (B) melsof
   - (C) flagatan
   - (D) gouperi
   - (E) milgoum

4. Which word means *a flower*?
   - (A) linabe
   - (B) ognath
   - (C) stitryic
   - (D) plathpe
   - (E) flagatan

5. Which word means *a room*?
   - (A) calno
   - (B) gouperi
   - (C) omheps
   - (D) erierdi
   - (E) stitryic

6. Which word means *a waterfall*?
   - (A) anstig
   - (B) browian
   - (C) wetowh
   - (D) imunmo
   - (E) gummilac

7. Which word means *a hand*?
   - (A) gummilac
   - (B) plafoun
   - (C) unblatri
   - (D) melsof
   - (E) flagatan

8. Which word means *a scarf*?
   - (A) omheps
   - (B) erierdi
   - (C) stitryic
   - (D) lymenori
   - (E) calno

9. Which word means *to buy*?
   - (A) imunmo
   - (B) linabe
   - (C) milgoum
   - (D) symproag
   - (E) anstig

10. Which word means *a building*?
    - (A) imunmo
    - (B) ognath
    - (C) milgoum
    - (D) lymenori
    - (E) flagatan

11. Which word means *young*?
    - (A) erierdi
    - (B) wetowh
    - (C) calno
    - (D) anstig
    - (E) plathpe

GO ON TO THE NEXT PAGE.

12. Which word means *a fruit*?
    (A) unblatri
    (B) linabe
    (C) gouperi
    (D) calno
    (E) plafoun

13. Which word means *a door*?
    (A) browian
    (B) ognath
    (C) anstig
    (D) imunmo
    (E) stitryic

14. Which word means *a wheelbarrow*?
    (A) gummilac
    (B) wetowh
    (C) plathpe
    (D) milgoum
    (E) plafoun

15. Which word means *a baby*?
    (A) unblatri
    (B) gouperi
    (C) plafoun
    (D) melsof
    (E) omheps

16. Which word means *a painting*?
    (A) lymenori
    (B) imunmo
    (C) calno
    (D) plafoun
    (E) browian

17. Which word means *a bird*?
    (A) linabe
    (B) plathpe
    (C) omheps
    (D) symproag
    (E) stitryic

18. Which word means *a school*?
    (A) erierdi
    (B) ognath
    (C) gummilac
    (D) wetowh
    (E) symproag

19. Which word means *angry*?
    (A) gummilac
    (B) anstig
    (C) wetowh
    (D) unblatri
    (E) omheps

20. Which word means *a stone*?
    (A) wetowh
    (B) plathpe
    (C) melsof
    (D) ognath
    (E) gummilac

GO ON TO THE NEXT PAGE.

Part 4
Verbal Reasoning
20 Questions, 15 Minutes

For questions 1–6, find the word that is a necessary part of the underlined word.

1. oven
    (A) heat
    (B) stone
    (C) bread
    (D) rack

2. scissors
    (A) paper
    (B) hair
    (C) cut
    (D) office

3. hat
    (A) black
    (B) felt
    (C) head
    (D) cowboy

4. knife
    (A) metal
    (B) edge
    (C) steak
    (D) kitchen

5. microphone
    (A) cord
    (B) music
    (C) announcement
    (D) sound

6. shallow
    (A) water
    (B) container
    (C) heat
    (D) depth

For questions 7–12, choose the word that should go below the line such that the words above the line and the words below the line have the same relationship.

7. breeze gust hurricane
    drizzle rain
    (A) weather
    (B) downpour
    (C) sun
    (D) snow

8. cup   quart gallon
    ounce pound
    (A) mile
    (B) flour
    (C) measure
    (D) ton

9. tie   bracelet belt
    neck   wrist
    (A) watch
    (B) waist
    (C) joint
    (D) jewelry

10. ankle knee elbow
    foot   leg
    (A) arm
    (B) finger
    (C) muscle
    (D) bone

11. feline lion cat
    canine wolf
    (A) mouse
    (B) jungle
    (C) dog
    (D) fur

GO ON TO THE NEXT PAGE.

12. <u>wood splinter log</u>
    bread crumb
    (A) baker
    (B) loaf
    (C) oven
    (D) jelly

For questions 13–17, find the statement that is true according to the information you are given.

13. John is taller than both Sam and Trudy. Trudy is taller than Cindy but not as tall as Eric. Cindy is taller than Walter and Alice.
    (A) Trudy is taller than Sam.
    (B) Alice is not as tall as Trudy.
    (C) Walter is taller than Alice.
    (D) Sam is not as tall as Eric.

14. Martina spent 3 hours studying the night before the math test. Carol did not study at all, but Carol always does her homework on time.
    (A) Martina will do better on the math test than Carol.
    (B) Martina studied more than Carol did the night before the math test.
    (C) Martina does not always turn in her homework on time.
    (D) Carol is better at math than Martina is.

15. Bob will either buy an ice cream cone or a cup of frozen yogurt. But he only buys frozen yogurt if he can have chocolate sprinkles. The store is out of chocolate sprinkles.
    (A) Bob will not buy anything.
    (B) Bob will buy an ice cream.
    (C) Bob will buy a frozen yogurt with chocolate syrup.
    (D) Bob will buy an ice cream with chocolate syrup.

16. Peter and Karen went to the movie theater. They bought their tickets before the movie started and went right into the theater. Peter bought some popcorn and a soda and then sat down to watch the movie. Halfway through the movie, Peter left the theater and did not return.
    (A) Peter was ill and went to the hospital.
    (B) Peter did not like the movie.
    (C) Peter did not see the end of the movie.
    (D) The popcorn gave Peter a stomachache.

17. Ron can type 13 pages per hour. Sylvia and Jean can type 8 pages per hour. Alex can type 4 pages per hour.
    (A) Jean can not type as fast as Ron can.
    (B) Alex makes lots of mistakes when he types.
    (C) Ron likes to type more than Sylvia does.
    (D) Alex only types with two fingers, while Sylvia uses all ten fingers.

For questions 18–20, choose the best answer.

18. kapalinagam means cargo ship
     ocamanagam means   passenger ship
     kapalimagal means cargo van

    Which of the following could mean passenger van?
    (A) ocamamagal
    (B) kapalipalaki
    (C) ocamapalaki
    (D) nagamocama

19. buluhati means painting of horses
     malahati means painting of cows
     buluonola means picture of horses

    Which of the following could mean a picture of cows?
    (A) bulumala
    (B) malanola
    (C) nolamala
    (D) bulukami

20. patohamari means apple juice
     cabohawano means orange pieces
     maxohapa means grape seeds

    Which of the following could mean apple seeds?
    (A) cabohamari
    (B) maxohawano
    (C) marihamari
    (D) hapahamari

GO ON TO THE NEXT PAGE.

Part 5
Reading Comprehension
40 Questions, 40 Minutes

Kangaroos are fascinating creatures because they are so different from other mammals. Unlike most mammals, kangaroos rear their young in a pouch and hop to get around. Their long, powerful hind legs are used for jumping, and their thick tail gives them balance. Their forelimbs are used almost like human hands. Despite these well-known characteristics, prevalent among all kangaroos, there are many lesser-known variations; some kangaroo species differ tremendously in such characteristics as habitat, color, social patterns, and size. For example, various species range in size from nine inches to more than eight feet.

The explanation often given for these odd features is that kangaroos are marsupials, and marsupials are a primitive form of mammal. This explanation, which may or may not be correct, is particularly popular among people who live in the Northern Hemisphere. Their view is reflected in the statements they make about the Virginia opossum, the only marsupial native to North America. The opossum is frequently described as a primitive animal, little changed since the time of the dinosaurs.

But even if the opossum can in some ways be considered a "living fossil," the same cannot be said of the kangaroo. These Australian marsupials have changed recently in order to adapt to a changing environment. Kangaroos evolved from small forest animals into creatures that live mainly in open spaces. This development was probably related to the spread of grassland areas in Australia between ten and fifteen million years ago.

1. Which of the following best describes what this passage is about?
   (A) a comparison of the opossum and the kangaroo
   (B) the competition between marsupials and dinosaurs
   (C) the evolutionary background of kangaroos
   (D) why kangaroos are not really mammals

2. The author of the passage would most likely believe that
   (A) opossums are smarter than kangaroos
   (B) dinosaurs ate kangaroo meat
   (C) kangaroos were once extinct
   (D) kangaroos are interesting animals

3. The author of this passage is most likely
   (A) a scientist
   (B) a hunter
   (C) an Australian
   (D) a physicist

4. According to the passage, kangaroos use their tails primarily to
   (A) defend themselves against predators
   (B) help them balance while they jump
   (C) communicate with other kangaroos
   (D) grasp small objects

5. The author says that kangaroos "range in size from nine inches to more than eight feet" in order to
   (A) shock the reader
   (B) demonstrate one way in which species of kangaroos can differ from each other
   (C) contradict earlier research on kangaroos
   (D) prove that not all kangaroos are important

6. The phrase "living fossil" refers to
   (A) a dinosaur
   (B) a kangaroo
   (C) an opossum
   (D) an Australian marsupial

7. The passage implies which of the following about the kangaroo's development?
   (A) The kangaroo has adapted to its surroundings more than some other marsupials
   (B) The kangaroo had a development almost identical to that of the opossum.
   (C) The kangaroo is native to North America
   (D) Kangaroos have been almost unchanged in the last one million years.

GO ON TO THE NEXT PAGE.

Abraham Lincoln was born in 1809 in a log cabin in Kentucky. In his early years he lived in Kentucky and Indiana. He did not attend many years of formal schooling, but he was very ambitious and taught himself through reading. Partly due to his poor upbringing, Lincoln was determined to promote equal economic opportunity for all people. When he was older, Lincoln moved to New Salem, Illinois, where he studied law and served in the state legislature. After he became a lawyer, he moved to Springfield, where he became an important and wealthy attorney.

Lincoln returned to politics with the repeal of the Missouri Compromise, which meant the threat of the expansion of slavery. In part due to the national attention he gained through a series of debates with Stephen A. Douglas, he moved to the forefront of the new Republican Party, and was soon elected President of the United States.

The Civil War began shortly after Lincoln took office. Despite his inexperience in military matters, he showed a keen understanding of military strategy. Lincoln always insisted that his main objective was to save the Union, but as it became clear that abolishing slavery would weaken the South, he began to give serious attention to the issue of emancipation.

Shortly after the Union victory and his re-election to office, Lincoln's life was cut short by an assassin's bullet. Lincoln remains, nevertheless, one of our greatest presidents. His rise from poverty to the White House exemplifies the American dream. He was a skillful politician, a natural leader, and bravely bore the weight of a war that almost ended the Union for which so many people had fought.

8. This passage is mostly about
   (A) how the Civil War was won by the North
   (B) the life of one the Presidents of the United States
   (C) where Abraham Lincoln was born
   (D) why Abraham Lincoln abolished slavery

9. According to the passage, Abraham Lincoln worked for equality in part due to
   (A) his religious beliefs
   (B) his poverty as a child
   (C) the advice of his wife
   (D) his dislike of the English monarchy

10. The author probably believes that Lincoln
    (A) was one of our most important presidents
    (B) lost the debates with Stephen Douglas
    (C) had an unhappy childhood.
    (D) was the wealthiest person in Springfield, Illinois.

11. According to the passage, Lincoln returned to politics from practicing law because of
    (A) the start of the Civil War
    (B) the repeal of the Missouri Compromise
    (C) the emancipation of the slaves
    (D) the Union victory

12. It can be inferred from the passage that Lincoln
    (A) had no sisters or brothers
    (B) did not like public speaking
    (C) did not command an army before the Civil War
    (D) wanted to return to Kentucky after his presidency.

13. Which of the following questions is answered in the passage?
    (A) In what year was Lincoln elected President?
    (B) Which political party did Lincoln belong to?
    (C) Why did the Civil War begin?
    (D) In what year did Lincoln die?

14. According to the passage, which of the following is true?
    (A) Lincoln's father died when he was young.
    (B) Lincoln was killed by one of his friends.
    (C) Lincoln was elected President more than once.
    (D) The Civil War would have been lost without Lincoln.

GO ON TO THE NEXT PAGE.

An Eskimo navigating in polar darkness and whiteouts makes use of many clues to find his way. When traveling on ice in the fog, the Eskimo uses the voices of seabirds against the cliffs and the sound of the surf at the edge of the ice. When he begins to travel over open terrain, he marks the angle of the wind and aligns the fur of his parka with the breeze. He notes the trend of any cracks in the ice as he crosses them. Sea ice cracks can reveal the presence of a cape or headland invisible in the distance, or they may confirm one's arrival at a known area.

Constant attention to such details, memories of the way the land looks, and stories told by other travelers are used together with the movements of animals, to keep the traveler on course. Searching for small but crucial clues can be exhausting for a person who does not know what to look for.

These navigational tools are still part of village life in the Arctic, used just as often today while traveling long distances by snowmobile as they were once by people traveling on foot. Such skills are still more critical for the success of a journey than even the best maps and navigation aids. Fogs and blizzards hide the reference points needed to navigate by map. Even compasses can't be relied on so close to the magnetic pole: the compass needle wanders aimlessly due to the proximity of the magnetic field. The most dependable sources of direction for most Eskimos, therefore, are the behavior of the wind and ocean currents, and such subtle clues as the flow of a river.

15. This passage is mostly
    (A) a comparison of modern and traditional methods of navigation
    (B) a description of traditional navigational techniques used by Eskimos
    (C) an explanation of the purpose of the migration of Eskimos
    (D) a discussion of advances in navigational equipment

16. Which of the following is *not* mentioned as a technique the Eskimos use for navigating?
    (A) consulting with the elders of the Eskimo community
    (B) examining cracks in the ice along the route
    (C) learning from the experiences of earlier travelers
    (D) using the angle of the wind to judge direction

17. According to the author, traditional navigational skills are still used by Eskimos because
    (A) traditional techniques are always superior to modern technology
    (B) Eskimos prefer not to travel too far from home
    (C) modern navigational equipment is too expensive for most Eskimos
    (D) traditional methods are sometimes more effective than sophisticated equipment

18. The last paragraph suggests that in the polar region navigation is complicated by the fact that
    (A) objects in the sky, such as stars, do not provide useful information
    (B) the summer moon affects ocean currents in unpredictable ways
    (C) accurate compass readings are difficult to obtain
    (D) wind and ocean currents change too quickly to be reliable

19. It can be inferred from the passage that
    (A) Eskimos live in the Antarctic.
    (B) Eskimo parkas are sometimes made with fur.
    (C) Eskimos do not have maps of their territory.
    (D) Eskimos always live in total darkness.

20. The author's attitude toward Eskimo navigation techniques is best described as
    (A) bored
    (B) angry
    (C) silly
    (D) respectful

GO ON TO THE NEXT PAGE.

It may seem to you as you gaze up into the night sky that the stars move from one night to the next. While the position of a star may vary a bit over the years, in general the movement of the stars is due to the rotation of the Earth, not the movement of the stars. The Earth rotates on its axis from west to east every day. Because you are not aware of the movement of the Earth, it looks to you as though the stars are moving from east to west in the sky. The only star that does not <u>appear</u> to have any motion is Polaris, or what is commonly called the North Star. The reason it does not appear to move is that it lies almost directly above the North Pole. Because its position is fixed, the North Star has long been used as a tool for navigation. No matter where you are, if you can locate the North Star, you can figure out which direction is North. Sailors out on the sea used it to find their way. Polaris is a very bright star, so it can be located easily.

21. The word <u>appear</u> in this passage most nearly means
    (A) seem
    (B) show up
    (C) reveal
    (D) occur

22. According to the passage, the reason we think that the stars move is due to
    (A) the distance between the Earth and the stars
    (B) the effect of the Sun
    (C) gravity
    (D) the rotation of the Earth

23. The North Star can be used for navigation because it
    (A) is very bright
    (B) is easy to locate
    (C) has a fixed position in the sky
    (D) is low on the horizon

24. According to the passage, the reason Polaris does not appear to move is that
    (A) it moves more slowly than the other stars
    (B) it is brighter than the other stars
    (C) it lies above the North Pole
    (D) it is farther away than other stars

25. According to the passage, most stars appear to move
    (A) from east to west
    (B) from west to east
    (C) toward the north
    (D) from north to south

26. This passage might be found in a
    (A) dictionary
    (B) textbook on astronomy
    (C) thesaurus
    (D) history book

GO ON TO THE NEXT PAGE.

A yurt is a kind of tent that the Mongols lived in year-round. It was designed specifically for the particular needs of the Mongol people. It was portable enough that it could be carried by a single pack animal. It could be set up or taken down in half an hour. And it could retain enough heat to keep its inhabitants warm during the <u>frigid</u> Mongolian winters.

The frame of a yurt is made from wooden poles, laced together with leather straps. The tops of these poles fit into slots in a wooden ring that forms the top of the structure. The ring is open in the center to allow air to flow in and smoke to flow out. When it rains, this hole can be covered with a piece of felt or animal skin.

To complete the yurt, large pieces of felt or animal hides are placed over the wooden frame. During especially cold months, several layers might be used to insure warmth. These pieces of felt are then <u>secured</u> to the frame using ropes.

If you ever meet a Mongol, however, don't ask to see his yurt. In fact, the word "yurt" is Russian; the Mongols themselves called the structure a "ger," which means "home."

27. The word <u>frigid</u> probably means
    (A) boring
    (B) frightening
    (C) very cold
    (D) dangerous

28. It can be inferred from the way the yurt is fashioned that the Mongols
    (A) had a large number of possessions
    (B) were a very peaceful people
    (C) moved around a great deal
    (D) grew up in large families

29. The yurts were probably warmed by using
    (A) the body heat of people who lived in them
    (B) hot water from nearby hot springs
    (C) a fire made inside the tent
    (D) heated rocks

30. The word <u>secured</u> probably means
    (A) attached
    (B) rescued
    (C) found
    (D) dried

GO ON TO THE NEXT PAGE.

The digestive system of the cow is complex and interesting. Unlike humans, who have a simple stomach, the cow has a large four-chambered stomach. Cows eat plants, primarily grasses, which are only partly digested in one of the four chambers, called the rumen. The cow will then regurgitate, or bring back up, the partially digested plant fibers in a small mass called "cud." The cud is chewed further and swallowed again, this time into the second chamber, called the reticulum. It passes then to the third and fourth chambers, until it is completely digested. It may sound unpleasant, but the cow is able to extract a maximum of nutrients from its food by digesting in this manner. The whole process may take more than three days.

31. The best title for this passage might be
    (A) The Cow's Great Gift to Man: Milk
    (B) Digestive Systems and their Purposes
    (C) The Diet of the Cow
    (D) The Digestive System of the Cow

32. According to the passage, the primary benefit of the cow's digestive system is that it
    (A) allows the cow to eat more slowly
    (B) doesn't require as much food as other digestive systems do
    (C) allows the cow to absorb more nutrients
    (D) is complex and original

33. The passage suggests that humans
    (A) depend on cows
    (B) do not have four-chambered stomachs
    (C) do not eat grass
    (D) require the same nutrients as cows do

34. Which of the following best describes the author's attitude toward the cow's digestive system?
    (A) The author admires the efficiency of the system
    (B) The author believes it is too complex
    (C) The author does not find it very interesting.
    (D) The author finds it very disgusting.

GO ON TO THE NEXT PAGE.

The first old "horseless carriages" of the 1880s may have been worthy of a snicker or two, but not the cars of today. The <u>progress</u> that has been made over the last one hundred years has been phenomenal. In fact, much progress was made even in the first twenty years—in 1903 cars could travel 70 mph. The major change from the old cars to today is the expense. Whereas cars were once a luxury that only the rich could afford, today people of all income levels own cars.

In fact, today there are so many cars that if they were to line up end to end, they would touch the moon. Cars are used for everyday transportation for millions of people, for recreation, and for work. Many people's jobs depend on cars—police officers, healthcare workers, and taxi drivers, to name a few.

One thing that hasn't changed is how cars are powered. The first cars ran on gas and diesel fuel just as today's cars do. Scientists have recently done a great deal of research on how to improve the design of cars, and this has made modern cars much more fuel efficient and less polluting than older cars.

35. The author uses the word <u>progress</u> to refer to
    (A) the ability of a car to move forward
    (B) technological advancements
    (C) new types of fuel
    (D) the low cost of the car

36. Which of the following is answered by the passage?
    (A) What are some jobs that make use of cars?
    (B) How much money is spent on cars today?
    (C) Where will the fuels of the future come from?
    (D) When will cars completely stop polluting?

37. This passage is primarily concerned with
    (A) the problem of fuel consumption
    (B) the invention of the car
    (C) the development of the car from past to present
    (D) the future of automobiles

38. Scientists devote much of their research today to
    (A) making cars that run faster
    (B) making more cars
    (C) making cars more affordable
    (D) making cars more fuel efficient

39. The author would probably agree that
    (A) cars are useful to many different kinds of people
    (B) cars cause more problems than they solve
    (C) early car owners were unfriendly people
    (D) we will never again be able to discover something as useful as the car

40. When discussing the early advances of the automobile, the author's tone could best be described as
    (A) proud
    (B) hesitant
    (C) doubtful
    (D) angry

GO ON TO THE NEXT PAGE.

Part 6—Mathematics Concepts and Applications
40 Questions, 35 Minutes

1. Which of the following is equal to $3 + 60 + \dfrac{2}{1000}$?
    (A) 63.002
    (B) 63.02
    (C) 36.02
    (D) 2063

2. For delivering newspapers, Polly earns $20 per month during the months of January through October. During the months of November and December, she earns $32 per month. What is Polly's average monthly income for the year?
    (A) $20
    (B) $21.50
    (C) $22
    (D) $22.50

3. A negative even number multiplied by a positive odd number will be
    (A) positive and odd
    (B) positive and even
    (C) negative and odd
    (D) negative and even

4. $\dfrac{0.246}{0.12} =$
    (A) 0.205
    (B) 2.05
    (C) 20.5
    (D) 205

5. $(3.0 \times 10^3) \times (5.3 \times 10^2) =$
    (A) 1.59×10^6
    (B) 1.59×10^5
    (C) 8.3×10^5
    (D) 8.3×10^6

6. What is the area of a circle with radius 5?
    (A) 5π
    (B) 10π
    (C) 25
    (D) 25π

7. The price of a notebook is reduced from $85.00 to $56.00. By approximately what percent is the price of the notebook decreased?
    (A) 15%
    (B) 23%
    (C) 29%
    (D) 34%

8. If the average of 2, 5, and x is equal to the average of 3 and x, what is the value of x?
    (A) 2
    (B) 3
    (C) 4
    (D) 5

9. Alicia receives $3.00 for every 50 papers she delivers on her paper route. If in the month of July she delivered 420 papers, how much money did she make in the month of July?
    (A) $25.20
    (B) $27.00
    (C) $32.30
    (D) $33.30

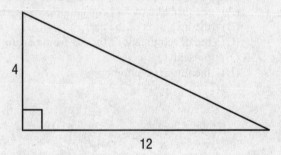

10. What is the area of the triangle above?
    (A) 16
    (B) 18
    (C) 22
    (D) 24

GO ON TO THE NEXT PAGE.

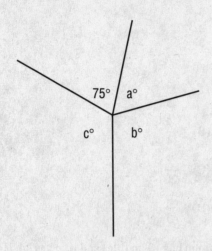

11. In the figure above, what is the value of $a + b + c$?
    (A)   105
    (B)   125
    (C)   235
    (D)   285

12. A record store increases the price of a $15 record by 20%. This new price is later reduced by 10%. What is the final price of the record?
    (A) $15.80
    (B) $16.20
    (C) $16.80
    (D) $18.00

13. Which of the following is the greatest?

    (A) $\dfrac{5}{11}$

    (B) $\dfrac{7}{13}$

    (C) $\dfrac{1}{3}$

    (D) $\dfrac{6}{15}$

14. How many factors do 16 and 56 have in common?
    (A)   2
    (B)   3
    (C)   4
    (D)   5

15. If $2x - 5 > 5x + 1$, which of the following gives the possible values of x?
    (A) $x < -2$
    (B) $x > -2$
    (C) $x < 2$
    (D) $x > 2$

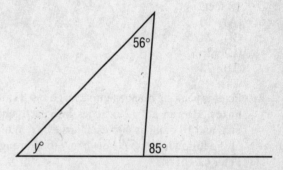

16. In the triangle above, what is the value of y?
    (A)   29
    (B)   39
    (C)   24
    (D)   66

17. How many multiples of 3 and 4 are between 1 and 50?
    (A)   2
    (B)   4
    (C)   6
    (D)   9

18. How many cubes with an edge of 1 inch can fit into a box of dimensions 5 inches by 8 inches by 3 inches?
    (A)   15
    (B)   24
    (C)   40
    (D)   120

GO ON TO THE NEXT PAGE.

19. Michelle made 20 sugar cookies and 50 chocolate chip cookies for a bake sale. Approximately what percent of the cookies she baked were sugar cookies?
    (A) 20%
    (B) 30%
    (C) 35%
    (D) 40%

20. If one gallon of paint can cover 3 square feet, how many gallons of paint will be needed to cover a rectangular wall that measures 12 feet by 18 feet?
    (A) 10
    (B) 24
    (C) 56
    (D) 72

21. Peter is packing oranges into 2 large and 8 small boxes. He can put 12 oranges into each small box, and 18 oranges into each large box. Which of the following shows how many total oranges Peter can pack?
    (A) $(2 \times 12) + (8 \times 18)$
    (B) $(12 \times 8) + (18 \times 2)$
    (C) $(2 \times 8) + (12 \times 18)$
    (D) $2(12 + 8 + 18)$

22. Louise has 8 pairs of socks in her drawer. 2 pairs are blue, 2 pairs are black, 3 pairs are red, and 1 pair is white. If she chooses one pair of socks at random from the drawer, what is the chance that the pair she draws will be black?

    (A) $\dfrac{1}{8}$

    (B) $\dfrac{1}{4}$

    (C) $\dfrac{3}{8}$

    (D) $\dfrac{1}{3}$

23. If $3x - 5 = 4x + 3$, what is the value of x?
    (A) −8
    (B) −5
    (C) 5
    (D) 8

24. $\dfrac{\frac{3}{4}}{\frac{3}{5}} =$

    (A) $\dfrac{4}{5}$

    (B) $\dfrac{5}{4}$

    (C) $\dfrac{9}{20}$

    (D) $\dfrac{9}{5}$

25. John has 18 marbles and Ken has 44. How many marbles must Ken give to John such that they have the same number of marbles?
    (A) 13
    (B) 18
    (C) 24
    (D) 32

26. Which of the following is equivalent to multiplying a number x by 5?
    (A) multiplying x by $\dfrac{10}{5}$
    (B) dividing x by $\dfrac{1}{5}$
    (C) multiplying x by $\dfrac{1}{5}$
    (D) dividing x by $\dfrac{5}{1}$

27. Which of the following leaves a remainder of 2 when divided by 3?
    (A) 25
    (B) 37
    (C) 44
    (D) 51

GO ON TO THE NEXT PAGE.

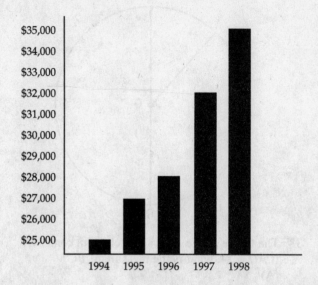

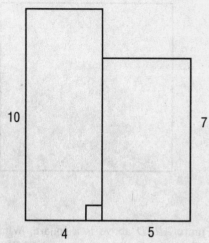

28. According to the chart above Amanda's salary increased by approximately what percent from 1994 to 1997?
    (A) 28%
    (B) 22%
    (C) 14%
    (D) 7%

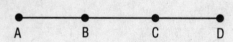

29. In the figure above, the distance between points B and C is 5. If B is the midpoint of AC and C is the midpoint of BD, what is the distance between A and D?
    (A) 5
    (B) 10
    (C) 15
    (D) 20

30. What is the perimeter of the figure above?
    (A) 26
    (B) 32
    (C) 38
    (D) 42

31. In a group of 50 adults and children, there are 18 more adults than children. How many adults are in the group?
    (A) 34
    (B) 32
    (C) 16
    (D) 18

32. If $2^x + 3^x = 97$ then $x=$
    (A) 2
    (B) 3
    (C) 4
    (D) 5

33. What is the sum of the distinct positive factors of 12?
    (A) 20
    (B) 27
    (C) 28
    (D) 36

GO ON TO THE NEXT PAGE.

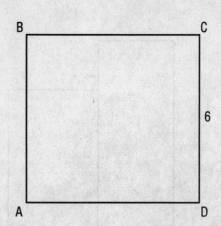

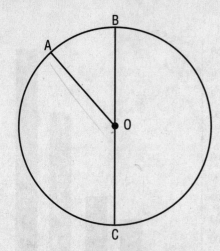

34. Figure *ABCD* above is a square. What is the difference between the area of *ABCD* and the perimeter of *ABCD*?
    (A) 8
    (B) 12
    (C) 16
    (D) 18

35. If $\frac{1}{5}$ of a number is 14, then $\frac{1}{2}$ of that number is

    (A) 35
    (B) 32
    (C) 30
    (D) 28

36. On Main Street, there are 2 red houses, 3 blue houses, and 5 white houses. What fractional part of the houses are blue?
    (A) 20%
    (B) 30%
    (C) 40%
    (D) 50%

37. $2\sqrt{3} + 3\sqrt{3} =$
    (A) 5
    (B) $5\sqrt{3}$
    (C) $6\sqrt{3}$
    (D) 15

38. The figure above shows a circle with center *O*. If *AO* = 14, what is the measure of *BC*?
    (A) 14
    (B) 24
    (C) 28
    (D) 32

39. If $-5 + 2(3a + 2b) = 4b - 2$ then *a* =

    (A) $\frac{1}{2}$

    (B) 2

    (C) 6

    (D) −1

40. $\frac{5^6}{5^2} =$
    (A) 4^5
    (B) 5^3
    (C) 5^4
    (D) 25^4

GO ON TO THE NEXT PAGE.

Part 7—Language Expression
40 Questions, 30 minutes

For questions 1–6, select the word or phrase that best completes the sentence.

1. I had not had time to fully practice my speech; _____ I went ahead and gave it.
    (A) therefore
    (B) because
    (C) nevertheless
    (D) moreover
    (E) instead

2. Many kinds of dogs are naturally good at fetching small objects; _____ the golden retriever was bred to bring back birds and small animals that were shot by hunters.
    (A) nonetheless,
    (B) for example,
    (C) yet,
    (D) in contrast,
    (E) besides,

3. I knew all the answers to the questions _____ I studied hard the night before the test.
    (A) but
    (B) although
    (C) because
    (D) even though
    (E) thus

4. Kimberly is an excellent chess player; _____ she was state champion last year, and will probably win again this year.
    (A) because,
    (B) instead,
    (C) in fact,
    (D) rather,
    (E) in general,

5. That was probably the _____ film I have seen all year.
    (A) more interesting
    (B) most interesting
    (C) much interesting
    (D) interestingest
    (E) interestingly

6. While some people have a great deal of patience for such matters, I'm sorry to say that Jack _____.
    (A) hasn't almost none
    (B) has scarcely none
    (C) has almost any
    (D) has hardly none
    (E) has almost none

For questions 7–12, choose the sentence that is correctly written.

7. (A) Remaining independent until the late 1800s, the US took Hawaii as a territory in 1900.
    (B) Hawaii remained independent until the late 1800s, and it became a US territory in 1900.
    (C) Hawaii remains independent until the late 1800s, and they became a US territory in 1900.
    (D) Hawaii having been independent until the late 1800s, became a US territory in 1900.
    (E) Becoming a US territory in 1900, Hawaii was keeping its independence up until the late 1800s.

8. (A) Importantly occasions such as birthdays should not be forgotten.
    (B) The importantest occasions should not be forgotten.
    (C) Birthdays are important occasions that should not be forgotten.
    (D) Occasions as importantly as birthdays should not be forgotten.
    (E) Being forgotten is not for important occasions such as birthdays.

GO ON TO THE NEXT PAGE.

9. (A) Rachel received the Premier Physicist award, which did outstanding work in the lab this year.
   (B) Rachel received the Premier Physicist award, whose work in the lab was outstanding this year.
   (C) The Premier Physicist award was given to Rachel this year, her work having been outstanding in this.
   (D) The Premier Physicist award, who was outstanding this year, was given to Rachel.
   (E) For her outstanding work in the lab this year, Rachel received the Premier Physicist award.

10. (A) In no other country do the symptoms of malnutrition appear more forcefully than in Rwanda.
    (B) In Rwanda, more so than in other countries, the symptoms of malnutrition are more forceful, it appears.
    (C) More so than in other countries, they appear to have the symptoms of malnutrition more forcefully in Rwanda.
    (D) In no other country more than they do in Rwanda do the symptoms of malnutrition appear more forcefully
    (E) The symptoms of malnutrition appear in Rwanda than other countries more forcefully

11. (A) Not understanding its importance, wrist pain is a symptom most people ignore.
    (B) Wrist pain is ignored by most people because of their not understanding its importance.
    (C) Most people, not understanding the importance of wrist pain and ignoring it.
    (D) Most people ignore wrist pain because they do not understand its importance.
    (E) A symptom ignored by most people not understanding its importance is wrist pain.

12. (A) A great deal of natural talent and grace, which are important qualities for figure skaters, are what Beverly has.
    (B) A great deal of natural talent and grace belongs to Beverly, which are important qualities for figure skaters.
    (C) Beverly has what are important qualities for figure skaters, which are a great deal of natural talent and grace.
    (D) Beverly has a great deal of natural talent and grace, which are important qualities for figure skaters.
    (E) A great deal of natural talent and grace, which are important qualities for figure skaters, belong to Beverly.

For questions 13–17, choose the sentence that uses verbs correctly.

13. (A) I ate lunch and then I go to math class.
    (B) Tomorrow I have seen a robin in the park.
    (C) Julie wants to go out at night and see some stars.
    (D) My mother said that there is only two pieces of cake left.
    (E) Mike wants his mother to driving him to school.

14. (A) Carol went to the store after work and then going to the gym.
    (B) The dog barked at the moon and runs around the yard.
    (C) In the morning we will all to go to the store and bought some milk.
    (D) Everyone appreciated Juan's hard work on the project.
    (E) I would never have bought that pen if I will have known how much it costs.

15. (A) A monkey that escaped from the zoo were seen last week in the park.
    (B) I have never seen an apple as large as yours.
    (C) Omar had already took a shower by the time I arrived .
    (D) Uma seeing a bear and ran away as fast as she could.
    (E) I know the story because I seen that film already.

GO ON TO THE NEXT PAGE.

16. (A) Henry cooked while Nancy serving dinner on the patio.
    (B) Just before class, James realized that he had forgotten his lunch.
    (C) My family will to travel to the Grand Canyon next year.
    (D) Alexander, dressed in his best suit, going to the party
    (E) The mountain had thrown tons of ash into the air before it had stopped exploding a few days later.

17. (A) The people at the zoo watches the lions.
    (B) Max trained his dog to bark, lie down, and then roll over.
    (C) My brother, who plays the piano, think that Beethoven was a genius.
    (D) David and Sally smiling while looking at family photographs.
    (E) Martin wanted eating all the cookies as soon as they were ready.

For questions 18–21, choose the underlined word that is the simple subject of the sentence.

18. While <u>he</u> was walking down the street, <u>David's</u>
    _A   _B
    <u>wallet</u> fell out of his <u>pocket</u> and into a <u>puddle</u>.
    _C   _D   _E

19. In an <u>emergency</u>, the <u>superintendent</u> of the
         _A   _B
    <u>building</u> will either fix the <u>problem</u> or call
    _C   _D
    <u>someone</u> who can.
    _E

20. On top of the <u>desk</u>, in the <u>box</u> with the wooden
                    _A   _B
    handle, lies <u>my</u> favorite <u>pair</u> of <u>scissors</u>.
                 _C   _D   _E

21. As <u>Linda</u> walked into the <u>room</u>, the <u>neighbor's</u>
       _A   _B   _C
    <u>dog</u> began to bark so loudly that it scared the <u>cat</u>.
    _D   _E

For questions 22–25, choose the underlined word or words that is the simple predicate (verb) of the sentence.

22. After <u>carefully</u> <u>studying</u> the dinosaur bones,
          _A   _B
    scientists <u>decided</u> that the <u>creature</u> probably
               _C   _D
    <u>lived</u> during the Cretaceous Period.
    _E

23. Since the children <u>ate</u> the cake, they <u>needed</u>
                        _A   _B
    something else <u>to sell</u> at the <u>bake</u> <u>sale</u>.
                    _C   _D _E

24. George Washington, who <u>led</u> the <u>fight</u> <u>against</u>
                           _A   _B   _C
    the British during the American Revolution,
    <u>became</u> the <u>first</u> President of the United States.
    _D   _E

25. Before I <u>saw</u> the <u>results</u> of the test we <u>took</u> on
             _A   _B   _C
    Tuesday, I <u>did not know</u> how well I <u>had done</u>.
               _D   _E

For questions 26–28, choose the sentence that best combines the two underlined sentences into one.

26. *Kevin wanted to become a policeman. Kevin became an architect instead.*
    (A) Kevin became an architect, wanted to become a policeman.
    (B) Though Kevin wanted to become a policeman, he became an architect instead.
    (C) Kevin, intending to be a policeman later, was an architect.
    (D) Kevin wanted to become a policeman but becomes an architect instead.
    (E) Kevin, having wanted to become a policeman, had become an architect instead.

GO ON TO THE NEXT PAGE.

27. *I wanted to go to the zoo on Sunday with my brother. So I did all my chores.*
    (A) Because I wanted to go to the zoo, I did all my chores on Sunday with my brother.
    (B) Because I wanted to go to the zoo on Sunday with my brother, I did all my chores.
    (C) Because I did all my chores, I wanted to go to the zoo on Sunday with my brother.
    (D) I did all my chores on Sunday, I wanted to go to the zoo with my brother.
    (E) I did all my chores, wanting to go to the zoo on Sunday with my brother.

28. *I was helping my father in the garage. I hurt my thumb.*
    (A) While my father was in the garage, I helped to hurt my thumb.
    (B) I was helping my father, in the garage I hurt my thumb.
    (C) I hurt my thumb, I was helping my father in the garage.
    (D) Helping my father in the garage, and hurting my thumb.
    (E) While I was helping my father in the garage, I hurt my thumb.

For questions 29–31, choose the topic sentence that best fits the paragraph.

29. _____ At first, people did not understand the idea of Impressionism, which emphasized the way that nature looked to a person who was viewing it. This made his artwork very controversial, and some people even refused to show his paintings at exhibitions. Later, people began to appreciate Monet's incredible talents, and he has become one of the most important artists of the last 200 years.
    (A) Most modern museums display a mix of classical and modern art.
    (B) The French city of Givenchy was home for many years to Claude Monet.
    (C) Claude Monet, a French painter, rarely used the colors black and gray.
    (D) Claude Monet was one of the founders of the artistic movement called Impressionism.
    (E) Several painters, such as Claude Monet, are known for painting several versions of the same scene.

30. _____ She supplied soldiers with bandages and medical supplies, food, and clean water. She helped search for survivors and cared for the wounded. Later, when she discovered the work of the Red Cross, she was instrumental in establishing the American chapter in 1881.
    (A) Clara Barton, an American humanitarian, cared a great deal for victims of natural disasters.
    (B) During the Civil War, Clara Barton performed deeds that earned her the title "Angel of the Battlefield."
    (C) Clara Barton discovered the Red Cross while traveling through Europe to help fight the Franco-Prussian war.
    (D) In her early years, Clara Barton worked as a schoolteacher before taking a job with the U.S. Patent Office.
    (E) During the civil war, soldiers did not receive very good health care.

GO ON TO THE NEXT PAGE.

31. _____. First, frogs have long hind legs with webbed feet. This makes it easy for them to hop or swim. Toads, on the other hand, have short and stubby legs that are better for walking. Moreover, frogs have smooth and slimy skin, because they tend to live in a wet environment. Toads, instead, have warty dry skin and prefer to live in arid environments.

   (A) Frogs are some of the most interesting creatures in the world.
   (B) Animals that live both in water and on land are called amphibians.
   (C) Though they may look similar, there are many differences between frogs and toads.
   (D) Frogs and toads have many similar features.
   (E) Living in the water has caused some animals to develop special features.

For questions 32–34, choose the sentences that best continue the topic sentence.

32. Chinua Achebe, born in Nigeria in 1930, has become one of the most important authors of the 20th century.

   (A) Many English-language authors come from Nigeria. Since Nigeria was once a British colony, many people speak English there.
   (B) He has had many different jobs. He has worked in radio, and taught in a university.
   (C) His novel *Things Fall Apart* is widely regarded as one of the great novels of the 20th century. He has published several other brilliant novels, as well as many important essays.
   (D) Most important authors of the 20th century have written novels. The novel is perhaps our most important art form today.
   (E) Achebe is very fond of his homeland. He goes back very frequently to see his family.

33. Hawaii has had an interesting history since it was first settled by Polynesians around the year 500.

   (A) One of Hawaii's main products is tropical fruit. Bananas, pineapples, and sugarcane are all grown in Hawaii.
   (B) Hawaii is sunny and has beautiful beaches. This is why thousands of tourists visit Hawaii every year.
   (C) Polynesian languages are very different from most western languages. The Hawaiian language is a descendent of one or more of these Polynesian languages.
   (D) The first westerner to discover Hawaii was British Captain James Cook. Hawaii remained independent until the late 1800s, and when it became a US territory, and later the 50th state of the United States.
   (E) In the year 500, Europeans were not yet aware that America existed. However, the Romans had spread through most of Europe, and even settled parts of Great Britain.

34. Biologists say that insects may be the most common life form on the planet.

   (A) Insects are an important source of food for some people. They have a great deal of protein and are easy to store.
   (B) They live in the air, in the soil, as well as in and on other animals. Ants alone are estimated to make up 10% of the total animal mass on earth
   (C) There are, however, many other common life forms. Algae and microscopic plankton can be found almost anywhere there is a body of water.
   (D) Insects are also one of the oldest life forms on earth. Many species of insect have been virtually unchanged for millions of years.
   (E) Many people are afraid of them, however. This is why there are so many products designed to kill insects.

GO ON TO THE NEXT PAGE.

COOP Practice Test 1

For questions 35–37, choose the sentence that does not belong in the paragraph.

35. ① It was never Ella Fitzgerald's intention to become a jazz singer. ② She had originally planned to be a dancer. ③ The arts of dancing and singing go back very far in human history. ④ But one day when she planned to dance in a talent show, she was so scared that she couldn't stand up straight. ⑤ She decided to sing instead, and her outstanding voice was noticed by a musician in the audience. ⑥ From there, she became famous very quickly, and is thought to be the greatest jazz singer of our time.
(A) Sentence 2
(B) Sentence 3
(C) Sentence 4
(D) Sentence 5
(E) Sentence 6

36. ① In 1980 Mount Saint Helens, in the state of Washington, became a volcano. ② It exploded for the first time in thousands of years. ③ The explosion was felt as far north as Seattle and as far south as Los Angeles. ④ The mountain threw tons of ash into the air before it stopped exploding a few days later. ⑤ Sometimes lava is used to make soap or other cleaning products. ⑥ Most geologists believe that Mount Saint Helens will not explode for many thousands of years to come. ⑦ But they admit that another explosion might occur at any time.
(A) Sentence 2
(B) Sentence 3
(C) Sentence 4
(D) Sentence 5
(E) Sentence 6

37. ① Nicolaus Copernicus was born on February 19, 1474. ② He first studied in Cracow, and then was sent to Italy to continue his education. ③ At first he studied law, but soon he became a scientist. ④ In the Middle Ages it was very easy to be a lawyer and a scientist at the same time. ⑤ Copernicus's most important contribution to science was the heliocentric (sun-centered) view of the universe. ⑥ This theory finally succeeded in displacing the old geocentric (earth-centered view of the universe that had persisted since the time of the Greeks.
(A) Sentence 2
(B) Sentence 3
(C) Sentence 4
(D) Sentence 5
(E) Sentence 6

GO ON TO THE NEXT PAGE.

For questions 38–40, choose the sentence that best fills the blank.

Marie Curie was one of the greatest scientists of all time. Among her many important works were her studies on radiation, and the discovery of the elements polonium and radium._____
Before her death in 1934 she founded the Curie Foundation in Paris and the Radium Institute in Warsaw to continue her work.

38. (A) Moreover, she was the first person to win two Nobel Prizes.
    (B) In contrast, her husband was also quite famous.
    (C) Nevertheless, she also had a well-educated sister.
    (D) She was born in Warsaw, Poland, in 1867.
    (E) Her family valued education very highly.

Many people believe that penguins live in the Arctic Circle, near the North Pole. _____. In fact, penguins live in the Antarctic, near the South Pole. They can also live in the islands of the Southern Hemisphere, some of which can be quite warm. But this is still nowhere near the North Pole.

39. (A) There are about 17 species of penguin.
    (B) Furthermore, there are many different kinds of penguins.
    (C) This is, however, simply not true.
    (D) For example, some penguins live in very mild climates.
    (E) Penguins are one of several birds that cannot fly.

Susan B. Anthony, born in 1820, was one of the strongest advocates for women's rights in America. It is thanks to her efforts that women obtained their civil rights. She fought most of her life for equality and for women's suffrage, or the right to vote. _____ Women did not get the vote until 1919, almost 13 years after her death.

40. (A) Unfortunately, she did not live to see her dream come true.
    (B) She was commemorated by a one-dollar coin in the 1980s.
    (C) As a young woman, she worked as a schoolteacher.
    (D) In addition, she spoke out against excessive drinking.
    (E) From her Quaker upbringing she learned to dislike slavery.

GO ON TO THE NEXT PAGE.

12

Answers and Explanations to COOP Practice Test 1

PART 1—SEQUENCES

1. **D** The sequence goes 1, 2, 3 and rotates from top to right to bottom, so the missing element should have four spots on the left.

2. **C** The first two elements have triangles on the outside and reversed inside shapes. Therefore the missing element should have spots on the outside and reversed inside shapes.

3. **A** From the first to second element, all the Os change to Xs and Xs change to Os. Therefore the missing element should have OOX.

4. **C** The first element has two lines, the next has three lines, and the next has four lines. The missing element should have five lines.

5. **A** The second element is what you would get if you flipped the first element upside down. The final element should be what you would get if you flipped the third element upside down.

6. **B** The first element has three black circles, the second has two black circles, and the third has one black circle. Therefore the missing element should have no black circles.

7. **B** The sequence should go 21 (+ 11) 32 (+ 6) 38 | 56 (+ 11) 67 (+ 6) 73 | 16 (+ 11) **27** (+ 6) 33.

8. **D** The sequence should go 63 (+ 2) 65 (− 2) 63 | 18 (+ 2) 20 (− 2) 18 | 52 (+ 2) 54 (− 2) **52**.

9. **B** The sequence should go 32 (÷ 2) 16 (÷ 2) 8 | 52 (÷ 2) 26 (÷ 2) 13 | 24 (÷ 2) **12** (÷ 2) 6.

10. **B** The sequence should go 2 (× 4) 8 (× 4) 32 | 3 (× 4) 12 (× 4) 48 | 1 (× 4) **4** (× 4) 16.

11. **A** The sequence should go 5 (+ 1) 6 (× 3) 18 | 2 (+ 1) 3 (× 3) 9 | 8 (+ 1) **9** (× 3) 27.

12. **A** The sequence should go 15 (+ 0) 15 (÷ 3) 5 | 24 (+ 0) 24 (÷ 3) 8 | 9 (+ 0) 9 (÷ 3) **3**.

13. **B** The sequence should go 6 (× 2) 12 (× 2) 24 | 8 (× 2) 16 (× 2) 32 | 2 (× 2) **4** (× 2) 8.

14. **D** Substitute numbers for letters to make it easier. The sequence should go 1 (+ 1) 2 (+ 1) 3 | 1 (+ 2) 3 (+ 2) 5 | 1 (+ 3) 4 (+ 3) 7 | 1 (+ 4) 5 (+ 4) 9, or A B C | A C E | A D G | **A E I**.

15. **A** Each element in the sequence begins with a letter that was the last letter in the previous element, so the missing element must begin with Q. Substitute numbers for letters; start with 5 because E is the fifth letter in the alphabet. The sequence should go 5 (+ 2) 7 (+ 2) 9 | 9 (+ 2) 11 (+ 2) 13 | 13 (+ 2) 15 (+ 2) 17 | 17 (+ 2) 19 (+ 2) 21, or E G I | I K M | M O Q | **Q S U** | U W Y.

16. **A** The number in the center increases by 1, so the missing element must have a 4 in it. The letters follow this pattern: 10 (+ 2) 12 | 13 (+ 2) 15 | 16 (+ 2) 18 | 19 (+ 2) 21 | 22 (+ 2) 24, or J L | M O | P R | **S U** | V X.

17. **B** The number at the end goes up by the power of 2 each time, so the missing element should have a **16** in it. The letters follow this pattern: 3 (− 1) 2 | 5 (− 1) 4 | 7 (− 1) 6 | 9 (− 1) 8 | 11 (− 1) 10, or C B | E D | G F | **I H** | K J.

18. **D** The sequence goes backward through the alphabet in blocks of four letters.

19. **A** The first and third letters of the sequence start with A and go down the alphabet; the second and fourth letters start with Z and go backward through the alphabet.

20. **C** The second letter in each element becomes the first letter in the next element, so the missing element should begin with an I.

PART 2—ANALOGIES

1. **B** A shoe is worn on a foot; a horseshoe is worn on a hoof.

2. **C** Bees live in a hive; fish live in a fish tank.

3. **A** Goggles protect the eyes; a helmet protects the head.

4. **B** A pencil is used to write on paper; chalk is used to write on a blackboard.

5. **C** A bus is a large car; a lion is a large cat.

6. **B** An apple grows on a tree; a raspberry grows on a bush.

7. **A** A suitcase is used to hold a shirt; a briefcase is used to hold a file.

8. **C** Bread is made from grain; jam is made from fruit.

9. **A** You use your eyes to look at a painting; you use your ear to hear music.

10. **D** An axe is used to cut a tree; a knife is used to cut a carrot.

11. **A** A button holds a shirt closed; laces hold a shoe closed.

12. **B** You use a toothbrush to brush your teeth; you use a hairbrush to brush your hair.

13. **B** A ring is worn around a finger; a necklace is worn around the neck.

14. **A** A stool is a kind of chair; a desk is a kind of table.

15. **D** A typewriter was used to write letters, but now people use computers; a carriage was used for transportation, but now people use cars.

16. **B** An umbrella protects against the rain; sunglasses protect against the sun.

17. **A** A vacuum is a machine that does the work of a broom; a sewing machine is a machine that does the work of a needle and thread.

18. **D** A pot is a small kettle; a cap is a small hat.

19. **A** A wristwatch is a small clock; a house is a small skyscraper.

20. **B** A caterpillar becomes a butterfly; an acorn becomes a tree.

PART 3 —MEMORY

1. D
2. E
3. C
4. D
5. E
6. A
7. B
8. D
9. C
10. B
11. A
12. D
13. D
14. A
15. A
16. E
17. A
18. D
19. E
20. C

PART 4—VERBAL REASONING

1. A An oven is used to heat things. It does not necessarily have to be made of stone, heat bread, or have a rack.

2. C Scissors are used to cut things. They can cut things besides paper and hair, and they do not have to be in an office.

3. C A hat is worn on the head. It may or may not be black, felt, or a cowboy hat.

4. B A knife has an edge for cutting. It may or may not be metal, used for steak, or found in a kitchen.

5. D A microphone is used to capture sound. It may or may not have a cord, capture music, or be used to make an announcement.

6. D Shallow means having very little depth. It may or may not describe the amount of water or space in a container, and it has nothing to do with heat.

7. **B** A breeze is a mild gust, and a gust is a mild hurricane. Drizzle is a light rain, and rain is a light downpour.

8. **D** Cup, quart, and gallon are measures of volume; ounce, pound, and ton are measures of weight.

9. **B** A tie goes around the neck; a bracelet goes around the wrist; a belt goes around the waist.

10. **A** An ankle is a joint in the foot; a knee is a joint in the leg; an elbow is a joint in the arm.

11. **C** A lion and a cat are kinds of feline; a wolf and a dog are kinds of canine.

12. **B** A small piece of wood is a splinter, and a large piece of wood is a log. A small piece of bread is a crumb, and a large piece of bread is a loaf.

13. **B** We know that Trudy is taller than Cindy, and Cindy is taller than Alice, so we know that Trudy is taller than Alice.

14. **B** All we know is that Martina studied for three hours and Carol did not study at all, so Martina studied more than Carol. None of the other choices is certain.

15. **B** We know that Bob will not buy a frozen yogurt since the store is out of sprinkles. Since we also know that he buys either an ice cream cone or frozen yogurt, we know he will buy an ice cream cone.

16. **C** All we know is that Peter left the movie theater and did not return, so he didn't see the end of the movie. None of the other choices is certain.

17. **A** We know that Jean types 8 pages per hour and Ron types 13 pages per hour. Therefore Jean types more slowly than Ron.

18. **A** Since *nagam* is in both words that mean ship, *nagam* means ship. Therefore, in the word *ocamanagam*, *ocama* must mean passenger. This narrows our choices to A and B. Since *kapali* is in both words that mean cargo, *kapali* means cargo. Therefore in *kapalimagal*, *magal* means van. The correct answer is *ocama* (passenger) *magal* (van).

19. **B** Because *bulu* appears in both words that mean horses, *bulu* means horses. Therefore, in *bulunola*, *nola* means picture. This narrows the choices to B and C. Since *hati* is in both words that mean painting, *hati* means painting. Therefore, in *malahati*, *mala* means cows. The correct answer is *mala* (cows) *nola* (picture).

20. **D** Apple seeds must have one part from *patohamari* (apple juice) and one part from *maxohapa* (grape seeds). The only choice that does so is D.

PART 5—READING COMPREHENSION

1. **C** Each paragraph of the passage discusses some aspect of the evolution of kangaroos.

2. **D** There is no evidence in the passage to support A, B, or C.

3. **A** The only person listed who would know about fossils and dinosaurs is a scientist.

4. **B** The first paragraph says that "their thick tail gives them balance."

5. **B** This quotation appears as an example for how "some kangaroo species differ."

6. **C** The words "living fossil" are used at the beginning of the last paragraph to describe an opossum.

7. **A** According to the last paragraph, the kangaroo has evolved a great deal, whereas the opossum has not (see the last sentence of the second paragraph).

8. **B** A, C, and D are only details of the passage. The whole passage discusses Lincoln's life, from his birth to his death.

9. **B** The passage says that "due to his poor upbringing, Lincoln was determined to promote equal economic opportunity for all people."

10. **A** There is no evidence to support B, C or D. The passage says, however, that Lincoln was "one of our greatest presidents."

11. **B** According to the passage, "Lincoln returned to politics with the repeal of the Missouri Compromise."

12. **C** The third paragraph says that Lincoln was inexperienced in military matters. We can therefore infer that he did not have the experience of commanding an army.

13. **B** According to the passage, he was a member of the Republican Party.

14. **C** The final paragraph says that he was killed just after "his re-election to office."

15. **B** Every paragraph discusses how an Eskimo can navigate without sight or tools.

16. **A** Every choice is mentioned somewhere in the passage except A.

17. **D** A is extreme, and there is no support in the passage for B or C. It does say in the final paragraph, however, that Eskimo methods sometimes work when modern technology is ineffective.

18. **C** According to the last paragraph, "compasses can't be relied on."

19. **B** There is no evidence in the passage to support A, C, or D. However, it does say that an Eskimo "aligns the fur of his parka with the breeze." Therefore, some parkas must be made with fur.

20. **D** The author speaks quite highly of the Eskimo techniques.

21. **A** Since the passage begins by saying that the stars "seem" to move and then uses the word *appear* in the same way, the word *appear* in this passage must mean "seem."

22. **D** The second sentence of the passage says that "the movement of the stars is due to the rotation of the earth."

23. **C**   The passage says that it can be used for navigation because "its position is fixed."

24. **C**   According to the passage, Polaris "lies almost directly above the North Pole."

25. **A**   The passage says that it seems "as though the stars are moving from east to west in the sky."

26. **B**   The only choice that would discuss the stars in depth is an astronomy text.

27. **C**   The word *frigid* follows a mention of a need "to keep its inhabitants warm." Therefore *frigid* must mean "very cold."

28. **C**   According to the first paragraph, the yurt was designed to be "portable" and to be "carried by a single pack animal."

29. **C**   The second paragraph says that the yurt was designed to allow "smoke to flow out." This means that there is smoke inside the yurt.

30. **A**   The word *secured* is used to discuss how the pieces of felt are attached to the frame of the yurt.

31. **D**   Since milk is never mentioned, A can be eliminated. B does not mention cows and is too general; C is only a detail of the passage.

32. **C**   According to the passage, "the cow is able to extract a maximum of nutrients from its food" with its special digestive system.

33. **B**   The passage says that cows are "unlike humans, who have a simple stomach."

34. **A**   D is extreme, and there is no evidence to support B or C. The first line, however, tells us that the author finds the cow's digestive system "interesting."

35. **B**   The word *progress* is used to describe the technological developments in the last hundred years.

36. **A**   The second paragraph says that police officers and taxi drivers make use of cars on the job.

37. **C**   A and B are only details, and D is not really discussed.

38. **D**   According to the final sentence of the passage, they devote research to making cars "more fuel-efficient and less polluting."

39. **A**   D is extreme, and there is no evidence in the passage to support B or C.

40. **A**   The author says in the first paragraph that the advances have been "phenomenal."

PART 6—MATHEMATICS CONCEPTS AND APPLICATIONS

1. **A**   3 + 60 alone makes 63, so C and D can be eliminated. Since the thousandth place is the third to the right of the decimal, $\frac{2}{1000} = 0.002$.

2. **C**   First, let's find Polly's total income for the year. She earns $20 per month for 10 months, or $200. Add to that her $32 from November and $32 from December, and her total income for the year is $264. To find the average, we divide this amount by 12 (the number of months).

3. **D**   Let's take –4 as our negative even number and 3 as our positive odd number. If we multiply them together we get –12, which is negative and even.

4. **B**   The easiest way to solve this is to move the decimals three places to the right, and we get $\frac{246}{120}$. If you like, you can estimate and see that this is just larger than 2, or you can do long division.

5. **A**   To solve 3.0×10^3 we move the decimal three places to the right, and get 3,000. To solve 5.3×10^2 we move the decimal two places to the right, and get 530. If we multiply these numbers together, we get 1,590,000. Already we can eliminate C and D. Which of A or B says 1,590,000? Take 1.59 and move the decimal point 6 places to the right.

6. **D**   The formula for the area of a circle is πr^2. Since the radius is 5, the area is 25π.

7. **D**   Percent decrease is always $\frac{difference}{original}$. The difference between the two prices is $29, and the original price of the notebook is $85. So the percent difference is $\frac{29}{85} = 0.34$, or 34%.

8. **D**   One easy way to solve this problem is to plug in the answer choices. Could x be 2? Is the average of 2, 5, and 2 equal to the average of 3 and 2? No. Could x be 3? Is the average of 2, 5, and 3 equal to the average of 3 and 3? No. Could x be 4? Is the average of 2, 5, and 4 equal to the average of 3 and 4? No. Could x be 5? Yes, because the average of 2, 5, and 5 is 4, and the average of 3 and 5 is 4.

9. **A**   We can set this up as a proportion: $\frac{50 \; papers}{\$3} = \frac{420 \; papers}{x}$. To solve for x, solve $\frac{420 \times 3}{50}$.

10. **D**   The area of a triangle is $\frac{1}{2}$ base × height. The base is 12 and the height is 4, so the area is 24.

11. **D**   We know that $a + b + c + 75 = 360$, so $a + b + c = 285$.

12. **B** First we need to find 20% of $15. Translate this as $\frac{20}{100} \times 15 = 3$. That means that the price is increased to $18. If that price is then reduced by 10%, that's $1.80 off.

13. **B** We can figure out which fraction is greatest by comparing them in pairs using the Bowtie. $\frac{7}{13}$ is larger than $\frac{5}{11}$, so A can be eliminated. $\frac{7}{13}$ is also larger than $\frac{1}{3}$. Finally, $\frac{7}{13}$ is larger than $\frac{6}{15}$.

14. **C** Let's begin by listing all the factors of 16 and 56. 16 can be factored as 1×16, 2×8, and 4×4. 56 can be factored as 1×56, 2×28, 4×14, and 7×8. They have the factors 1, 2, 4, and 8 in common.

15. **A** We can solve for x by first subtracting $5x$ from each side. This gives us $-3x - 5 > 1$. If we add 5 to each side, this becomes $-3x > 6$. Now we need to divide each side by -3. When you divide by a negative number, you need to change the direction of the inequality.

16. **A** The angle inside the triangle next to 85 must be 95 degrees, because their sum is 180. Now the angles inside the triangle are 95 and 56. The sum of the angles inside a triangle must equal 180, so the third angle must be 29.

17. **B** It's very hard to count multiples up to 50. There must be an easier way. What are the first multiples of 3? 3, 6, 9, 12, and 15. What are the first multiples of 4? 4, 8, 12, and 16. What do you notice? Their first common multiple is 12. Therefore the question is really asking how many 12s there are between 1 and 50. This is a much simpler question: 12, 24, 36, 48.

18. **D** The easiest way to solve this is to find the volume of the large box. Volume is length $\times$ width $\times$ height $= 5 \times 8 \times 3 = 120$. Each small cube has volume $1 \times 1 \times 1 = 1$.

19. **B** Michelle made 70 cookies. Of those 70 cookies, 20 were sugar. The question is what percent of the total cookies were sugar? You can translate the question as $\frac{x}{100} \times 70 = 20$. To solve for x, multiply each side by 100 and divide by 70. This gives you 28%. The closest is B.

20. **D** First we need to find out how many square feet the wall measures: $12 \times 18 = 216$ square feet. Each gallon of paint covers 3 square feet, so we will need $\frac{216}{3}$ gallons of paint.

21. **B** Let's take the small boxes first. We have 8 small boxes with 12 oranges each. That makes 8×12 oranges in the small boxes. Only B has (8×12) in it.

22. **B** Since Louise has 8 total pairs, and we want to know the probability of drawing one of the 2 black pairs, we set up the fraction $\frac{2}{8}$, which is the same as $\frac{1}{4}$.

23. **A**   To get all the x's on one side, subtract $4x$ from each side. This gives us $-x - 5 = 3$. Now let's add 5 to each side: $-x = 8$.

24. **B**   You can rewrite this as $\frac{3}{4} \div \frac{3}{5}$. To divide fractions, flip the second fraction and multiply them: $\frac{3}{4} \times \frac{5}{3} = \frac{15}{12} = \frac{5}{4}$.

25. **A**   The best way to solve this problem is by plugging in the answer choices. Start with A. If Ken gives 13 marbles to John, then Ken will lose 13 marbles and John will gain 13 marbles. Ken will then have 31 and John will have 31.

26. **B**   Let's plug in a number for x to make this problem easier. Let's say that x is 10. The question now reads: Which of the following is equivalent to multiplying 10 by 5? The answer is 50. Which of the answer choices also says 50? B does, because if we divide 10 by $\frac{1}{5}$, we get 50.

27. **C**   Plug in the answer choices until we find the one that leaves a remainder of 2. 25 divided by 3 leaves a remainder of 1, so A isn't the answer. 37 divided by 3 leaves a remainder of 1, so B isn't the answer. 44 divided by 3 leaves a remainder of 2, so C is the answer.

28. **A**   Amanda's salary increased from \$25,000 to \$32,000. Percent increase is calculated by $\frac{difference}{original}$. In this case the difference in salary is \$7,000 over the original %25,000: $\frac{7,000}{25,000} = 28\%$.

29. **C**   If BC is 5 and B is the midpoint of AC, then AB is also 5. Likewise, if C is the midpoint of BD, then CD is also 5.

30. **C**   The side of the rectangle opposite side 4 must also be 4; the side of the rectangle opposite side 5 must also be 5, and the remaining side must be 3 because the two sides on the right of the figure make 10.

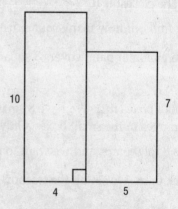

Therefore the perimeter of the whole figure is $5 + 4 + 10 + 4 + 3 + 5 + 7 = 38$.

31. **A** Plug in the answer choices until we find the right answer. Could the number of adults be 34? The problem says that there are 18 more adults than children, so if there are 34 adults there will be 16 children. Does this make a total of 50? Yes.

32. **C** Plug in the answer choices until we find the value for x that works in the equation. Could x be 2? $2^2 + 3^2$ is 13, not 97. Let's try 3: $2^3 + 3^3$ is 35. How about 4? $2^4 + 3^4$ is 97.

33. **C** Let's begin by finding the factors of 12. 12 can be written 1×12, 2×6, and 3×4. Now we need to find the sum of these factors: $1 + 12 + 2 + 6 + 3 + 4 = 28$.

34. **B** Since this is a square, the perimeter is $6 + 6 + 6 + 6$, or 24, and the area is 6×6, or 36. The difference between 24 and 36 is 12.

35. **A** If $\frac{1}{5}$ of a number is 14, then that number must be 14×5, or 70. Now the problem wants us to take $\frac{1}{2}$ of 70, which is 35.

36. **B** There are a total of 10 houses, of which 3 are blue. If 3 out of 10 are blue, then $\frac{3}{10}$, or 30%, are blue.

37. **B** When the number under the root symbol is the same, you can add them together: $2\sqrt{3} + 3\sqrt{3} = 5\sqrt{3}$.

38. **C** AO is a radius of the circle. If the radius is 14, then the diameter (which is twice the radius) is 28.

39. **A** First let's multiply out the left side of the equation. This gives us $-5 + 6a + 4b = 4b - 2$. If we subtract $4b$ from each side, we get $-5 + 6a = -2$. Now we can add 5 to each side, which gives us $6a = 3$. By dividing 6 from each side, we get $a = \frac{1}{2}$.

40. **C** Let's write these exponents out and then reduce. 5^6 is the same as $5 \times 5 \times 5 \times 5 \times 5 \times 5$. 5^2 is the same as 5×5. So we can rewrite the expression as $\frac{5 \times 5 \times 5 \times 5 \times 5 \times 5}{5 \times 5}$. If we reduce, we are left with $5 \times 5 \times 5 \times 5$, or 5^4.

PART 7—LANGUAGE EXPRESSION

1. **C** Since you would not normally give a speech when you hadn't practiced, these two ideas express a contrast. Therefore the word in the blank should be a word like *but*. The closest is C.

2. **B** The second phrase expands on the idea of the first, so we need a same-direction word such as B.

3. **C** Since the second phrase explains why the first occurred, the best choice is C.

4. C   Since the second phrase continues the idea of the first, we need a same-direction word such as A or C. A does not work in this context.

5. B   A and B are the only valid comparative forms; B is the best, since the sentence discusses the best film of the whole year.

6. E   A, B, and D are double negatives, so they can be eliminated. We do need something that expresses that Jack has no patience, so E is the best.

7. B   D and E are awkward, and C has two different verb tenses. A makes it sound as if the US remained independent instead of Hawaii.

8. C   In A, B, and D the word *important* is misplaced or in the wrong form. E is illogical.

9. E   A, B, and D make it sound as if the award was doing the work, and the second phrase of C is awkward.

10. A   B and D are redundant, the pronoun "they" is unclear in C, and E is illogical.

11. D   C is a fragment, and A, B, and E are awkward.

12. D   All the other choices are awkward and unidiomatic.

13. C   A, B, and D have problems of verb tense. E has an incorrect verb form.

14. D   All the other choices have problems of parallelism or verb tense.

15. B   A has a problem of subject/verb agreement, C and E have incorrect verb forms, and D has a problem of parallelism.

16. B   A and D are sentence fragments, C has an unnecessary *to* before the verb, and E has a problem of verb tense.

17. B   A and C have problems of subject/verb agreement, D is a fragment, and E has an incorrect verb form.

18. C   Since the opening phrase begins with "While," nothing in that phrase can be the main subject.

19. B   In this sentence it is the superintendent who does the acting.

20. D   The opening phrases tell us where the pair (of scissors) lies.

21. D   The opening phrase tells us when the dog began to bark.

22. C   The main idea is "scientists decided."

23. B   The first phrase begins with "Since," so the verb "ate" is not the main verb.

24. D   The main idea is "George Washington . . . became the first President."

25. D   Since the first phrase begins with "Before," none of its verbs are the main verb. The main idea is "I did not know."

26. B   A is a fragment, C changes the meaning of the original sentences, and D and E have problems of verb tense.

27. B   A and E change the meaning of the original sentences, C is illogical, and D is a comma splice.

28. **E** D is a fragment; A, B, and C are awkward or illogical.

29. **D** Since the rest of the paragraph discusses Impressionism and Monet, the most plausible choice is D.

30. **B** The following sentences discuss ways in which Clara Barton helped soldiers during a war. Therefore, the opening sentence should introduce this.

31. **C** The rest of the paragraph discusses the differences between frogs and toads.

32. **C** This topic sentence discusses how Achebe was an "important author." The only choice that discusses this idea is C.

33. **D** This topic sentence mentions Hawaii's "interesting history." The sentences that follow should expand on the idea of history.

34. **B** This topic sentence mentions how common insects are. The sentences that expand on this idea are in B.

35. **B** This paragraph discusses Ella Fitzgerald. Therefore, sentence 3 does not fit.

36. **D** All of the sentences in this paragraph are about Mount Saint Helens except sentence 5.

37. **C** This paragraph is about Copernicus with the exception of sentence 4.

38. **A** The sentences around the blank discuss Curie's accomplishments. Therefore, the sentence that fills the blank should also discuss an accomplishment.

39. **C** Just after the blank there is a correction of a false opinion. Therefore the blank should introduce this contrast with a word like *but* or *however*.

40. **A** After the blank we see that Anthony's project did not succeed until after her death. The blank should introduce this contrast.

12

The Princeton Review
COOP Practice Test 2

COOP Practice Test 2
Memory
(12 Minutes)

You have 12 minutes to memorize the following definitions for these imaginary words.

A doveki is soup

A cholka is a shoe

A socopa is a friend

Tanytor means to sing

Ununti is bread

A lababse is a table

A mulethi is a spoon

A verdid is a ship

An oukew is a nose

A doomys is a fence

Dered means to swim

A leceen is a bottle

A nemtee is a piece of chalk

A radilo is a family

Nopradig means happy

A padnom is a vegetable

Anadi is the color blue

A kice is a typewriter

Sunanta is paper

A honixu is a stick

GO ON TO THE NEXT PAGE.

Part 1
Sequences
20 Questions, 15 Minutes

Choose the letter that shows what should fill the blank in the sequence

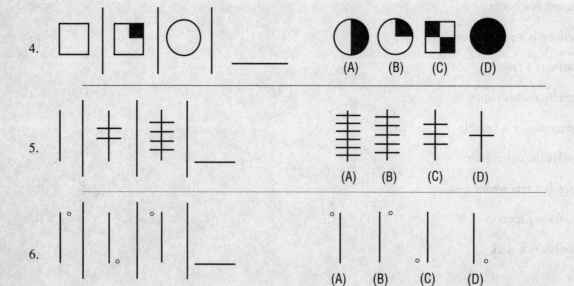

1. $\dfrac{x}{y}$ | $\dfrac{y}{x}$ | $\dfrac{p}{q}$ | ____

$\dfrac{p}{x}$ $\dfrac{p}{y}$ $\dfrac{q}{p}$ $\dfrac{q}{x}$
(A)   (B)   (C)   (D)

2. BBBA | BBAA | BAAA | ____

BABA   AAAA   ABBB   ABBA
(A)   (B)   (C)   (D)

3. △○○△ | ○△△○ | +□□+ | ___

□++□   □+□+   □○○□   △++△
(A)   (B)   (C)   (D)

4.

(A)   (B)   (C)   (D)

5.

(A)   (B)   (C)   (D)

6.

(A)   (B)   (C)   (D)

GO ON TO THE NEXT PAGE.

7. 34 46 49 | 8 20 23 | 57 __ 72   (A) 63   (B) 65   (C) 69   (D) 70

8. 31 28 35 | 17 14 21 | 36 __ 40   (A) 30   (B) 33   (C) 35   (D) 39

9. 66 66 22 | 18 18 6 | 27 __ 9   (A) 5   (B) 9   (C) 27   (D) 53

10. 8 6 12 | 17 15 30 | 6 __ 8   (A) 4   (B) 6   (C) 8   (D) 12

11. 6 18 19 | 3 9 10 | 4 __ 13   (A) 8   (B) 12   (C) 16   (D) 20

12. 3 12 6 | 12 48 24 | 8 __ 16   (A) 12   (B) 24   (C) 32   (D) 36

13. 11 33 33 | 6 18 18 | 13 __ 39   (A) 13   (B) 18   (C) 39   (D) 45

14. A1B2 | A2B3 | A3B4 | ____ | A5B6   (A) A5B5   (B) A5C6   (C) A4B4   (D) A4B5

15. ABC | FGH | KLM | ___ | UVW   (A) PQR   (B) RST   (C) UVW   (D) XYZ

GO ON TO THE NEXT PAGE.

16. AZA | BYB | CXC | ___ | EVE   (A) DYD   (B) DWD   (C) WDW   (D) XDX

17. GHF | IJH | KLJ | ____ | OPN   (A) LMN   (B) NML   (C) MNL   (D) KML

18. ABDE | FGIJ | KLNO | _____ | UVXY   (A) MNPR   (B) PRST   (C) PQST   (D) MNRS

19. BDFH | FHJL | JLMP | _____ | RTVX   (A) MPRT   (B) MPTV   (C) MNPT   (D) MNRV

20. B9LG | C12M | HD15NI | _____ | F21PK   (A) E16OI   (B) E18OJ   (C) E19PL   (D) E20QJ

GO ON TO THE NEXT PAGE.

Part 2
Analogies
20 Questions, 7 Minutes

For the following questions, look at the pictures in the top two boxes. Then choose the picture that should go in the empty box so that the bottom two pictures have the same relation as the top two pictures.

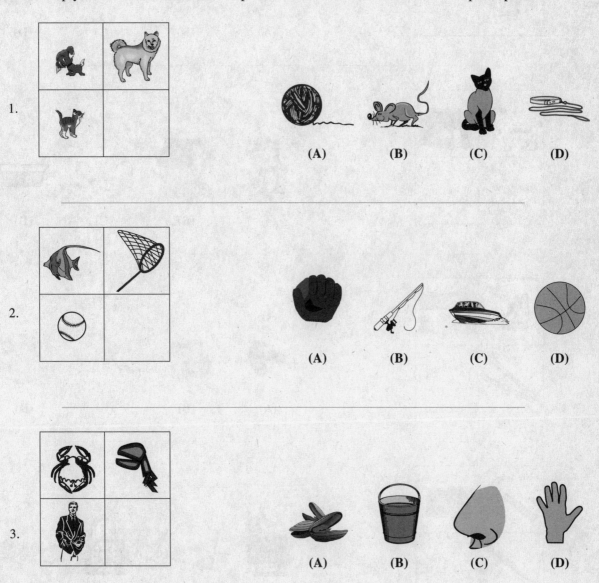

GO ON TO THE NEXT PAGE.

4.   (A)   (B)   (C)   (D)

5.   (A)   (B)   (C)   (D)

6.   (A)   (B)   (C)   (D)

7.   (A)   (B)   (C)   (D)

GO ON TO THE NEXT PAGE.

8.

(A) (B) (C) (D)

9.

(A) (B) (C) (D)

10.

(A) (B) (C) (D)

11.

(A) (B) (C) (D)

GO ON TO THE NEXT PAGE.

12.

(A)   (B)   (C)   (D)

13.

(A)   (B)   (C)   (D)

14.

(A)   (B)   (C)   (D)

15.

(A)   (B)   (C)   (D)

GO ON TO THE NEXT PAGE.

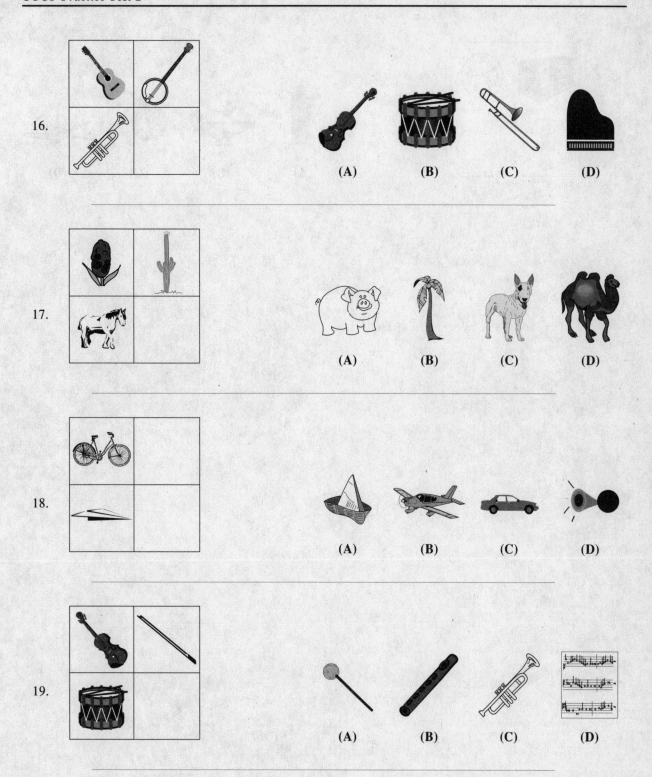

16.

(A)   (B)   (C)   (D)

17.

(A)   (B)   (C)   (D)

18.

(A)   (B)   (C)   (D)

19.

(A)   (B)   (C)   (D)

GO ON TO THE NEXT PAGE.

20.

(A)   (B)   (C)   (D)

GO ON TO THE NEXT PAGE.

Part 3
Memory
20 Questions, 5 Minutes

The following questions ask you about the words you memorized at the beginning of this test. Choose the word that means the same as the underlined word or phrase.

1. Which word means *bread*?
   (A) radilo
   (B) doomys
   (C) mulethi
   (D) ununti
   (E) sunanta

2. Which word means *a shoe*?
   (A) doomys
   (B) ununti
   (C) radilo
   (D) cholka
   (E) sunanta

3. Which word means *a friend*?
   (A) nopradig
   (B) kice
   (C) oukew
   (D) lababse
   (E) socopa

4. Which word means *a table*?
   (A) nemtee
   (B) doveki
   (C) padnom
   (D) honixu
   (E) lababse

5. Which word means *soup*?
   (A) kice
   (B) socopa
   (C) leceen
   (D) doveki
   (E) nemtee

6. Which word means *to sing*?
   (A) verdid
   (B) anadi
   (C) dered
   (D) cholka
   (E) tanytor

7. Which word means *a spoon*?
   (A) dered
   (B) socopa
   (C) mulethi
   (D) padnom
   (E) ununti

8. Which word means *a typewriter*?
   (A) lababse
   (B) nemtee
   (C) honixu
   (D) kice
   (E) oukew

9. Which word means *a nose*?
   (A) honixu
   (B) mulethi
   (C) ununti
   (D) oukew
   (E) nopradig

10. Which word means *a bottle*?
    (A) tanytor
    (B) dered
    (C) radilo
    (D) sunanta
    (E) leceen

11. Which word means *to swim*?
    (A) dered
    (B) ununti
    (C) oukew
    (D) anadi
    (E) padnom

GO ON TO THE NEXT PAGE.

12. Which word means *a stick*?
    (A) cholka
    (B) honixu
    (C) tanytor
    (D) verdid
    (E) dered

13. Which word means *a piece of chalk*?
    (A) socopa
    (B) nemtee
    (C) leceen
    (D) verdid
    (E) honixu

14. Which word means *a family*?
    (A) radilo
    (B) doveki
    (C) socopa
    (D) mulethi
    (E) padnom

15. Which word means *happy*?
    (A) nopradig
    (B) tanytor
    (C) leceen
    (D) anadi
    (E) oukew

16. Which word means *a vegetable*?
    (A) mulethi
    (B) sunanta
    (C) padnom
    (D) verdid
    (E) doveki

17. Which word means *the color blue*?
    (A) cholka
    (B) anadi
    (C) lababse
    (D) doomys
    (E) nopradig

18. Which word means *a ship*?
    (A) verdid
    (B) doveki
    (C) nemtee
    (D) radilo
    (E) anadi

19. Which word means *paper*?
    (A) doomys
    (B) leceen
    (C) sunanta
    (D) kice
    (E) tanytor

20. Which word means *a fence*?
    (A) cholka
    (B) lababse
    (C) nopradig
    (D) doomys
    (E) kice

GO ON TO THE NEXT PAGE.

Part 4
Verbal Reasoning
20 Questions, 15 Minutes

For questions 1–6, find the word that is a necessary part of the underlined word.

1. <u>dentist</u>
   (A) toothbrush
   (B) office
   (C) nurse
   (D) teeth

2. <u>dictionary</u>
   (A) picture
   (B) word
   (C) history
   (D) bookshelf

3. <u>refrigerator</u>
   (A) cold
   (B) ice
   (C) food
   (D) kitchen

4. <u>melody</u>
   (A) sound
   (B) piano
   (C) beauty
   (D) orchestra

5. <u>feline</u>
   (A) jungle
   (B) attack
   (C) speed
   (D) cat

6. <u>humidity</u>
   (A) summer
   (B) thermometer
   (C) water
   (D) cleanliness

For questions 7–12, choose the word that should go below the line such that the words above the line and the words below the line have the same relationship.

7. <u>cool   cold   frigid</u>
   warm   hot
   (A) temperature
   (B) scalding
   (C) air
   (D) water

8. <u>second   minute   hour</u>
   day   month
   (A) clock
   (B) year
   (C) time
   (D) holiday

9. <u>eye   tongue   hand</u>
   sight   taste
   (A) arm
   (B) touch
   (C) finger
   (D) hear

10. <u>bush   vine   tree</u>
    berry   grape
    (A) carrot
    (B) apple
    (C) raisin
    (D) leaf

11. <u>feathers   fur   scales</u>
    bird   bear
    (A) fur
    (B) animal
    (C) dog
    (D) fish

GO ON TO THE NEXT PAGE.

12. <u>annoyed</u>   <u>angry</u>   <u>enraged</u>
content   happy
    (A) ecstatic
    (B) feeling
    (C) sad
    (D) bored

For questions 13–17, find the statement that is true according to the information you are given.

13. Martin's class can go to Europe this summer only if they get a group rate. To get a group rate, at least 20 people must sign up for the trip. Martin's class is eventually able to go to Europe this summer.
    (A) More than 30 people signed up for the trip.
    (B) Group rates are common for class trips.
    (C) No fewer than 20 people signed up for the trip.
    (D) Martin had to convince many of his friends to sign up for the trip.

14. David, Alice, and Marsha belong to their high school's track team. Alice can run 6 miles per hour. David can run 7 miles per hour. Marsha can run 7 miles per hour.
    (A) David and Alice are the fastest runners on the team.
    (B) Alice is a better student than Marsha.
    (C) David and Marsha tied for first place at last week's race.
    (D) Marsha can run faster than Alice.

15. John has more marbles than Tabatha. Cindy has fewer marbles than Larry. Peter has more marbles than Tabatha. Julie has more marbles than Larry.
    (A) Julie has more marbles than Cindy.
    (B) John has more marbles than Larry.
    (C) Tabatha has more marbles than Julie.
    (D) Cindy has more marbles than Tabatha.

16. To be allowed to swim in the pool during recess, each student has to pass a swim test. To pass the test, a student must be able to swim 3 laps of the pool. Carlos can swim 4 laps of the pool, John can swim 5 laps, and Erwin can swim 2 laps.
    (A) Carlos likes to swim more than Erwin.
    (B) Carlos, John, and Erwin can swim during recess.
    (C) Carlos may swim during recess but Erwin cannot.
    (D) John can swim faster than Carlos but not as fast as Erwin.

17. On a recent math test, Alex got a higher score than Scott and Lucy. Scott got a higher score than Petra and Janice. Lucy got a higher score than Marcus and Wendy.
    (A) Janice got a higher score than Lucy.
    (B) Wendy and Petra got the same score.
    (C) Petra got a failing grade on the math test.
    (D) Wendy got a lower score than Alex.

For questions 18–20, choose the best answer.

18. calajobo means window shade
calamala means lamp shade
agaajobo means window cleaner

    Which of the following could mean lamp cleaner?
    (A) agaacala
    (B) agaamala
    (C) calaalam
    (D) malamala

19. poyoakoo means cat hair
noonakoo means dog hair
noonaala means dog food

    Which of the following could mean cat food?
    (A) noonmola
    (B) poyoaala
    (C) poyonoon
    (D) aalapana

20. cimthacana means run quickly
lathawa means eat slowly
lathacana means run slowly

    Which of the following could mean eat quickly?
    (A) lathacim
    (B) lacana
    (C) cimcana
    (D) cimthawa

GO ON TO THE NEXT PAGE.

Part 5
Reading Comprehension
40 Questions, 40 Minutes

Most people know that the ancient Egyptians mummified their dead. But few people know the details of how or why a mummy was made.

The point of mummification was to remove all of the parts of the body that could <u>decompose</u> to ensure that the remaining parts lasted forever. This was important to the Egyptians, who believed that parts of a person's soul needed a body to live in. If the body were to rot and disappear, the soul would be left homeless for eternity. To prevent the body from rotting, all the water had to be removed and all the bacteria had to be killed.

The process of embalming took more than sixty days. First, most of the internal organs had to be removed. The embalmer would break the corpse's nose and pull out the brain. He would then make an incision in the abdomen to remove the stomach, intestines, lungs, and liver. These were then salted, dried, and placed in jars that were buried with the body. The heart, which the Egyptians believed to be the source of consciousness, was often salted, dried, and placed back inside the body.

After the organs were removed, the body was doused with alcohol. This served to kill the bacteria in the body. The body was then salted, which dried out the skin. Finally the whole body was wrapped in waxed bandages to form a waterproof casing around the body.

1. The word <u>decompose</u> in the passage most nearly means
    - (A) sing
    - (B) rot
    - (C) get wet
    - (D) frighten

2. According to the passage, about how long did it take to make a mummy?
    - (A) less than one month
    - (B) one month
    - (C) two months
    - (D) a year

3. This passage is mostly about
    - (A) the process of mummification
    - (B) the organs of the human body
    - (C) Egyptian religious beliefs
    - (D) why mummies are so small

4. It can be inferred from the passage that another word for mummification is
    - (A) salting
    - (B) embalming
    - (C) dousing
    - (D) incision

5. According to the passage, the Egyptians mummified their dead in order to ensure that
    - (A) the dead person would be protected from wolves
    - (B) the dead person's soul would have a home
    - (C) nobody would rob the dead person's grave
    - (D) the dead person's organs would not be lost

6. According to the passage, all of the following organs were put into jars except
    - (A) heart
    - (B) liver
    - (C) lungs
    - (D) intestine

7. It can be inferred from the passage that which of the following can cause a corpse to rot?
    - (A) wax
    - (B) sand
    - (C) salt
    - (D) bacteria

GO ON TO THE NEXT PAGE.

Like so many of his famous compatriots, Phineas Taylor Barnum came of good old New England <u>stock</u>. His ancestors were among the builders of the colonies of Massachusetts and Connecticut. His father's father, Ephraim Barnum, was a captain in the War of the Revolution, and was distinguished for his valor and fervent patriotism. His mother's father, Phineas Taylor, was locally noted as a wag and practical joker. His father, Philo Barnum, was in turn a tailor, a farmer, a storekeeper, and a country tavernkeeper, and was not particularly prosperous in any of these callings.

Philo Barnum and his wife, Irena Taylor, lived in Bethel, Connecticut, and there, on July 5, 1810, their first child was born. He was named Phineas Taylor Barnum after his maternal grandfather, and the latter, in return for the compliment, bestowed upon his first grandchild at his christening the title-deeds of a "landed estate," five acres in extent known as Ivy Island and situated in that part of Bethel known as the "Plum Trees."

In his early years the boy led the life of the average New England farmer's son of that period. He drove the cows to and from the pasture, shelled corn, weeded the garden, and "did up chores." As he grew older he rode the horse in plowing corn, raked hay, wielded the shovel and the hoe, and chopped wood. At six years old he began to go to school—the typical district school. "The first date," he once said, "I remember inscribing upon my writing-book was 1818." The ferule, or birch-rod, was in those days the assistant schoolmaster, and young P.T. Barnum made its acquaintance. He was, however, an apt and ready scholar, particularly excelling in mathematics. One night, when he was ten years old, he was called out of bed by his teacher, who had made a wager with a neighbor that Barnum could calculate the number of feet in a load of wood in five minutes. Barnum did it in less than two minutes, to the delight of his teacher and the astonishment of the neighbor.

8. The word <u>stock</u> in this passage most nearly means
   (A) soup
   (B) merchandise
   (C) ancestors
   (D) money

9. P.T. Barnum's paternal grandfather was
   (A) a soldier in the Revolutionary War
   (B) a practical joker
   (C) a farmer
   (D) a shopkeeper

10. According to the passage, P.T. Barnum's father
   (A) did many things and was good at none of them
   (B) was one of the best teachers in the state
   (C) was a farmer
   (D) was a captain

11. According to the passage, Barnum was particularly good at
   (A) physics
   (B) mathematics
   (C) biology
   (D) chemistry

12. It can be inferred from the passage that Barnum was named after
   (A) his father
   (B) his mother
   (C) his mother's father
   (D) his father's father

13. Barnum's early years were spent primarily learning
   (A) how to become a farmer
   (B) how to be a mathematician
   (C) how to lead a circus
   (D) how to be a soldier

14. When the passage says "The ferule, or birch-rod, was in those days the assistant schoolmaster," this probably means that in the early 1800s
   (A) the birch-rod was the subject of much scientific study
   (B) school assignments were written on birch-rods
   (C) birch-rods were used to punish students who misbehaved
   (D) assistant schoolmasters resembled birch-rods

GO ON TO THE NEXT PAGE.

Alfred Wegener was one of many scientists whose theories were proven only after his death. Wegener was born in 1880 in Berlin. Wegener loved the outdoors and was always fascinated by the formation of the continents. However, in his early years he chose to study the stars.

Shortly after receiving his doctorate in astronomy, Wegener started studying the more <u>mundane</u> topic of the weather. He experimented with kites and balloons, even setting a world record for staying <u>aloft</u> for fifty-two hours straight. His appointment to the University of Marburg brought him considerable attention and status in the academic community.

Wegener, however, never lost interest in the formation of the continents. He noticed that though they were now far apart, it looked as if the continents fit together like puzzle pieces. Perhaps, he theorized, they were parts of one large continent at some point in the distant past. In 1912 he proposed his theory of continental drift. According to this theory, the continents broke apart millions of years ago and have drifted apart ever since then.

Many scientists at the time rejected Wegener's ideas. It was only in the 1960s, approximately thirty years after his death, that other scientists finally proved the correctness of Wegener's theory.

15. The word <u>mundane</u> in this passage most nearly means
    (A) loud
    (B) rare
    (C) ordinary
    (D) complicated

16. It can be inferred from the passage that Wegener died in approximately what year?
    (A) 1880
    (B) 1930
    (C) 1950
    (D) 1960

17. According to the passage, Wegener first came to believe that the continents were all part of one large land mass because
    (A) he read a book by a famous scientist that said so
    (B) the continents all had similar names
    (C) the outlines of the continents seemed to fit together
    (D) most scientists rejected the idea

18. It can be inferred from the passage that astronomy is the study of
    (A) weather
    (B) stars
    (C) continents
    (D) oceans

19. The word <u>aloft</u> in this passage most nearly means
    (A) airborne
    (B) asleep
    (C) flat
    (D) quiet

20. This passage is mostly about
    (A) Alfred Wegener's childhood
    (B) how to make a hot-air balloon
    (C) a scientist and his theory
    (D) why the continents have drifted apart

GO ON TO THE NEXT PAGE.

Bison and buffalo are not the same animals. For years, the American bison were mistakenly referred to as buffalo. Buffalo are actually found in Asia, Africa, and South America. Bison roamed the Northern American western plains by the millions just a couple of centuries ago. Because they were so widely hunted, however, their numbers fell greatly. In fact, as of a century ago, there were only about 500 left. They were <u>deemed</u> near extinction, but due to conservation efforts, their numbers have increased. There are approximately 50,000 bison living today in protected parks. Though they may never be as abundant as they once were, they are not in danger of extinction as long as they remain protected.

21. The passage implies that the primary difference between buffalo and bison is
    (A) their geographic location
    (B) their size
    (C) their number
    (D) when they lived

22. The primary purpose of this passage is to
    (A) discuss the origin of the word *buffalo*
    (B) promote conservation efforts
    (C) describe some of the history of the American bison
    (D) explain why people confuse bison and buffalo

23. According to the passage, the reason that American bison are no longer near extinction is
    (A) lack of interest in hunting them
    (B) conservation efforts
    (C) loss of value of their fur
    (D) the migration of the animals

24. The word <u>deemed</u> in this passage most closely means
    (A) found
    (B) rarely
    (C) thought
    (D) eaten

25. According to the passage, what can be hoped for as long as American bison are protected?
    (A) They will be as plentiful as they once were.
    (B) They will disturb the delicate ecological balance in the plains.
    (C) They will probably not die out.
    (D) They will face even greater dangers.

GO ON TO THE NEXT PAGE.

During the early years of the twentieth century, large cities such as London and Paris had short-haul stagecoaches to carry passengers to and from the suburbs. These vehicles were, however, not well adapted to the needs of a short journey. The coaches were difficult to enter and exit, and would often ruin passengers' clothing. One French visitor to London complained bitterly after a two-hour trip in such a coach in 1810, "I never saw anything so ill managed." To add insult to injury, the fares were exorbitantly high.

An improved vehicle was finally invented by another Frenchman, Stanislaus Baudry, who entered the transport business more by accident than by design. In 1823, he was the owner of a bathhouse in the suburb of Nantes, and to oblige his customers he ran a coach from the town center out to his establishment. Before long Baudry found that many of his passengers had no intention of bathing, but simply wanted a ride to the outskirts of the city. This gave him the idea of starting regular suburban services with vehicles designed to allow passengers to get on and off without stepping too much on each other's toes. Baudry's original coach started its journey from outside the shop of M. Omnes, whose motto "Omnes omnibus"—"Omnes for everyone"—is generally supposed to have resulted in the name "omnibus" being chosen for the name of the new vehicle.

26. Which of the following is the main idea of this passage?
   (A) the differences in public transport in Paris and London
   (B) the future of public transportation
   (C) the early history of public vehicles
   (D) the disadvantages of travel by coach

27. Which of the following is a reason for the unpopularity of short-haul stagecoaches?
   (A) the unpleasant appearance of the coaches
   (B) the difficulty of stopping the coaches once they started
   (C) the way in which the coaches hurt the horses that pulled them
   (D) the difficulty of getting in and out of the coaches

28. This passage probably comes from
   (A) a dictionary
   (B) a textbook on small business
   (C) a history of urban transportation
   (D) the diary of a nineteenth-century Frenchman

29. According to the passage, Stanislaus Baudry is best described as a
   (A) patriotic Englishman
   (B) perceptive businessman
   (C) social reformer
   (D) city planner

30. The "omnibus" differed from other forms of transportation primarily because it
   (A) was used more in Europe than in the United States
   (B) has remained almost unchanged to the present day
   (C) was the cheapest form of transportation
   (D) was designed to carry passengers on short journeys

GO ON TO THE NEXT PAGE.

Krakatau, earlier misnamed Krakatoa, an island located in the Sundra Strait between Sumatra and Java, disappeared on August 27, 1883. It was destroyed by a series of powerful volcanic eruptions. The most violent blew upward with an estimated force of 100–150 megatons of TNT. The sound of the explosion traveled around the world, reaching the opposite end of the earth near Bogota, Colombia, whereupon it bounced back to Krakatau and then back and forth for seven recorded passes over the earth's surface. The audible sounds, resembling the distant cannonade of a ship in distress, carried southward across Australia to Perth, northward to Singapore, and westward 4,600 kilometers to Rodriques Island in the Indian Ocean. This was the longest recorded distance traveled by any airborne sound in history.

The eruptions lifted more than 18 cubic kilometers of rock and other material into the air. Most of the tephra, as it is called by geologists, quickly rained back down to earth, but a residue of sulfuric-acid aerosol and dust boiled upward as high as 50 kilometers. It remained in the stratosphere, where for several years it created brilliant red sunsets and "Bishop's rings," visible circles surrounding the sun.

31. This passage is mostly
   (A) an explanation of the atmospheric phenomenon of Bishop's rings
   (B) a comparison of a volcanic eruption to the force of a bomb
   (C) a discussion of a volcanic eruption of enormous power
   (D) a discussion of the effect of volcanic activity on the stratosphere

32. The author mentions "the distant cannonade of a ship in distress" in order to
   (A) describe a ship damaged by a volcanic eruption
   (B) show that sound travels very quickly over water
   (C) help illustrate the sound made by the Krakatau eruption
   (D) illustrate the distance traveled by the volcano's heat wave

33. The author's tone in the passage can best be described as
   (A) scientific
   (B) critical
   (C) optimistic
   (D) annoyed

34. The brilliant sunsets mentioned in the passage were caused by
   (A) gas and dust drifting in the stratosphere
   (B) the detonation of 100 megatons of TNT
   (C) an increase in the sun's temperature after the eruption
   (D) vibrations from the sound waves created by the explosion

35. It can be inferred from the passage that Krakatau is nearest to
   (A) Perth
   (B) Bogota
   (C) Java
   (D) Rodriques Island

GO ON TO THE NEXT PAGE.

William, Duke of Normandy, conquered England in 1066. One of the first tasks he undertook as king was the building of a fortress in the city of London. Begun in 1066 and completed several years later by William's son, William Rufus, this structure was called the White Tower.

The Tower of London is not just one building, but an 18-acre complex of buildings. In addition to the White Tower, there are nineteen other towers. The Thames River flows by one side of the complex, and a large moat, or shallow ditch, surrounds it. Once filled with water, the moat was drained in 1843 and is now covered with grass.

The Tower of London is the city's most popular tourist attraction. A great deal of fascinating history has taken place within its walls. The tower has served as a fortress, a royal residence, a prison, the royal mint, a public records office, an observatory, a military barracks, a place of execution, and a city zoo. Today, it houses the crown jewels and a great deal of English history.

36. The primary purpose of this passage is to
   (A) discuss the future of the Tower of London
   (B) explain why the Tower was used as a royal residence
   (C) argue that the Tower is an inappropriate place for the crown jewels
   (D) discuss the history of the Tower of London

37. The Tower of London was used for all of the following except
   (A) a place where money was minted
   (B) a royal residence
   (C) a place of religious pilgrimage
   (D) a place where executions were held

38. Which of the following questions is answered by the passage?
   (A) How much money does the Tower of London collect from tourists each year?
   (B) In what year did construction of the Tower begin?
   (C) What type of stone was used to make the Tower of London?
   (D) Who was the most famous prisoner in the Tower?

39. The author's tone in this passage can best be described as
   (A) confused
   (B) objective
   (C) emotional
   (D) envious

40. The author would probably agree that
   (A) the Tower of London is useful only as a tourist attraction
   (B) the Tower of London could never be built today
   (C) the Tower of London has a complex history
   (D) the prisoners at the Tower were generally well treated

GO ON TO THE NEXT PAGE.

Part 6—Mathematics Concepts and Applications
40 Questions, 35 Minutes

1. During the month of March, Nancy ran $14\frac{1}{2}$ miles. During the month of April, she ran $8\frac{3}{4}$ miles. What is the difference between the distance she ran during the month of March and the distance she ran during the month of April?

   (A) $5\frac{3}{4}$ miles

   (B) 6 miles

   (C) $6\frac{1}{4}$ miles

   (D) $6\frac{3}{4}$ miles

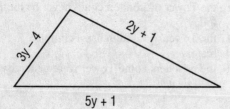

2. What is the perimeter of the triangle above?
   (A) $10y + 2$
   (B) $10y - 2$
   (C) $7y + 2$
   (D) $4y - 2$

3. $2\frac{1}{2}$ is how many times greater than $1\frac{1}{2}$?

   (A) $1\frac{2}{3}$
   (B) $1\frac{1}{3}$
   (C) 2
   (D) $2\frac{1}{2}$

4. What is the value of x in the figure above?
   (A) 90
   (B) 60
   (C) 45
   (D) 30

5. A telephone call costs $2.35 for the first minute and 15 cents for each additional minute. What is the cost of an 8-minute call?
   (A) $3.55
   (B) $3.40
   (C) $3.25
   (D) $3.10

6. What is the sum of the distinct prime factors of 48?
   (A) 5
   (B) 6
   (C) 12
   (D) 36

7. Which of the following is equal to $42.2678 \times 1,000$?
   (A) 4.22678×10^3
   (B) 4.22678×10^4
   (C) 4.22678×10^5
   (D) 4.22678×10^6

GO ON TO THE NEXT PAGE.

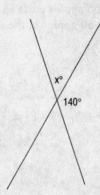

8. What is the value of *x* in the figure above?
    (A) 30
    (B) 40
    (C) 45
    (D) 60

9. $(4 \times \frac{1}{100}) + (3 \times \frac{1}{10}) + (2 \times \frac{1}{1000}) + 5 =$
    (A) 4.325
    (B) 5.234
    (C) 5.342
    (D) 5.432

10. If $2(x + 2x) > -6$, what is the range of possible values of *x*?
    (A) $x > -1$
    (B) $x > 1$
    (C) $x < -1$
    (D) $x < 1$

11. $4^4 \times 4^5 =$
    (A) 4^1
    (B) 4^9
    (C) 4^{20}
    (D) 16^9

12. $\frac{25}{27} \times \frac{9}{5} =$
    (A) $\frac{34}{32}$
    (B) $\frac{5}{4}$
    (C) $\frac{5}{3}$
    (D) $\frac{3}{5}$

13. John puts $5,000 into a savings account that gives him 4% simple interest every year. If John makes no deposits or withdrawals, how much money will be in John's account at the end of one year?
    (A) $5,004
    (B) $5,040
    (C) $5,020
    (D) $5,200

14. While driving to the amusement park, the Claffeys' car travels an average of $\frac{1}{2}$ mile every minute. At this rate, how many hours will it take to drive 40 miles?
    (A) $1\frac{1}{3}$
    (B) $2\frac{1}{2}$
    (C) 20
    (D) 80

GO ON TO THE NEXT PAGE.

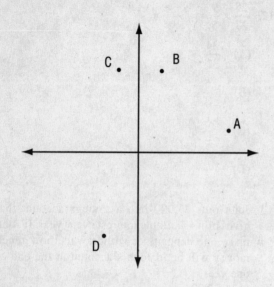

15. Which of the points on the graph above could have the coordinates (2,7)?
    (A) point A
    (B) point B
    (C) point C
    (D) point D

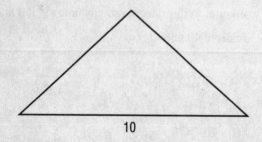

16. If the area of the triangle above is 40, what is its height?
    (A) 4
    (B) 8
    (C) 10
    (D) 12

17. If $4x - 9 = x + 6$, then $x =$
    (A) 1
    (B) 3
    (C) 4
    (D) 5

18. A basket of 5 apples costs $8. How much will it cost to buy 60 apples at the same rate?
    (A) $40
    (B) $60
    (C) $86
    (D) $96

19. $13 + 2 \times 9 + 1 - (2 - 8) =$
    (A) 26
    (B) 38
    (C) 76
    (D) 84

20. Nine years ago, Mack was half as old as he is now. How old is Mack now?
    (A) 9
    (B) 12
    (C) 15
    (D) 18

21. At a local clothing store, two shirts and a pair of shorts cost $19.25. If five shirts cost $28.50, what is the price of a pair of shorts?
    (A) $5.50
    (B) $7.65
    (C) $7.75
    (D) $7.85

22. $3\frac{3}{4}\% =$
    (A) 3.75
    (B) 0.0375
    (C) 0.00375
    (D) 0.000375

23. If $x = 3$, then $3x^2$ is how much less than $(3x)^2$?
    (A) 0
    (B) 6
    (C) 36
    (D) 54

GO ON TO THE NEXT PAGE.

24. Walter's card collection contains football cards and baseball cards. If he has 120 football cards and 80 baseball cards, what fractional part of his collection is made up of baseball cards?
    (A) 15%
    (B) 20%
    (C) 40%
    (D) 66%

25. What is the volume of a cube with sides that are 3 inches?
    (A) 3 in^3
    (B) 6 in^3
    (C) 9 in^3
    (D) 27 in^3

26. $4.5 \div 0.02 =$
    (A) 90
    (B) 180
    (C) 185
    (D) 225

27. A grain silo has dimensions 25 feet by 6 feet by 12 feet. If the silo can be filled with grain at a rate of 4 cubic feet per minute, how many minutes will it take to fill the silo?
    (A) 120
    (B) 250
    (C) 450
    (D) 600

28. $3\frac{1}{2} \times 6\frac{1}{2} =$
    (A) $9\frac{1}{2}$
    (B) 18
    (C) $22\frac{3}{4}$
    (D) $27\frac{1}{4}$

29. If a circle has a radius of 4, what is the ratio of its area to its circumference?
    (A) 2:1
    (B) 3:1
    (C) 4:1
    (D) 5:3

30. In 1997, Cindy sold 120 newspapers. In 1998, she sold 200. The number of newspapers Cindy sold increased by approximately what percent from 1997 to 1998?
    (A) 40%
    (B) 50%
    (C) 66%
    (D) 80%

31. If $\frac{1}{3}$ of a number is 32, then $\frac{3}{4}$ of that number is
    (A) 16
    (B) 32
    (C) 64
    (D) 72

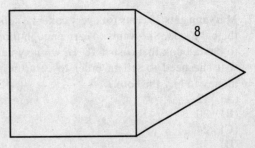

32. The figure above consists of a square and an equilateral triangle. What is the perimeter of the figure above?
    (A) 24
    (B) 40
    (C) 64
    (D) 80

33. How many multiples of 3 and 5 are between 1 and 32?
    (A) 0
    (B) 1
    (C) 2
    (D) 3

34. Terence has an average of 80 on his four science tests. If on the first three tests he scored 76, 77, and 78, what did he score on the fourth test?
    (A) 83
    (B) 85
    (C) 87
    (D) 89

GO ON TO THE NEXT PAGE.

35. If one of the angles in a right triangle is 65, what is the measure of the smallest angle in the triangle?
    (A) 15
    (B) 25
    (C) 35
    (D) 65

36. Lewis has a bowl of red and blue marbles. The ratio of blue marbles to red marbles is 5:2. If he has a total of 70 marbles in the bowl, how many blue marbles does he have?
    (A) 20
    (B) 30
    (C) 40
    (D) 50

37. Maryann gets 75 cents for every cake she sells at the bake sale. She wants to earn enough money to buy a book that costs $18. How many cakes will she need to sell in order to earn enough money to buy the book?
    (A) 12
    (B) 20
    (C) 24
    (D) 32

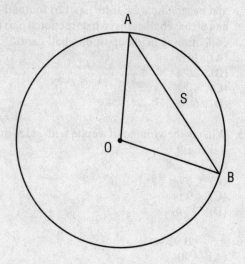

38. The figure above shows a circle with center O. If $OA = 4$, what is the perimeter of triangle OAB?
    (A)   9
    (B) 11
    (C) 13
    (D) 15

39. If $x + x = x \times x$, which of the following could be the value of x?
    (A) 1
    (B) 2
    (C) 3
    (D) 4

40. If $\dfrac{1}{\dfrac{1}{x}} = \dfrac{3}{4}$ then $x =$

    (A) $\dfrac{3}{4}$

    (B) $\dfrac{4}{3}$

    (C) 3
    (D) 4

GO ON TO THE NEXT PAGE.

Part 7—Language Expression
40 Questions, 30 minutes

For questions 1–6, select the word or phrase that best completes the sentence.

1. Sometimes words come to mean something very different than what they used to mean; _____ the word "terrific" used to mean "causing great fear" and now means "wonderful."
    (A) nonetheless,
    (B) for example,
    (C) yet,
    (D) in contrast,
    (E) besides,

2. John has won an incredible number of trophies; _____ he has won more of them than anyone else in the history of his school.
    (A) because,
    (B) instead,
    (C) in fact,
    (D) rather,
    (E) in general,

3. _____ I had never seen him before, I knew who he was by the sound of his voice.
    (A) Truly
    (B) Although
    (C) Because
    (D) Meanwhile
    (E) Moreover

4. Telly is a world-class athlete who can run _____ than anyone else on our team.
    (A) quick
    (B) more quickly
    (C) as quickly
    (D) most quickly
    (E) quicklier

5. I'm sure that I _____ see anything like that again.
    (A) won't never
    (B) will not never
    (C) will never
    (D) won't hardly ever
    (E) never will not

6. Patricia is the _____ person I have ever known.
    (A) intelligently
    (B) intelligenter
    (C) much intelligent
    (D) mostly intelligently
    (E) most intelligent

For questions 7–12, choose the sentence that is correctly written.

7. (A) The zookeepers bathed the monkeys fed them and returned them to their cages.
    (B) The zookeepers bathed the monkeys, fed them, and returned them to their cages.
    (C) The zookeepers bathed the monkeys; fed them; and returned them to their cages.
    (D) The zookeepers: bathed the monkeys, fed them and returned them to their cages.
    (E) The zookeepers, bathed the monkeys, fed them, and returned them to their cages.

8. (A) Many people learn best by reading than others learn best by listening.
    (B) Many people learn best by reading, while others learn best by listening.
    (C) Many people, who learn better by reading, others learn best by listening.
    (D) Many people learn better by reading as others who learn by listening.
    (E) Many people who learn best by reading are others who learn best by listening.

9. (A) A green salad, for lunch every day, is what Marinda likes to eat.
    (B) For lunch every day, a green salad is eaten by Marinda.
    (C) For lunch every day, a green salad is what Marinda likes to eat.
    (D) Marinda likes to eat a green salad every day for lunch.
    (E) Marinda likes for lunch to eat a green salad every day.

GO ON TO THE NEXT PAGE.

10. **(A)** Many historians believe that the first helicopter was drawn by Leonardo da Vinci.
    (B) Leonardo da Vinci, it is believed by many historians, was the one who drew the first helicopter.
    (C) The first helicopter, believed by many historians, was drawn by Leonardo da Vinci.
    (D) The one who drew the first helicopter, which was believed by many historians, was Leonardo da Vinci.
    (E) The first helicopter, it is believed by many historians, which were drawn by Leonardo da Vinci.

11. **(A)** In Colorado, many people spend their winter vacation, which is famous for its ski resorts.
    (B) Famous for its ski resorts, it is winter vacation that most people spend in Colorado.
    (C) Many people spend their winter vacation in Colorado, which is famous for its ski resorts.
    (D) Many people, famous for its ski resorts, spend their winter vacation in Colorado.
    (E) Spending their winter vacation in Colorado, which is famous for its ski resorts, are many people.

12. **(A)** Walter lost my hat and since he is my best friend I gave him mine.
    (B) Walter, who is my best friend, lost his hat, so I gave him mine.
    (C) I gave my hat to my best friend Walter because he lost his hat.
    (D) My hat was what I gave to Walter, my best friend, because he lost his hat.
    (E) My best friend Walter lost his hat, so I gave him mine.

For questions 13–17, choose the sentence that uses verbs correctly.

13. **(A)** Jules asked his sister to helping him with his math homework.
    (B) By noon, the temperature had rose to almost 100 degrees in the desert.
    (C) If I will not get lost, I would be there on time.
    (D) I thought I had closed the door, but perhaps I was wrong.
    (E) Martin ran down the stairs and tripping over the cat.

14. **(A)** Tomorrow is a holiday, so we will not be able to to go the bank.
    (B) Larry saw his friend on the street corner and greets him.
    (C) When Emily stepped out of the car she will realize that it is raining.
    (D) Running through the hallway, Howard dropping his books.
    (E) Karen eats her breakfast and was watching television.

15. **(A)** It was hard to believe that Paul comes to the party and didn't say hello.
    (B) I will not go to Paris until I can speak French.
    (C) Last night I go to bed early, but I still woke up late this morning.
    (D) If you turn in your paper on time, you will have gotten a better grade.
    (E) Just after his birth, Jonas would move to Korea with his family.

16. **(A)** A passing bicyclist seeing the accident.
    (B) Last year, Gisele won the science prize and receives an award.
    (C) When the audition was over, the girls walked home together.
    (D) I wasn't hungry because I have ate all my dessert before dinner.
    (E) Anna picked up the dog and shows it to her mother.

17. **(A)** John being happy to help his mother with the dishes.
    (B) Annie fell down on a rock and torn her shirt.
    (C) Last week, Laura finally has the answer to her question.
    (D) After school, we went to the park to play soccer.
    (E) Tomorrow I will finally seen the end of the movie.

GO ON TO THE NEXT PAGE.

For questions 18–21, choose the underlined word that is the simple subject of the sentence.

18. Despite the cold <u>weather</u>, <u>John's</u> <u>family</u> decided
                    A   B   C
    to stay an extra <u>week</u> at the <u>hotel</u>.
               D   E

19. The haunted <u>house</u>, which was built by <u>students</u>
               A   B
    in my <u>class</u> at our local community <u>center</u>, scared
           C   D
    even my <u>father</u>.
            E

20. Even though <u>we</u> worked on the <u>house</u> as fast as
              A   B
    <u>we</u> could, the <u>roof</u> was not finished until the last
    C   D
    <u>day</u> of the month.
    E

21. While my <u>brother</u> had never seen the <u>movie</u>
            A   B
    before, my <u>sister</u> had seen it several <u>times</u> at
             C   D
    <u>camp</u>.
    E

For questions 22–25, choose the underlined word or words that is the simple predicate (verb) of the sentence.

22. Since his brother <u>moved</u> away, Manny
                   A
    <u>has discovered</u> that he <u>needs</u> <u>to do</u> more <u>work</u>
      B   C   D   E
    around the house.

23. Always <u>ready</u> <u>to do</u> his part of the <u>housework</u>,
            A   B   C
    Sam <u>helped</u> his mother <u>wash</u> the dishes after
        D   E
    dinner.

24. After John <u>finished</u> his <u>homework</u>, he <u>went</u> to
             A   B   C
    the library <u>to read</u> a <u>mystery</u> novel.
             D   E

25. Of the people I <u>interviewed,</u> all of whom
                    A
    <u>had been chosen</u> by my teacher, most <u>wanted</u>
          B   C
    <u>to move</u> <u>to Florida</u>.
     D   E

For questions 26–28, choose the sentence that best combines the two underlined sentences into one.

26. <u>Patricia practiced the piano. Later, Patricia watched a movie.</u>
    (A) Patricia practiced the piano, and then later Patricia watched a movie.
    (B) Patricia practiced the piano, and later watched a movie.
    (C) Patricia practiced the piano, watched a movie.
    (D) Patricia practiced the piano while she watched a movie.
    (E) Practicing the piano while watching a movie was what Patricia did later.

27. <u>Last week I ate a pomegranate for the first time. I thought the pomegranate was delicious.</u>
    (A) Last week I ate a pomegranate for the first time, I thought it was delicious.
    (B) Deliciously I ate a pomegranate last week for the first time.
    (C) For the first time, last week, I thought it was delicious when I ate a pomegranate.
    (D) Last week I ate a delicious pomegranate, and thought it was the first time.
    (E) Last week I ate a pomegranate for the first time, and thought it was delicious.

28. <u>My mother was born in Illinois. My mother is a doctor.</u>
    (A) My mother, who was born in Illinois, is a doctor.
    (B) My mother, is a doctor, was born in Illinois.
    (C) My mother was born in Illinois and my mother is a doctor.
    (D) In Illinois my mother was born and is a doctor.
    (E) Born in Illinois, a doctor is what my mother is.

GO ON TO THE NEXT PAGE.

For questions 29–31, choose the topic sentence that best fits the paragraph.

29. _____ Galileo was born in the town of Pisa, Italy. His first studies were in medicine at Pisa University. Later he moved to Padua to become professor of mathematics. While in Padua, he perfected the refracting telescope, which he used to find the moons of Jupiter. He also verified Copernicus's theory that the planets revolve around the sun and not around the earth.
   (A) Galileo was happy to remain in his hometown of Pisa for his studies.
   (B) Galileo Galilei was one of history's greatest minds.
   (C) At that time, there were several great universities in Italy.
   (D) Galileo's father was very supportive of his son's studies.
   (E) The Leaning Tower of Pisa is one of the world's most famous buildings.

30. _____ At adulthood they will often grow to weigh 7 tons. The only animals bigger than the elephant live in the water, which helps to support their weight and regulate their body temperature.
   (A) Few animals are more social than the elephant.
   (B) All mammals, including elephants, give birth to live young.
   (C) The elephant is the largest animal that lives on land.
   (D) One of the challenges for any animal is to stay warm in the winter and cool in the summer.
   (E) Aquatic animals have fewer problems than land animals.

31. _____ Crocodiles have longer and thinner jaws than alligators do. Alligators live in fresh water in lakes, rivers, or marshes. Crocodiles, on the other hand, prefer to live in salty or brackish water. While both animals need warm climates, the crocodile is very sensitive to cold, and therefore lives in tropical regions.
   (A) Crocodiles and alligators are some of the fiercest animals on earth.
   (B) Crocodiles differ from alligators in a number of ways.
   (C) The southern regions of the United States are home to many interesting creatures.
   (D) Alligators and crocodiles have many similar features.
   (E) Crocodiles are not very common in America.

For questions 32–34, choose the sentences that best continue the topic sentence.

32. Since the founding of the country, Massachusetts has been the home of a great number of humanitarians, writers, and patriots.
   (A) To many people's surprise, Massachusetts also has the country's biggest crop of cranberries. It also produces a great deal of fruit and dairy products.
   (B) President John Adams, Susan B. Anthony, Clara Barton, and Emily Dickinson all lived in Massachusetts for a good part of their lives. Benjamin Franklin also resided there.
   (C) The Boston Tea Party, often considered the start of the American Revolution, took place in Boston, Massachusetts. Citizens dumped crates of tea into Boston Harbor to protest British taxation.
   (D) Many great battles of the American Revolution took place in and around Boston, Massachusetts. The battles at Lexington and Concord were among the most important of the war.
   (E) Humanitarians are people who do good things to help other people live better lives.

GO ON TO THE NEXT PAGE.

33. Maya Angelou is not only a brilliant poet, but she is also a gifted public speaker.
    (A) She is often asked to give lectures at colleges across the country. She was even asked to recite her poetry at the presidential inauguration of Bill Clinton.
    (B) She has been nominated for many awards, including a Pulitzer Prize. Her screenplay *Georgia, Georgia* has also been produced as a film.
    (C) She was born in 1928 and was introduced to literature by her grandmother. She first tried her hand at theater before beginning to write poetry.
    (D) Learning to be a good speaker is important to becoming a good poet. Poets are often asked to read their works in public.
    (E) Many people have a hard time speaking in public, but almost anyone can learn to do it well.

34. While commonly considered a vegetable, the tomato is actually more closely related to fruits than it is to most vegetables.
    (A) It is very important to eat a lot of fruits and vegetables every day. At least 5 servings are required for a healthy diet.
    (B) Tomato soup and juice are delicious. They are also good for you.
    (C) The tomato is made into many kinds of sauces and dips, such as salsa and ketchup. It is also usually eaten on salads and hamburgers.
    (D) Tomatoes come in all sizes and shapes. Some are as small as strawberries, while others are as large as oranges.
    (E) The tomato grows on a vine, like grapes and strawberries. Moreover, it is a good source of vitamin C, like citrus fruits.

For questions 35–37, choose the sentence that does not belong in the paragraph.

35. ① Salman Rushdie is one of today's most famous authors. ② He was born in 1947 in Bombay, India, in the same year that India gained its independence from England. ③ One of his early novels, *Shame,* was praised by critics as one of the best books of the twentieth century. ④ In 1980, he wrote *Midnight's Children*, which won the prestigious Booker Prize. ⑤ Many good books have never received the Booker Prize. ⑥ Rushdie continues to write his own special brand of literature which retells true stories from a fantastic point of view. ⑦ He still lives in England, where he lives a quiet life away from the public eye.
    (A) sentence 2
    (B) sentence 3
    (C) sentence 4
    (D) sentence 5
    (E) sentence 6

36. ① One of the most amazing natural events that you can witness is a cyclone. ② Cyclones develop when air begins to spiral inward around a low-pressure area, creating a kind of whirlpool of air. ③ Without air, most land animals could not survive. ④ Some strong tropical cyclones pick up such speed and power that they become hurricanes. ⑤ These are the most violent kind of cyclones, and they can do a great deal of damage when they encounter an inhabited island or coastline. ⑥ They can cause floods and wind damage, and may even be deadly.
    (A) sentence 2
    (B) sentence 3
    (C) sentence 4
    (D) sentence 5
    (E) sentence 6

GO ON TO THE NEXT PAGE.

37. ☐ One of the most widespread musical instruments in the Middle Ages was the lute, a stringed instrument in the same family as the guitar. ☐ The lute took many different forms over the years, of varying sizes and shapes. ☐ Two variations on the lute were the chitarrone and the theorbo. ☐ The chitarrone took its name from the Italian word *chitarra*, meaning guitar. ☐ Many other musical terms also come from the Italian language. ☐ In later years, the chitarrone and theorbo were mainly used to accompany vocal groups and for the theater.

   (A) sentence 2
   (B) sentence 3
   (C) sentence 4
   (D) sentence 5
   (E) sentence 6

For questions 38–40, choose the sentence that best fills the blank.

38. Learning a foreign language is a marvelous and rewarding experience._____
For example, you can read great books in their original versions. You can travel with much greater ease in foreign countries. And you can converse with interesting people who you might never have been able to speak with before.

   (A) One of the most popular foreign languages to learn is French.
   (B) Knowing a foreign language allows you to do many fascinating things.
   (C) It is true that many people find it difficult to learn languages.
   (D) Most people in the world begin to learn a foreign language in grade school.
   (E) Everybody should try to learn at least one foreign language.

39. One of this century's most important American painters was Jackson Pollock. His highly abstract style broke with the artistic tradition of drawing figures and shapes. _____
These might look to the untrained eye like random splatters and smears. But once you begin to study Pollock's art, you begin to see and appreciate the emotion, intensity, and feeling that went into the creation of these huge masterpieces.

   (A) Instead, Pollock threw or dripped his paint, creating dribbles and splotches.
   (B) Most painters prefer to draw things that resemble photographs.
   (C) Pollock was born in 1912 and died in 1956.
   (D) Furthermore, there was recently a major exposition of his work in Washington, DC.
   (E) One of the major influences on Pollock was the work of Pablo Picasso.

40. Many animals use camouflage to hide from other animals. Camouflage means that the animal's colors are very similar to the colors in its environment, so it blends in and is difficult to see. _____ There are also many species of butterflies that have wings colored to look like flowers or plants.

   (A) For instance, some insects are long and thin, and resemble tree branches.
   (B) In fact, some of them are poisonous and therefore are safe from predators.
   (C) For example, there are beetles that can eat almost anything, including tree bark.
   (D) On the other hand, some birds can fly high into the air where they are difficult to catch.
   (E) Nevertheless, some animals use colors as a way to attract a mate.

GO ON TO THE NEXT PAGE.

14

Answers and Explanations to COOP Practice Test 2

PART 1—SEQUENCES

1. **C**   The second element reverses the top and bottom of the first, so the missing element should reverse the top and bottom of the third.

2. **B**   The first element has one A, the second has two As, and the third has three As, so the missing element should have four As.

3. **A**   The second element reverses the elements of the first—the triangles change to circles and the circles to triangles. Therefore, the missing element should reverse the elements of the third.

4. **B**   The second element is the same as the first but fills in one-quarter of the figure. Therefore, the missing element should be the same as the third, with one-quarter filled in.

5. **A**   The first element has one line, the second has three lines, and the third has five lines, so the missing element should have seven lines to follow the pattern of adding two lines.

6. **C**   The second element moves the dot from top to bottom on the right side, so the missing element should move the dot from top to bottom on the left side.

7. **C**   The sequence should go 34 (+ 12) 46 (+ 3) 49 | 8 (+ 12) 20 (+ 3) 23 | 57 (+ 12) **69** (+ 3) 72.

8. **B**   The sequence should go 31 (− 3) 28 (+ 7) 35 | 17 (− 3) 14 (+ 7) 21 | 36 (− 3) **33** (+ 7) 40.

9. **C**   The sequence should go 66 (+ 0) 66 (÷3) 22 | 18 (+ 0) 18 (÷3) 6 | 27 (+ 0) **27** (÷3) 9.

10. **A**   The sequence should go 8 (− 2) 6 (× 2) 12 | 17 (− 2) 15 (× 2) 30 | 6 (− 2) **4** (× 2) 8.

11. **B**   The sequence should go 6 (× 3) 18 (+ 1) 19 | 3 (× 3) 9 (+ 1) 10 | 4 (× 3) **12** (+ 1) 13.

12. **C**   The sequence should go 3 (× 4) 12 (÷ 2) 6 | 12 (× 4) 48 (÷ 2) 24 | 8 (× 4) **32** (÷ 2) 16.

13. **C**   The sequence should go 11 (× 3) 33 (+ 0) 33 | 6 (× 3) 18 (+ 0) 18 | 13 (× 3) **39** (+ 0) 39.

14. **D**   The A and B do not change; only the numbers increase: 1 2 | 2 3 | 3 4 | **4 5** | 5 6.

15. **A**   The sequence gives three letters, then skips two, then gives the next three letters. The letters follow this pattern: 1 2 3 | 6 7 8 | 11 12 13 | 16 17 18 | 21 22 23, or ABC | FGH | KLM | **PQR** | UVW.

16. **B**   The outside letters start with A and go forward through the alphabet; the inside letter starts with Z and goes backward through the alphabet.

17. **C**   The middle letter of each element becomes the last letter of the next element. So the last letter of the missing element must be L, and the middle letter must be N. Use numbers in place of letters to make it clearer: 7 8 6 | 9 10 8 | 11 12 10 | 13 14 12 | 15 16 14, or GHF | IJH | KLJ | **MNL** | OPN.

18. **C**   The sequence has a missing letter in the middle of each element. Again, numbers will help clarify: 1 2 4 5 | 6 7 9 10 | 11 12 14 15 | 16 17 19 20 | 21 22 24 25, or ABDE | FGIJ | KLNO | **PQST** | UVXY.

19. **A**   The last two letters of one element become the first two letters of the next element. So the missing element must begin with **MP** and end with **RT**.

20. **B**   The number in the middle goes up by 3. Therefore, the missing element must have an **18** in the middle.

PART 2—ANALOGIES

1. **C** A puppy is a young dog; a kitten is a young cat.

2. **A** A net is used to catch a fish; a baseball glove is used to catch a baseball.

3. **D** A crab holds things with a claw; a human holds things with a hand.

4. **A** A vase is used to hold flowers; a pot is used to hold a plant.

5. **B** A horse lives in a stable; a dog lives in a doghouse.

6. **C** You put on skates to travel on ice; you put on skis to travel on snow.

7. **A** You use a hammer to make a house; you use a paintbrush to make a painting.

8. **B** A boxer attacks with his fists; a bee attacks with its stinger.

9. **A** An astronaut travels in a rocket; a sailor travels on a ship.

10. **C** A cowboy wears cowboy boots; a ballet dancer wears ballet shoes.

11. **A** A mask is worn on the face; a shoe is worn on the foot.

12. **C** A belt is worn around the waist; a scarf is worn around the neck.

13. **B** A can opener is used to open a can; a key is used to open a lock.

14. **A** A glove protects the hand; a thimble protects a finger.

15. **B** You use a spoon to eat soup; you use a fork to eat pasta.

16. **C** A guitar and a banjo are both stringed instruments; a trumpet and a trombone are both wind instruments.

17. **D** A cactus is a plant that lives in the desert; a camel is an animal that lives in the desert.

18. **B** A motorcycle is a motorized bicycle; a propeller plane is a motorized paper airplane.

19. **A** You play a violin with a bow; you play a drum with a mallet.

20. **B** A digital clock is a modern wind-up clock; a light bulb is a modern oil lamp.

PART 3—MEMORY

1. **D**

2. **D**

3. **E**

4. **E**

5. **D**

6. **E**

7. C
8. D
9. D
10. E
11. A
12. B
13. B
14. A
15. A
16. C
17. B
18. A
19. C
20. D

PART 4—VERBAL REASONING

1. **D** A dentist is someone who cares for your teeth. A dentist may or may not use a toothbrush, work in an office, or have a nurse.

2. **B** A dictionary gives definitions of words. It may or may not have pictures or sit on a bookshelf, and it does not give information on history.

3. **A** A refrigerator keeps things cold. It may or may not make ice, have food in it, or be in the kitchen.

4. **A** A melody is a series of sounds. It may or may not be played on a piano, be beautiful, or be played by an orchestra.

5. **D** Feline means having to do with cats. It has nothing to do with jungles, attacks, or speed.

6. **C** Humidity means having a lot of water. It may or may not occur in summer and has nothing to do with thermometers or cleanliness.

7. **B** Something very cool is cold and extremely cool is frigid. Something very warm is hot and extremely warm is scalding.

8. **B** Seconds make up a minute, and minutes make up an hour. Days make up a month, and months make up a year.

9. **B** An eye has the sense of sight, the tongue has the sense of taste, and a hand has the sense of touch.

10. **B** A berry is a fruit that grows on a bush, a grape is a fruit that grows on a vine, and an apple is a fruit that grows on a tree.

11. **D** A bird has feathers, a bear has fur, and a fish has scales.

12. **A** Angry means very annoyed, and enraged means very angry. Happy means very content, and ecstatic means very happy.

13. **C** Since Martin's class does go to Europe, they must have gotten the group rate, so they must have at least 20 people signed up for the trip. None of the other choices is certain.

14. **D** Since Alice can run 6 miles per hour and Marsha can run 7 miles per hour, Marsha can run faster than Alice. None of the other choices is certain.

15. **A** Since Julie has more marbles than Larry and Larry has more marbles than Cindy, we know that Julie has more marbles than Cindy.

16. **C** Since Carlos can swim more than 3 laps and Erwin can only swim 2, we know that Carlos can swim during recess but Erwin cannot.

17. **D** Since Alex got a higher score than Lucy and Lucy got a higher score than Wendy, we know that Alex got a higher score than Wendy.

18. **B** Since cala is in both words that mean shade, cala must mean shade. Therefore in calamala, mala means lamp, so the correct answer must have the word mala in it. This eliminates A and C. D repeats the word mala, so it is also not the answer.

19. **B** Since akoo appears in both words meaning hair, akoo means hair. Therefore in poyoakoo, poyo means cat. Therefore the correct answer must be B or C. Since noon is in both words that mean dog, noon must mean dog. Therefore C can be eliminated.

20. **D** Since lath is in both words that mean slowly, lath means slowly. Therefore in lathawa, awa means eat. The answer must have awa in it, and only D does.

PART 5—READING COMPREHENSION

1. **B** The word *decompose* is used in the passage in contrast to "lasted forever."

2. **C** The passage says that it took "more than sixty days." The closest choice is C.

3. **A** Every paragraph in the passage discusses some aspect of making a mummy.

4. **B** The beginning of the third paragraph calls this process "embalming."

5. **B** The first paragraph states that "a person's soul needed a body to live in."

6. **A** The third paragraph says that all the organs but the heart were put into jars; the heart was "placed back inside the body."

7. **D** According to the last paragraph, the body was doused in alcohol "to kill the bacteria." We can infer that bacteria might cause the body to rot.

8. **C** In the first paragraph, the word *stock* is followed immediately by "His ancestors."

9. **A** According to the passage, he was "a captain in the War of the Revolution."

10. **A** The first paragraph says that he was "a tailor, a farmer, a storekeeper, and a country tavernkeeper, and was not particularly prosperous in any of these callings."

11. **B** The third paragraph says that he excelled "in mathematics."

12. **C** According to the second paragraph, he was named "after his maternal grandfather."

13. **A** At the beginning of the third paragraph it states that he "drove the cows to and from the pasture, shelled corn," and performed other farming duties.

14. **C** This phrase is used in contrast to the sentence that follows, which says that Barnum was a good student. Therefore the "birch-rod" must refer to something to do with bad students.

15. **C** In the passage, the word *mundane* is used to describe the weather as opposed to astronomy. This makes C the most likely choice.

16. **B** The final paragraph says that the 1960s were about thirty years after his death. Therefore, he must have died around 1930.

17. **C** In the third paragraph it states that Wegener noticed that "the continents fit together like puzzle pieces."

18. **B** The end of the first paragraph says that Wegener "chose to study the stars"; the next sentence states that he got his degree in astronomy.

19. **A** In the second paragraph the word *aloft* is used to describe a balloon.

20. **C** Every paragraph of the passage discusses Alfred Wegener. A is too narrow.

21. **A** According to the passage, bison live in North America while buffalo live in Asia and Africa.

22. **C** The paragraph discusses how bison were originally plentiful in America, that they faced extinction, and how they are now protected. This best supports C.

23. **B** The passage states that "due to conservation efforts, their numbers have increased."

24. **C** The only choice that makes sense if replaced with the word *deemed* is C.

25. **C** The final sentence of the paragraph says that "they are not in danger of extinction."

26. **C** The first sentence of this passage mentions transportation in the early years of large cities, and the rest of the passage discusses this idea.

27. **D** According to the first paragraph, they "were difficult to enter and exit."

28. **C** Only C would discuss developments in transportation in cities.

29. **B** The second paragraph says that he was a businessman who owned a bathhouse and took advantage of a need for short-distance transportation.

30. **D** There is no evidence to support A, B, or C. However, the omnibus arose out of a problem with short-distance vehicles.

31. **C** The passage discusses the eruption at Krakatau and the results.

32. **C** The end of the first paragraph talks about how loud and powerful the sound of the explosion was.

33. **A** There is no evidence for B, C, or D.

34. **A** According to the second paragraph, they were caused by "a residue of sulfuric-acid aerosol and dust."

35. **C** The opening line of the passage states that Krakatau is "between Sumatra and Java."

36. **D** The passage begins with the origin of the Tower and discusses its uses through the years.

37. **C** A, B, and D are mentioned in the passage.

38. **B** The first paragraph says that construction on the Tower was begun in 1066.

39. **B** There is no evidence to support A, C, or D. The author simply describes the facts of the Tower.

40. **C** A and B are extreme and can be eliminated. D is never discussed.

PART 6—MATHEMATICS CONCEPTS AND APPLICATIONS

1. **A** To find the difference between $14\frac{1}{2}$ and $8\frac{3}{4}$, first subtract the whole number portion: $14 - 8 = 6$. Now subtract the fractional part. To solve $\frac{1}{2} - \frac{3}{4}$, use the Bowtie. Multiply the bottom numbers together to get 8, which goes on the bottom of each of the new fractions. Then we multiply up and diagonally: $2 \times 3 = 6$ and $4 \times 1 = 4$. Our problem now becomes $\frac{4}{8} - \frac{6}{8}$, which is equal to $-\frac{2}{8}$, or $-\frac{1}{4}$. When we subtract this from 6, we get $5\frac{3}{4}$.

2. **B** The perimeter is the sum of the sides, or $(3y - 4) + (2y + 1) + (5y + 1)$.

3. **A** You could solve this by dividing $2\frac{1}{2}$ by $1\frac{1}{2}$, but there is an easier way: Plug in the answer choices starting with A, and see which choice times $1\frac{1}{2}$ gives us $2\frac{1}{2}$. Is $1\frac{2}{3}$ times $1\frac{1}{2}$ equal to $2\frac{1}{2}$? Yes.

4. **C** The right angle in the triangle measures 90 degrees. Therefore, the other two angles must measure a total of 90 degrees. Since the triangle is isosceles, the two remaining angles must split the 90 degrees evenly. They are both therefore 45 degrees.

5. **B** The first minute will cost $2.35. The other 7 minutes will cost 15 cents each, or $7 \times 0.15 = \$1.05$.

6.   A   First find the factors of 48: 1×48, 2×24, 3×16, 4×12, and 6×8. How many of these are prime? Only 2 and 3.

7.   B   To multiply by 1,000 you move the decimal three places to the right: $42.2678 \times 1,000$ becomes 42,267.8. Now figure out which choice is equal to this. For A, move the decimal three places to the right to match the exponent of 10, and you get 4,226.78. A can't be the answer. For B, move the decimal four places to the right to match the exponent of 10, and get 42,267.8.

8.   B   Since x and 140 are on the same line, their sum must be 180: $180 - 140 = 40$.

9.   C   Let's break this down into pieces. The first term is $(4 \times \frac{1}{100})$. This is the same as 4 in the hundredths place, or 0.04. We could figure out the decimal equivalents of the other parts, but we don't have to do that much work: The only choice that has a 4 in the hundredths place is C.

10. A   To solve for x, first we need to multiply out the left side, which gives us $2x + 4x = 6x$. The inequality now reads $6x > -6$. Now divide each side by 6.

11. B 4^4 is the same as $4 \times 4 \times 4 \times 4$. 4^5 is the same as $4 \times 4 \times 4 \times 4 \times 4$. If we multiply them together we get $4 \times 4 \times 4 \times 4 \times 4 \times 4 \times 4 \times 4 \times 4$, or 4^9.

12. C   To make this math work easier, don't forget to reduce first. We can reduce 25 and 5, as well as 9 and 27, and we get $\frac{5}{3} \times \frac{1}{1}$, or $\frac{5}{3}$.

13. D   To find the amount of interest, we need to calculate 4% of $5,000. This translates as $\frac{4}{100} \times 5000$. Cancel out two zeros, and you get 4×50, or $200. Add this to his original deposit.

14. A   If the car travels $\frac{1}{2}$ mile every minute, then it travels 1 mile every 2 minutes. To travel 40 miles will then take 80 minutes, or $1\frac{1}{3}$ hours.

15. B   Coordinate (2,7) must have a positive x- and positive y-coordinate. This eliminates C and D. Since the x-coordinate is smaller than the y-coordinate, the point will be high on the y-axis.

16. B   The area of a triangle $= \frac{1}{2}$ base $\times$ height. We know that the base is 10. If the area is 40, then $40 = \frac{1}{2} 10 \times$ height. So $40 = 5 \times h$. Divide each side by 5 to solve for the height.

17. D First put all the xs on the left side of the equation. We can do this by subtracting x from each side, which leaves us with $3x - 9 = 6$. Now add 9 to each side, to get $3x = 15$. Finally, we divide each side by 3 to get $x = 5$.

18. D To solve this, set up a proportion. $\dfrac{5\ apples}{\$8} = \dfrac{60\ apples}{x}$. To solve we cross multiply 60×8 and then divide by 5.

19. B For this question, make sure to follow the order of operations. First, do what is in parentheses: $2 - 8 = -6$. Now we have $13 + 2 \times 9 + 1 - (-6)$. Next, solve $2 \times 9 = -18$. This gives us $13 + 18 + 1 - (-6)$. Now add straight across. (Don't forget that (-6) is the same as $+6$!)

20. D Solve this by plugging in the answer choices. If Mack is 9, then 9 years ago he was 0 years old. Does that make him half as old as he is now? No. If Mack is 12, then 9 years ago he was 3. Does that make him half as old as he is now? No. If Mack is 15, then 9 years ago he was 6. Does that make him half as old as he is now? No. If Mack is 18, then 9 years ago he was 9. This makes him half as old as he is now.

21. D If five shirts cost \$28.50, then each shirt costs one-fifth of that, so divide \$28.50 by 5 to get \$5.70. Multiply that number by 2 to see that shirts cost \$11.40. Since two shirts and a pair of shorts cost \$19.25, then the shorts must cost \$19.25 − \$11.40, or \$7.85.

22. B $3\dfrac{3}{4}\%$ is the same as 3.75%. Remember that % is the same as dividing by 100. Therefore, this equals $\dfrac{3.75}{100}$. To divide by 100, we move the decimal two places to the left.

23. D Let's put 3 in place of x and solve for each expression: $3(3^2) = 27$ and $(3 \times 3)^2 = 81$. The difference is $81 - 27 = 54$.

24. C Walter has a total of $120 + 80 = 200$ baseball cards. Of these cards, 80 of them are baseball cards. Therefore, the fractional part of his collection that are baseball cards is $\dfrac{80}{200}$, which can be reduced to $\dfrac{40}{100}$, or 40%.

25. D The volume of a cube is length × width × height. The length, width, and height of this cube are each 3, so the volume is $3 \times 3 \times 3 = 27$.

26. D Rewrite this expression as $\dfrac{04.5}{0.02}$. If we move the decimal on top and on bottom two places to the right, we get $\dfrac{450}{2} = 225$.

27. C First, let's find the volume of the silo, which will tell us how much grain it can hold. It can hold a total of $25 \times 6 \times 12 = 1,800$ cubic feet of grain. If it is being filled at a rate of 4 cubic feet every minute, divide 1,800 by 4 to find how many minutes it will take to fill the silo.

28. C To make it easier to multiply these fractions, put them in standard form. $3\frac{1}{2}$ is the same as $\frac{7}{2}$ ($2 \times 3 + 1 = 7$), and $6\frac{1}{2}$ is the same as $\frac{13}{2}$ ($2 \times 6 + 1 = 13$). Now multiply $\frac{7}{2} \times \frac{13}{2} = \frac{91}{4}$, or $22\frac{3}{4}$

29. A The area of a circle is πr^2 and the circumference is $2\pi r$. If a circle has a radius of 4, its area is 16π and its circumference is 8π. The ratio of 16π to 8π is the same as 2:1.

30. C Percent increase is always figured by taking the difference over the original amount. The difference between the number of papers that Cindy sold in 1997 and 1998 is 80. The original number she sold in 1997 was 120. Therefore her percentage increase was $\frac{80}{120} = \frac{2}{3}$, or 66%.

31. D If $\frac{1}{3}$ of a number is 32, then the original number must be $3 \times 32 = 96$. $\frac{3}{4}$ of 96 is 72.

32. B Since the triangle is equilateral, all of its sides are 8. Since one of its sides is also a side of the square, the square must also have sides of 8. Therefore the perimeter is equal to 3 sides of the square plus 2 sides of the triangle, each of which are 8: $5 \times 8 = 40$.

33. C First, look at the multiples of 5. They are 5, 10, 15, 20, 25, and 30. How many of these are also multiples of 3? Only 15 and 30 are.

34. D Use the average circle to figure out this problem. If Terence averaged 80 on 4 tests, the sum total of his results on his tests must have been 4×80, or 320. The three tests given have a sum of 231, so $320 - 231$ is his score on his final test.

35. B Since the triangle is a right triangle, one of the angles is 90. If the other angle is 65, then the sum of these two angles is 155. Since there are 180 angles in a triangle, the third angle must measure 25 degrees.

36. D If the ratio of blue to red marbles is 5:2, this means that 5 out of every 7 is blue and 2 of every 7 is red. This means that we can set up a proportion: $\frac{blue}{total}\frac{5}{7} = \frac{x}{70}$. By cross multiplying we see that there must be 50 blue marbles out of the 70 total marbles.

37. C To find how many 75-cent cakes she needs to sell to make $18, divide $18 by $0.75. To make the division easier, move the decimal point two places to the right: $\frac{1800}{75} = 24$.

38. C Since $OA = 4$, then OB is also 4, since all radii are the same length. This makes the perimeter $4 + 4 + 5$.

39. B Plug in the answer choices, starting with A. When $x = 1$, is $1 + 1 = 1 \times 1$? No. When $x = 2$, is $2 + 2 = 2 \times 2$? Yes.

40. A $\dfrac{1}{\frac{1}{x}}$ is the same as $1 \div \dfrac{1}{x}$, which is the same as $1 \times \dfrac{x}{1}$, or just x.

PART 7—LANGUAGE EXPRESSION

1. B Since the second phrase continues the idea of the first, we need a same-direction word.

2. C Since the second phrase continues the idea of the first, we need a same-direction word such as A or C, and A is illogical.

3. B Since the two phrases express a contrast, we need an opposite-direction word.

4. B Only B and C are valid comparative forms. Since the comparison is completed with the word *than*, only B works.

5. C All the other choices are double negatives and can be eliminated.

6. E Only E is a valid comparative form.

7. B A is a run-on sentence, and D and E put punctuation between the subject and the verb. A comma should be used to separate items in a list, so B is the best.

8. B All the other choices are awkward or illogical.

9. D B is in the passive voice, and A, C, and E are awkward.

10. A B, C, D are in the passive voice, and E does not have a main verb.

11. C B, D, and E are awkward or illogical; A says that the winter vacation is famous for its ski resorts, which doesn't make sense.

12. E A, B, and D are awkward, and C is redundant.

13. D A and B have invalid verb forms, C has a tense problem, and the verbs in E are not in parallel form.

14. A B, C, and E have problems of verb tense, and D has no main verb.

15. B All the other choices have problems of verb tense.

16. C A is a fragment, B and E have problems of verb tense, and D uses an invalid verb form.

17. D A is a fragment, and B, C, and E have problems of verb tense.

18. C It is the family that has decided to stay an extra week.

19. A The word *house* is the thing that scared my father.

20. D The opening phrase gives only additional information, since it begins with "Even though." The main idea is "the roof was not finished."

21. C Since the word *brother* is in a phrase with the word *while*, it cannot be the main subject.

22. **B**   The word *moved* is in a phrase with the word *since*, so it can be eliminated.

23. **D**   The opening phrase describes Sam, who helped his mother.

24. **C**   The verb finished is in a phrase with the word *after*, so it can be eliminated. The main idea is "John . . . went to the library."

25. **C**   The main sentence states that people "wanted" something (namely, to move to Florida).

26. **B**   A is redundant, C is a comma splice, D changes the meaning of the original sentences, and E is awkward.

27. **E**   A, B, and C are awkward, and D is illogical.

28. **A**   B is awkward, C and E are redundant, and D changes the meaning of the original sentences.

29. **B**   Since the rest of the sentences discuss Galileo's life and discoveries, the first sentence should introduce him in a general way.

30. **C**   The rest of the paragraph discusses the size of elephants, so the first sentence should discuss their size.

31. **B**   This paragraph mentions how crocodiles and alligators differ. The first sentence should introduce this idea.

32. **B**   The opening sentence mentions writers and patriots. Only B expands on this idea.

33. **A**   This topic sentence mentions public speaking. Only A and D discuss this; however, D does not mention Maya Angelou.

34. **E**   The opening sentence says that the tomato is a fruit. E discusses the relationship between tomatoes and fruits.

35. **D**   This paragraph discusses the works of Salman Rushdie, but sentence 5 does not.

36. **B**   Every sentence of this paragraph talks about cyclones except sentence 3.

37. **D**   While this paragraph discusses various forms of the lute, sentence 5 discusses the origin of musical terms.

38. **B**   The sentence following the blank gives an example of things you can do with a foreign language. Therefore, the sentence that fills the blank should say that you can do things with foreign languages.

39. **A**   The sentence following the blank refers to things that look like random splatters, so the sentence that fills the blank should mention things that look like splatters.

40. **A**   The sentence that precedes the blank talks about camouflage; only A gives an example of camouflage.

PART III

Cracking the HSPT

15

What is the HSPT?

The High School Placement Test (HSPT) is a 2-hour, five-section test designed to help high schools make admissions decisions. Your score of 200 to 800 will be based on how many of the 298 questions you get right. The HSPT is fairly vocabulary-intensive, so concentrate on chapter 16 and begin learning vocabulary as soon as possible.

Along with the basic HSPT, you may be offered an optional test in Catholic religion, science, or mechanical aptitude. The score on these optional tests does not count toward your HSPT score, and very few schools ask for them, so we won't cover these areas in this book.

Here is the format of the HSPT.

- Verbal skills (16 minutes)

- Quantitative skills (30 minutes)

- Reading comprehension and vocabulary (25 minutes)

- Mathematics (45 minutes)

- Language (25 minutes)

Be sure to review chapter 1 of this book ("General Test-Taking Skills") to learn the basic techniques that will help you score high on the HSPT—and most any standardized test. Also review An Introduction for Students for a basic strategy of how to approach this book. Chapters 15 to 21 will take you through each of the test sections in detail, and will review all of the types of problems you'll see. Make sure to take the practice tests in the back of the book and study the explanations to find out which areas you need to review the most to earn a high score on the HSPT. Good luck!

16
Vocabulary

Improving your vocabulary is one great way to improve your score on the HSPT. Several questions rely heavily on your knowledge of the meaning of words, and the more words you know, the better your chances of getting the question right.

If you're picking up this book well in advance of the test, that's great! It's never too early to start working on your vocabulary. Get started now, and try to learn five to ten new words each day between now and the test.

If you're near the test date, the first thing you should do is to look up and learn all the words you find in the HSPT practice tests in this book. If you have time remaining, learn the words in our Hit Parade, which are taken from other tests of approximately the same grade level. The Hit Parade words are grouped into basic categories. Write these words on flash cards (write the word on the front of an index card, then write the definition and a sample sentence on the back), carry them around with you, and learn them! They're probably a little harder than the words you're used to—but think how much you'll be able to really impress (or annoy) your friends.

Here are three hints to help you learn words:

- **Read a lot.** Read as much as you can. By reading, you'll find new words you don't know and see many more words used in the right context, and not just on vocab lists (which is often enough to help you get the correct answer).
- **Create sample sentences.** If you make flash cards, be sure to write a sentence using the word on your cards so that you learn the word in context.
- **Use these words.** Use them whenever you can. By using them—either in writing assignments or in conversation—you'll remember them.

THE PRINCETON REVIEW HIT PARADE

Good Things

    antidote: something that counteracts a poison
    competent: qualified, able
    authentic: genuine, real
    altruistic: doing good for others
    benevolence: goodness
    astute: sharp, shrewd
    aspirant: someone reaching for something
    placate: to quiet down, to appease
    ingenuity: inventiveness
    congenial: agreeable
    adept: skillful
    jubilant: joyful
    sustain: to keep alive

Bad Things

    deficient: lacking
    brash: bold
    irate: enraged
    abdicate: to give up authority or power

recalcitrant: disobedient
insolent: disrespectful, rude
debilitating: weakening, harmful
animosity: hostility
delicate: fragile, easily broken
contaminated: dirtied, polluted
rickety: flimsy, weak
banal: unoriginal, boring
insipid: lacking flavor or interest, dull
plight: predicament, bad situation
mar: to spoil, to mark

Just So-So

vacant: empty
mediocre: average, ordinary
mundane: ordinary
erratic: changing, unreliable
meager: very small or few, not enough
superficial: only on the surface, not very deep or insightful
conventional: traditional, ordinary

Ways to Speak

brusque: short in speech to the point of rudeness
reprimand: to scold, to criticize
repudiate: to renounce, to down
decree: to command
ratify: to approve (usually a law)
debunk: to prove false
jeer: to make fun of

Ways to Act

incompetent: unable to do something properly
pedantic: overly scholarly, boring
pugnacious: hostile
choleric: irritable
belligerent: hostile, warlike
ravenous: extremely hungry

Things to Do

yearn: to long for, to want very badly
analyze: to study carefully
scrutinize: to study carefully
contort: to twist, to deform
prohibit: to prevent
hinder: to prevent, to hold back

17

Verbal Skills

WHICH ONE IS NOT LIKE THE OTHERS?

Several of the questions in the verbal skills section of the HSPT will give you four words and ask you which word does not belong with the other words. Here's a typical example:

1. Which word does *not* belong with the others?

   A) pencil
   B) chalk
   C) ruler
   D) pen

Here's how to crack it

All of the choices will usually have something to do with each other—in this case, each of these objects is something that you might use at school. So we have to find something else that three of these words have in common. Then we'll know which one of them is the one that does *not* belong.

The best way to approach this is to make a sentence. Think of a sentence that will tell us what three of the words have in common.

A pencil, a pen, and chalk are all things you can write with.

A ruler, however, is not something you can write with. Therefore, the answer is C.

COMMON TRICKS

In the above example, the words all seemed related because they were all things you might find at school. We had to make a more exact sentence to figure out which one did not belong. There are two other common ways that a word will seem like it belongs with the others, even when it doesn't.

Read the following question:

2. Which word does *not* belong with the others?

   A) shovel
   B) hammer
   C) tool
   D) screwdriver

What kind of sentence could we make for this problem?

A shovel, a hammer, and a screwdriver are all kinds of tools.

In this case, tool is related to shovel, hammer, and screwdriver because these objects are all kinds of tools. However, it does not belong with the others because the words *shovel*, *hammer*, and *screwdriver* are names for tools; the word *tool* is the name of a category, not a name for a tool. This makes C the best answer.

Now try this one:

3. Which word does *not* belong with the others?

   A) trunk
   B) tree
   C) branch
   D) leaf

What kind of sentence could you make for this question?

A branch, a leaf, and a trunk are all parts of a tree.

All of the words in this problem seem to fit together because they are all related to trees. However, the words *branch, leaf,* and *trunk* all refer to parts of a tree; the word *tree* does not refer to a part of a tree. Therefore, the answer is B.

That's all there is to it!

ANALOGIES

WHAT IS AN ANALOGY?

An analogy is just a fancy word that means two pairs of objects have the same relationship. For instance, kittens/cat and puppies/dog are analogies. Each pair of words has the same relationship: Kittens are baby cats, just as puppies are baby dogs. On the HSPT, the way you express this analogy is by saying "Cat is to kittens as dog is to puppies."

Your job will be to complete the analogy to make a sentence like the one above. Here's an example of how an analogy question will appear on the HSPT.

4. Apple is to fruit as beef is to
   A) restaurant
   B) vegetable
   C) meat
   D) cow

Here's how to crack it

Make a sentence

Just as with the last question type, the best way to figure out the relationship between words is to make a sentence. In this case, to find the relationship between the first two words, we should make a sentence with them. Then we can try to use that same sentence for each of the answer choices to see which one fits best.

Step 1: Cross out the words "is to" and "as."
Step 2: Make a sentence using the first two words in the problem. In this case, we can make the sentence "An apple is a kind of fruit."
Step 3: Try using the same sentence with each of the answer choices and see which one works best. So you'd say, "Beef is a kind of _____."

Is beef a kind of restaurant? No, so cross off A. Is beef a kind of vegetable? No, so cross off B. Is beef a kind of meat? Yes. Is beef a kind of cow? No, so cross off D.

The best answer is C. It is the only choice that works with the sentence we made to define the words *apple* and *fruit.*

Making good sentences

Of course, some sentences you can make are more helpful than others. If we had said, "Apple and fruit both have five letters," that wouldn't have been very useful to us in solving the problem.

When you make a sentence for the first two words, try to use one word to define the other. For example, the sentence "An apple is a kind of fruit" defines what an apple is.

HSPT ANALOGY EXERCISE (ANSWERS ARE ON PAGE 246)

Try making sentences from the following words.

mansion / house	_____
leaf / tree	_____
desert / sand	_____
engine / automobile	_____
bread / baker	_____
brush / painter	_____

SYNONYMS AND ANTONYMS

Other questions in the verbal skills section will ask you to identify synonyms and antonyms of words. A synonym is a word that has the same meaning as another word. Here's a trick that should help you remember: **s**ynonym = **s**ame. An antonym is a word that has the opposite meaning of another word.

Here's an example of a synonym problem.

5. Hinder most nearly means

   A) look up
   B) play
   C) hold back
   D) protect

Here's how to crack synonyms

If you know the meaning of the word:

Step 1: Cover the answer choices with your hand. If you read the answer choices first, you might get confused.

Step 2: State what the word means to you in your own words.

Step 3: Uncover the answer choices and see which choice most closely matches what you said.

In this case, let's cover up the word *hinder*. In your own words, what does it mean? Maybe you came up with something like "stop" or "prevent." Now uncover the answer choices and see which best matches your word. Chances are good that you came up with something very close to hold back; therefore, the answer is C.

If you "sort of" know what the word means:

Maybe you have a sense of what the word means but can't quite put your finger on it. Perhaps you can think of a saying that uses the word—even if you're not sure what the word means—and you should still be able to get the right answer or at least come up with a good guess. If either of these is the case, use the "side of the fence" trick. This is when you ask yourself whether the word is a positive word or a negative word. If the word is positive, you can eliminate any words that are not positive. If the word is negative, you can eliminate any words that are not negative.

Take a look at the following example.

6. Pretentious most nearly means

   A) intelligent
   B) arrogant
   C) inventive
   D) hidden

If you have a sense of the word *pretentious*—perhaps you've heard someone criticized as a really pretentious person—you may know that pretentious is a bad thing to be. It's a negative word. Since this question is asking for a synonym of the word *pretentious*, we know that the correct answer has to be another negative word.

Even if we don't know what *pretentious* means, we know that A and C are positive words, so they can be eliminated. D really isn't positive or negative. If you know that B is also a negative word, you should guess B, which is the correct answer.

Here's how to crack antonyms

If you know the meaning of the word:

Step 1: Cover the answer choices with your hand. If you read the answer choices first, you might get confused.

Step 2: State what the word means to you in your own words.

Step 3: Uncover the answer choices and see which choice most closely matches what you said.

If you "sort of" know what the word means:

Maybe you have a sense of what the word means but can't quite put your finger on it. Perhaps you can think of a saying that uses the word—even if you're not sure what the word means—and you should still be able to get the right answer or at least come up with a good guess. If either of these is the case, use the "side of the fence" trick. This is when you ask yourself whether the word is a positive word or a negative word. If the word is positive, you can eliminate any words that are not positive. If the word is negative, you can eliminate any words that are not negative.

Try this example:

7. Courteous means the *opposite* of

A) honest
B) unconcerned
C) rude
D) jealous

If you have a sense of the word *courteous*, you may know that it's a positive word. Since this question is asking us for an antonym, we know that the correct answer has to be a negative word.

Even if we don't know what the word *courteous* means, we know that A is another positive word, so eliminate it. Remember that we're looking for the opposite. B really isn't positive or negative, so it probably isn't the answer. If you can get no further with this problem, you can take a great guess between C and D. (In fact, the answer is C.)

What if you have no idea what a word means?

Regardless of whether it's a synonym or antonym question, if you really have no idea what the word means, take your best guess and move on to the next question. Your time will be better spent on other problems in this section.

TRUE OR FALSE QUESTIONS

For a true or false question, you will be asked to read two sentences that describe people, places, or things. The third sentence will be something that we might or might not know for sure. Your job is to figure out whether the final sentence is true, false, or uncertain.

WHAT DO "TRUE," "FALSE," AND "UNCERTAIN" MEAN?

Look at these two statements.

- Jason scored a 92 on his math test.

- Lisa scored a 96 on her math test.

There are many things you might assume to be true, given these two statements. Here are some of them.

- Lisa is a better student than Jason.

- Lisa knows math better than Jason.

- Lisa and Jason are in the same math class.

However, none of these choices really has to be true. Sure, they might be true, but we don't really know. These statements are all uncertain, since we can't know 100 percent that they are true or false. Lisa might not be a better student than Jason—maybe she just got lucky on this test, or maybe in most other subjects she scores much worse than Jason. Lisa might not be better at math—maybe she's just taking an easier math class than Jason is taking. We don't whether they're in the same math class. We don't even know whether they're in the same grade or the same school! We can't make any assumptions on these questions.

> What is something that we are certain is *true* given the information above?
> Lisa scored higher on her math test than Jason scored on his math test.

> And what is something we are certain is *false* given the information above?
> Lisa scored lower on her math test that Jason scored on his math test.

HOW TRUE OR FALSE QUESTIONS APPEAR ON THE HSPT

Read the following question.

8. Mary collected more shells than Carrie and Tim. Tim collected more shells than Tracy. Mary collected more shells than Tracy. If the first two statements are true, then the third is

   A) true
   B) false
   C) uncertain

Here's how to crack it

The best way to approach true or false questions is to make a diagram.

Let's make a diagram showing who has more shells, putting those with the most shells to the left. We know that Mary collected more shells than Carrie and Tim. We can draw this:

$$M \geq C \ Tim$$

We also know that Tim collected more than Tracy. So we can add this fact to our diagram

$$M \geq C, \text{Tim}$$
$$\text{Tim} \geq \text{Tracy}$$

Since we know that Mary has more than Tim, and that Tim has more than Tracy, we know that Mary has more than Tracy, so the third statement is **true**.

Now try this one:

Mary collected more shells than Carrie and Tim. Tim collected fewer shells than Tracy. Mary collected more shells than Tracy. If the first two statements are true, then the third is:

A) true
B) false
C) uncertain

We can diagram the first sentence of this question the same way as before:

$$M \geq C, \text{Tim}$$

We now add the second sentence, which says that Tracy has more shells than Tim

$$M \geq C$$
$$\text{Tracy} > \text{Tim}$$

We know that Mary has more than Carrie and Tim, and that Tracy has more than Carry and Tim, but we don't know whether Mary or Tracy has more shells. We only know that they each have more than Carry and Tim do. Therefore the third statement is **uncertain**.

Now try some sample problems:

HSPT VERBAL SKILLS EXERCISE (ANSWERS ARE ON PAGE 246)

1. Which word does *not* belong with the others?

   A) sad
   B) lonely
   C) feeling
   D) upset

2. Which word does *not* belong with the others?

   A) oregano
   B) parsley
   C) spice
   D) pepper

3. Company is to president as army is to

   A) battle
   B) general
   C) soldier
   D) weapon

4. Gigantic is to large as hilarious is to

   A) serious
   B) interesting
   C) insulting
   D) funny

5. Conquer most nearly means

   A) defeat
   B) fear
   C) dislike
   D) calm

6. Fortify means the *opposite* of

   A) load
   B) weaken
   C) sail
   D) clean

7. Compel most nearly means

   A) see
   B) force
   C) ask
   D) hope

8. Opaque means the *opposite* of

   A) dirty
   B) clear
   C) normal
   D) late

9. Alex bought more apples than Barry and Marcia. Marcia bought more apples than Elisa and Kim. Alex bought more apples than Kim. If the first two statements are true, then the third is

   A) true
   B) false
   C) uncertain

10. Alex bought more apples than Barry. Barry bought more apples than Marcia and Elisa. Elisa bought more apples than Alex. If the first two statements are true, then the third is

    A) true
    B) false
    C) uncertain

11. Alex bought more apples than Barry and Marcia. Elisa bought more apples than Marcia. Alex bought more apples than Elisa. If the first two statements are true, then the third is

    A) true
    B) false
    C) uncertain

18

Quantitative Skills

Most of the questions in this section require you to do some amount of arithmetic. Let's take a moment to review the basics.

MATH VOCABULARY

Term	Definition	Examples
integer	any number that does not contain either a fraction or a decimal	−4, −1, 0, 9, 15
positive number	any number greater than zero	$\frac{1}{2}$, 1, 4, 101
negative number	any number less than zero	$-\frac{1}{2}$, −1, −4, −101
even number	any number that is evenly divisible by two	−2, 0, 2, 8, 24 (note: 0 *is* even)
odd number	any number that is not evenly divisible by two	−1, 1, 5, 35
prime number	any number that is evenly divisible only by one and itself	2, 3, 5, 7, 11, 13 (note: 1 is *not* a prime number)
sum	the result of addition	The sum of 6 and 2 is 8.
difference	the result of subtraction	The difference between 6 and 4 is 2.
product	the result of multiplication	The product of 3 and 4 is 12.

HSPT MATH VOCABULARY EXERCISE (ANSWERS ARE ON PAGE 246)

1. How many integers are there between −4 and 5?
2. How many positive integers are there between −4 and 5?
3. What is the sum of 6, 7, and 8?
4. What is the product of 2, 4, and 8?

ORDER OF OPERATIONS

How would you do the following problem?
$$4 + 5 \times 3 - (2 + 1)$$

Whenever you have a problem such as this, remember the rule.

Please Excuse My Dear Aunt Sally

Believe it or not, this sentence tells you the order in which you should solve the above problem. This stands for:

Parentheses
Exponents
Multiplication and Division (from left to right)
Addition and Subtraction (from left to right)

Therefore we need to solve the parentheses first.

$$4 + 5 \times 3 - (2 + 1)$$

becomes

$$4 + 5 \times 3 - 3$$

Next, we do multiplication and division to get

$$4 + 15 - 3$$

Finally, we add and subtract to get our final answer of 16.

HSPT ORDER OF OPERATIONS EXERCISE (ANSWERS ARE ON PAGE 247)

1. $15 - 5 + 3 = $ ___
2. $15 - 2 \times 3 = $ ___
3. $2 \times (2 + 3) - 5 = $ ___
4. $20 + 3 \times 5 + 10 = $ ___
5. $(3 + 6) \times 3 \times 4 = $ ___

FRACTIONS

A fraction is just another way of representing division. For instance, $\frac{2}{5}$ actually means two divided by five (which is 0.4 as a decimal). Another way to think of this is to imagine a pie cut into five pieces: $\frac{2}{5}$ means two out of the five pieces. The parts of the fraction are called the numerator and the denominator.

The numerator is the number on top; the denominator is the number on the bottom.

$$\frac{\text{numerator}}{\text{denominator}}$$

REDUCING FRACTIONS

Often you'll need to reduce your fractions after you have made a calculation. This means that you want to make the numbers as small as possible. To reduce a fraction, simply divide top and bottom by the same number. Don't spend too long trying to figure out the best number to divide by; use 2, 3, or 5, and keep dividing until you can't divide anymore.

For example, if you have the fraction $\frac{42}{18}$, we can divide the top and bottom each by 3 to get $\frac{14}{6}$. Then we can divide top and bottom by 2 and get $\frac{7}{3}$. It can't be reduced any further than this, so this is your final answer.

ADDING AND SUBTRACTING FRACTIONS

To add or subtract fractions, the fractions have to have a common denominator. This means that they have to have the same number on the bottom (the denominators need to be the same). If the fractions already have a common denominator, you can add or subtract them by adding or subtracting the numbers on top.

$$\frac{4}{7} + \frac{2}{7} = \frac{6}{7}$$

If the fractions do not have a common denominator, the easiest way to add or subtract them is to use the Bowtie.

Step 1: Multiply the two bottom numbers together. Their product goes on the bottom of your two new fractions.

Step 2: Multiply diagonally from the bottom left to the top right. Write this product on the top right.

Step 3: Multiply diagonally from the bottom right to the top left. Write this product on the top left.

See—it looks like a bowtie! Now you have two fractions with a common denominator, and you can add or subtract them.

For example:

① $\dfrac{1}{2} \xrightarrow{\ +\ } \dfrac{1}{3}$ $\overline{6} + \overline{6}$

② $\dfrac{1}{2} \xrightarrow{\ +\ } \dfrac{1}{3}$ $\dfrac{}{6} + \dfrac{2}{6}$

③ $\dfrac{1}{2} \xleftarrow{\ +\ } \dfrac{1}{3}$ $\dfrac{3}{6} + \dfrac{2}{6} = \dfrac{5}{6}$

MULTIPLYING AND DIVIDING FRACTIONS

To multiply fractions, multiply straight across the top and bottom.

$$\frac{3}{5} \times \frac{1}{3} = \frac{3 \times 1}{5 \times 3} = \frac{3}{15}$$

To divide fractions, flip the second fraction and multiply.

$$\frac{3}{5} \div \frac{1}{3} = \frac{3}{5} \times \frac{3}{1} = \frac{9}{5}$$

HSPT FRACTIONS EXERCISE (ANSWERS ARE ON PAGE 247)

1. Reduce $\dfrac{12}{60} = $ ___

2. $\dfrac{3}{8} + \dfrac{2}{3} = $ ___

3. $\dfrac{3}{4} - \dfrac{2}{3} = $ ___

4. $\dfrac{3}{5} \times \dfrac{3}{2} = $ ___

5. $\dfrac{1}{3} \div \dfrac{1}{2} = $ ___

DECIMALS

Remember that decimals are just another way of writing fractions. Be sure to know the names of all the decimal places.

$$3 \quad 4 \cdot 8 \quad 5 \quad 7$$

tens — units — tenths — hundredths — thousandths

ADDING DECIMALS

To add decimals, just line up the decimal places and add.

$$
\begin{array}{r}
24.05 \\
+ \; 12.23 \\
\hline
36.28
\end{array}
$$

SUBTRACTING DECIMALS

To subtract decimals, just line up the decimal places and subtract.

$$
\begin{array}{r}
24.05 \\
-\ 12.23 \\
\hline
11.82
\end{array}
$$

MULTIPLYING DECIMALS

To multiply decimals, count the total number of digits to the right of the decimal point in the numbers you are multiplying. Then multiply the numbers without the decimal points. Once you have your answer, add back into the new number all of the decimal places you removed from the first two numbers.

To solve 0.2×3.4, remove two decimal places and multiply.

$$
\begin{array}{r}
34 \\
\times\ 2 \\
\hline
68
\end{array}
$$

Now put back the two decimal places we removed to get 0.68.

DIVIDING DECIMALS

To divide decimals, move the decimal places in both numbers the same number of places to the right until you are working with only integers. But unlike when you're multiplying decimals, you don't have to put the decimals back in when you're dividing.

$$3.4 \div 0.2 = 34 \div 2 = 17$$

CONVERTING DECIMALS TO FRACTIONS

Remember that multiplying by 10 means the same thing as moving the decimal point one place to the right, and dividing by 10 means the same thing as moving the decimal points one place to the left.

$$9 \div 10 = \frac{9}{10} = 0.9$$

$$5 \div 100 = \frac{5}{100} = 0.05$$

This is why the first place to the right of the decimal is called "tenths" and the second place to the right is called "hundredths." Nine tenths = $0.9 = \frac{9}{10}$. Five hundredths = $0.05 = \frac{5}{100}$. So to convert a decimal to a fraction, all you need to do is change the numbers after the decimal to their fraction form.

$$5.24 = 5 + \frac{2}{10} + \frac{4}{100}$$

HSPT DECIMALS EXERCISE (ANSWERS ARE ON PAGE 247)

1. $2.43 + 5.25 =$ ___

2. $5.75 - 3.12 =$ ___

3. $1.5 \times 3 =$ ___

4. $2.5 \times 0.5 =$ ___

5. $2.5 \div 0.5 =$ ___

6. What is 6.32 in fraction form? ___

EXPONENTS, SCIENTIFIC NOTATION, AND SQUARE ROOTS

Exponents are just a short way of writing multiplication. 3^2 means to multiply two 3s together: 3×3. Likewise, 3^4 means to multiply four 3s together: $3 \times 3 \times 3 \times 3$. On the HSPT you will not see very complex exponents, so the best way to solve them is to write them out longhand and multiply.

Scientific notation is also a short way of writing big numbers. Whenever you see a number such as 3.44×10^2, this means that you should move the decimal point to the right the same number of places as the exponent to the 10. In this case, you move the decimal two places to the right (10^2), and you get 344. Likewise, 4.355×10^2 is just another way of writing 435.5.

Square root is just the opposite of raising a number to the second power. $\sqrt{4} = 2$, since $2^2 = 4$. On the HSPT you will not have very big square roots. Your best bet is simply to memorize these common ones.

$$\text{Since } 2^2 = 4, \quad \sqrt{4} = 2.$$
$$\text{Since } 3^2 = 9, \quad \sqrt{9} = 3.$$
$$\text{Since } 4^2 = 16, \quad \sqrt{16} = 4.$$
$$\text{Since } 5^2 = 25, \quad \sqrt{25} = 5.$$

HSPT EXPONENTS, SCIENTIFIC NOTATION, AND SQUARE ROOTS EXERCISE (ANSWERS ARE ON PAGE 247)

1. $4^3 =$ ___

2. $2^4 =$ ___

3. $3.4 \times 10^2 =$ ___

4. $5.23 \times 10^4 =$ ___

5. $\sqrt{4} + \sqrt{16} =$ ___

SOLVE FOR X

To solve an equation, you want to get the variable (the x) on one side of the equation and put everything else on the other side.

To get only the variable on one side, follow these two steps.

Step 1: Move elements around using addition and subtraction. Put the variables on one side of the equation and numbers on the other. As long as you do the same operation on both sides of the equal sign, you aren't changing the value of the variable.

Step 2: Divide both sides of the equation by the coefficient, which is the number in front of the variable. If that number is a fraction, multiply everything by the denominator.

For example:

$$3x + 5 = 17$$

$$\frac{3x + 5 = 17}{-5 \quad -5}$$

Subtract 5 from each side.

$$\frac{3x = 12}{\div 3 \quad \div 3}$$

Divide 3 from each side.

$$x = 4$$

Always remember the rule of equations: *Whatever you do to one side of the equation, you must also do to the other side.*

HSPT SOLVE FOR X EXERCISE (ANSWERS ARE ON PAGE 248)

1. If $4x = 20$ then $x =$ ___

2. If $4x + 3 = 31$ then $x =$ ___

3. If $6 = 8x + 4$ then $x =$ ___

4. If $4x - 3 = 3x$ then $x =$ ___

PERCENT TRANSLATION

Everyone knows how easy it is to make a simple mistake on a percent problem. Should you write "5% of 100" as $\frac{5}{100}$ or as $\frac{100}{5}$ or as something else? To make sure to avoid silly mistakes, here's a foolproof method for solving percent questions. Any percent problem can be translated word for word into an equation if you know the mathematical equivalent of the English words. For instance, "percent" means the same thing as "divide by 100," and "of" means the same thing as "multiply." Therefore, "5% of 100" can be written as $\frac{5}{100} \times 100$, which equals 5.

The chart below shows you the mathematical translation of the English words you will probably see. To solve any percent question, read the problem back to yourself and replace the words on the left side of the chart with the math symbols on the right. Then you can easily solve.

Percent	$\div 100$
Of	$\times$
What	x (or any variable)
Is, Are, Equals	$=$

Here is an example:

20% of $50 =$

$$20\% \quad \text{of} \quad 50$$

$$\frac{20}{100} \times 50$$

5 is what percent of 80?

$$5 \quad \text{is what percent of} \quad 80$$

$$5 = \frac{x}{100} \times 80$$

$$5 = \frac{x}{100} \times 80$$

HSPT PERCENT TRANSLATION EXERCISE (ANSWERS ARE ON PAGE 248)

1. 30% of $60 = $ ___

2. 40% of $200 = $ ___

3. 15 is what percent of 60? ___

4. What is 25% of 10% of 200? ___

COMPUTATION QUESTIONS

Several of the questions on the HSPT will ask you to perform basic arithmetic computations. Don't worry about variables here; you won't see any—just addition, subtraction, multiplication, and division. The trick here is to work carefully and in bite-size pieces to make sure that you don't make any careless errors.

Here's an example of a computation question.

10. What number is 4 more than $\frac{1}{4}$ of 32?

   A) 6
   B) 8
   C) 10
   D) 12

The most common mistakes in computation problems stem from trying to do the whole problem at once. Let's just take it one step at a time—in bite-size pieces—and get the right answer. First, let's solve $\frac{1}{4}$ of 32. $\frac{1}{4}$ of 32 is 8. So now the question reads: What number is 4 more than 8? 4 + 8 = 12. The answer is D.

If you are careful and have mastered your basic arithmetic, these questions shouldn't give you too much trouble.

HSPT COMPUTATION EXERCISE (ANSWERS ARE ON PAGE 248)

1. What is three times the difference of 75 and 30?

2. What is $\frac{1}{8}$ of the sum of 50 and 14?

3. What is 16 more than half of 30?

4. What number is 160% of 40?

5. What number is 2 more than the difference of 6^2 and 5^2?

SERIES QUESTIONS

A series is a list of numbers that follow a pattern. For instance, the numbers 2, 4, 6, 8 make a series because each number is 2 more than the number before it. On the HSPT, several questions will show you a series with a blank in it and ask you to figure out what number should fill the blank. What you need to do is to figure out the pattern.

To see how to solve one, let's look at the following example.

11. What number should come next in this series: 1, 5, 9, __?

Here's how to crack it

Between the numbers, write the number that—by performing an operation like adding, subtracting, multiplying, or dividing—takes you from the first number to the next and so on.

$$\begin{array}{ccccc} & +4 & & +4 & \\ 1 & & 5 & & 9 \quad \underline{} \end{array}$$

Since each number is 4 more than the previous number, the next number in the series must be 13.

Sometimes you will need to try more than one kind of operation between each pair of numbers. On more complicated problems, you may need to try subtraction, multiplication, and division.

Here's another example.

12. What number should come next in this series: 7, 5, 12, 10, 17, __?

$$
\begin{array}{ccccccccc}
& -2 & & +7 & & -2 & & +7 & & -2 \\
7 & & 5 & & 12 & & 10 & & 17 & & \underline{\quad}
\end{array}
$$

Since the series goes (– 2) then (+ 7), then next element should be 2 less than 17, or 15.

Try this one.

13. What number should come next in this series: 2, 4, 5, 10, 11, 22, __?

$$
\begin{array}{ccccccccccc}
& \times 2 & & +1 & & \times 2 & & +1 & & \times 2 & & +1 \\
2 & & 4 & & 5 & & 10 & & 11 & & 22 & & \underline{\quad}
\end{array}
$$

This series goes (×2) then (+ 1), so the next element should be 1 more than 22, or 23.

Sometimes the blank will be in the middle of the series rather than at the end. Follow the same technique, and double-check your answer by making sure that the number you put in the blank works with the number(s) that follow.

14. What number should fill the blank in this series:
3, 5, 10, 12, 24, __, 52?

$$
\begin{array}{ccccccccccc}
& +2 & & \times 2 & & +2 & & \times 2 & & +2 & & \times 2 \\
3 & & 5 & & 10 & & 12 & & 24 & & \underline{\quad} & & 52
\end{array}
$$

This series goes (+ 2) then (×2), so the missing number should be 2 more than 24, or 26. We can double-check this by making sure that $26 \times 2 = 52$, which it does.

That's all there is to series questions! Now give it a try.

HSPT SERIES EXERCISE (ANSWERS ARE ON PAGE 248)

1. 4, 8, 12, 16, 20, __?

2. 38, 32, 26, 20, __?

3. 6, 12, 16, 32, 36, 72, __?

4. 10, 5, 15, 10, 20, 15, __?

5. 7, 14, 12, 24, 22, 44, __?

6. 8, 16, 20, 40, __, 88?

7. 20, 18, 25, 23, __, 28?

COMPARISON PROBLEMS

The rest of the problems in this section of the HSPT will ask you to compare three values or three quantities.

Here's an example of a question that asks you to compare three values.

15. Examine (a), (b), and (c) and find the best answer.

(a) $\dfrac{6}{10}$

(b) $\dfrac{44}{100}$

(c) $\dfrac{9}{100}$

A) $a > b > c$
B) $a = b = c$
C) $b > a = c$
D) $b > a > c$

Here's how to crack it

Solve for the values of (a), (b), and (c). You may be asked to perform some simple arithmetic operations or do simple geometry. (For the geometry review, see chapter 20).

In this case, (a) = 0.6, (b) = 0.44, and (c) = 0.09.

Once you have the values for (a), (b), and (c), carefully look at the answer choices to see which accurately represents their relationships. Use the Process of Elimination to cross off any choices that you know are wrong, and be sure to read carefully!

Since (a) is the largest, we can eliminate answers B, C, and D. Therefore, A is the answer.

Here's an example of a question that asks you to compare three quantities.

16. Examine (a), (b), and (c) and find the best answer.

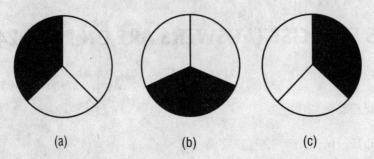

(a)   (b)   (c)

A) (a) is more shaded than (b)
B) (a) is less shaded than (b) and more shaded than (c)
C) (c) is more shaded than both (a) and (b)
D) (a), (b), and (c) are equally shaded

In this case, you should inspect circles (a), (b), and (c). Figure out what the relationship is among them, and use Process of Elimination to find the best choice. Since (a) and (b) are equally shaded, A and B can be eliminated. Since (b) and (c) are equally shaded, C can also be eliminated. Therefore, D must be the answer.

HSPT COMPARISON EXERCISE (ANSWERS ARE ON PAGE 249)

1. Examine (a), (b), and (c) and find the best answer.

   (a) $2(9 - 5)$
   (b) $(2 \times 9) - 5$
   (c) $2 \times 9 - 5$

   A) (a) is greater than (b) and (c)
   B) (a) is equal to (b) and less than (c)
   C) (b) and (c) are equal and greater than (a)
   D) (a), (b), and (c) are equal

2. Examine (a), (b), and (c) and find the best answer.

   (a) 40% of 60
   (b) 60% of 40
   (c) 50% of 90

   A) (a) is greater than (b) and (c)
   B) (a) is equal to (b) and less than (c)
   C) (b) and (c) are equal and greater than (a)
   D) (a), (b), and (c) are equal

3. Examine (a), (b), and (c) and find the best answer.

   (a) 2.3×10^2
   (b) 2,300
   (c) 2.3×10^3

   A) (a) is greater than (b) and (c)
   B) (a) is equal to (b) and less than (c)
   C) (b) and (c) are equal and greater than (a)
   D) (a), (b), and (c) are equal

4. Examine (a), (b), and (c) and find the best answer.

   (a) the area of a square with side 6
   (b) the perimeter of a square with side 6
   (c) half the area of a square with side 8

   A) (a) is greater than (b) and (c)
   B) (a) is equal to (b) and less than (c)
   C) (b) and (c) are equal and greater than (a)
   D) (a), (b), and (c) are equal

5. Triangle *ABC* is isosceles. Angle *a* measures 40 degrees. Find the best answer.

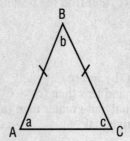

A) *a* is greater than *b* + *c*
B) *a* is less than *b* + *c*
C) *a* is equal to *b* + *c*
D) *a*, *b*, and *c* are all equal

19

Reading Comprehension and Vocabulary

A WORD ABOUT TIMING

This section of the HSPT combines two different question types: reading comprehension and reading vocabulary. How should you spend your time?

The reading vocabulary questions are very much like the synonym questions we discussed in chapter 17. You should go through them very quickly, since you probably either know the word or you don't. This means that you should spend the majority of your time on the reading comprehension. Slow down, take your time, and get your points on reading comprehension, because taking extra time on vocabulary probably won't help. Of your 25 minutes, you should plan to spend 20 minutes on reading comprehension and only the last 5 on vocabulary.

HOW TO THINK ABOUT READING COMPREHENSION

Reading the passages on the HSPT is different from most other kinds of reading that you will do in school. You might think that you have to read slowly enough to learn all the information in the passage. But there is much more information in the passage than you can learn in a short time, and you will be asked about only a few facts from the passage. So trying to understand all of the facts in the passage is not the best use of your time.

Most importantly, you don't get points for understanding everything in the passage. You only get points for answering questions correctly. Therefore, we're going to teach you the best strategy to get you the most correct answers.

There is one more important thing to know, which works to your advantage: *The answer to every question can be found somewhere in the passage.* All you've got to do is find it. This means that you should think of reading comprehension like a treasure hunt: You need to use clues in the questions to find the answers in the passage and earn your points.

STRATEGY FOR ATTACKING READING COMPREHENSION

Step 1: Read the passage and label each paragraph. Don't try to learn every single fact in the passage; you can always go back later. It is important only to get a general idea of what each paragraph talks about.

Step 2: Answer the general questions based on your paragraph labels.

Step 3: Answer the specific questions by looking back at the passage and finding the answer.

Important! In steps 2 and 3, answer your questions by using Process of Elimination. The test-writers will often try to disguise the correct answer by using different words that mean basically the same thing as the words used in the passage. You might not recognize these words right away as the ones used in the passage. Why do the test-writers do this? If they gave you the exact same words straight out of the passage, that would be too easy. So your best bet is to cross off the choices that you know are wrong and pick from the choices that are left.

Now let's look at each step in more detail.

STEP 1: LABEL YOUR PARAGRAPHS

Every good treasure hunt needs a map, which will help you locate the answers in the passage. The best way to make a map is to label your paragraphs as you read. This will help you understand the main idea of the passage and at the same time make it easier to locate facts in the passage while you're reading.

After you finish each paragraph, stop for a moment and ask yourself, "What is this paragraph about?" Try to summarize the idea of this paragraph in seven or eight words, and quickly write this summary in the margin. This way you'll have a guide to important parts of the passage when you have to answer a question.

After you have read the entire passage, take a moment and ask yourself, "What is this whole passage about?" Write a one-sentence summary at the bottom of the page. This will help you answer any main-idea questions you may see.

Try doing step 1 for the following passage:

> Contrary to popular belief, the first European known to lay eyes on America was not Christopher Columbus or Amerigo Vespucci, but a little-known Viking named Bjarni Herjolfsson. In the summer of 986, Bjarni sailed from Norway to Iceland, heading for the Viking settlement where his father Heriulf resided.

_____

> When he arrived in Iceland, Bjarni discovered that his father had already sold his land and estates and set out for the latest Viking settlement on the subarctic island called Greenland. Discovered by an <u>infamous</u> murderer and criminal named Eric the Red, Greenland lay at the limit of the known world. Dismayed, Bjarni set out for this new colony.

_____

> Since the Vikings traveled without a chart or compass, it was not uncommon for them to lose their way in the unpredictable northern seas. Beset by fog, the crew lost their bearings. When the fog finally cleared, they found themselves before a land that was level and covered with woods. They traveled farther up the coast, finding more flat, wooded country. Farther north, the landscape revealed glaciers and rocky mountains. Without knowing it, Bjarni had arrived in North America.

_____

> Though Bjarni realized this was an unknown land, he was no intrepid explorer. Rather, he was a practical man who had simply set out to find his father. Refusing his crew's request to go ashore, he promptly turned his bow back to sea. After four days' sailing, Bjarni landed at Herjolfsnes on the southwestern tip of Greenland, the exact place he had been seeking all along.

_____

> What is this whole passage about?   _____

Your labels and passage summary should look something like this.

Paragraph 1: America was first visited by Bjarni Herjolfsson.
Paragraph 2: Herjolfsson wanted to follow his father to Greenland.
Paragraph 3: He got lost and ended up at America.
Paragraph 4: He turned around and finally reached Greenland.

Summary: How Bjarni Herjolfsson got lost and saw America before anyone else.

Now we have a good picture of the overall point of the passage, and we should be able to look back and find any details we need. So let's turn to the questions.

STEP 2: ANSWER THE GENERAL QUESTIONS

It's usually best to answer the general questions first. These questions ask you about the passage as a whole. There are several types of general questions, and they look like this.

Main Idea/Purpose
The passage is mostly about
The main idea of this passage is
The best title for this passage would be
The purpose of this passage is to
The author wrote this passage in order to

Tone/Attitude
The author's tone is best described as
The attitude of the author is one of

General Interpretation
The author would most likely agree that
It can be inferred from the passage that
The passage implies that
You would probably find this passage in a
This passage is best described as

To answer a main idea/purpose question, ask yourself, "What did the passage talk about most?" Look at the choices and cross off anything that was not discussed or that was only a detail of the passage.

To answer a tone/attitude question, ask yourself, "How does the author feel about the subject?" Cross off anything that doesn't agree with the author's view.

To answer a general interpretation question, ask yourself, "Which answer sounds most like what the author said?" Cross off anything that was not discussed in the paragraph or that does not agree with the author's view.

Let's take a look at some general questions for this passage.

1. The passage is mostly about

   A) the Vikings and their civilization
   B) the waves of Viking immigration
   C) sailing techniques of Bjarni Herjolfsson
   D) one Viking's glimpse of America

To answer this question, let's look back at our labels and our summary of the passage. We said that the main idea of the passage was how Bjarni Herjolfsson got lost and saw America before anyone else. A and B are about the Vikings in general and not about Herjolfsson, so they can be eliminated. C is about Herjolfsson, but his sailing techniques are not really discussed. This makes D the best choice.

2. Which of the following can be inferred from the passage?
   A) The word *America* was first used by Herjolfsson.
   B) Herjolfsson's discovery of America was an accident.
   C) Herjolfsson was helped by Native Americans.
   D) Greenland and Iceland were the Vikings' most important discoveries.

You should make quick work of this problem using Process of Elimination. The passage never says anything about Native Americans, so C can be eliminated. Also, it doesn't say that Herjolfsson ever used the word *America*, so you can cross off A. (If you're not positive whether this is true or not, quickly skim back and double-check this in the passage.) We're already down to two choices. D is an extreme choice— meaning it uses strong language that makes something absolutely true or false—due to the word *most*, so it probably is not the answer. If you check the passage, you can see that D is never stated. Therefore B is the best choice.

STEP 3: ANSWER THE SPECIFIC QUESTIONS

Specific questions ask you about a fact or detail mentioned in the passage. For these questions, look back at the passage to find your answer. These are the different kinds of specific questions.

Fact
  According to the passage
  According to the author
  Which of these questions is answered by the passage?
  Vocabulary in Context

The word <u>pilfer</u> probably means
  What does the passage mean by <u>pilfer</u>?

Specific Interpretation/Purpose
  The author mentions Mother Goose in order to
  From the information in the passage, Mother Goose would probably

To answer a fact question, look back at the passage and find the lines that mention the thing you are asked about. Use your passage labels to find the information quickly, or simply skim until you find it. Reread those lines to see exactly what the passage says. Then look for a choice that best restates what the passage says. Cross off anything that is never stated or that says the opposite of the information in the passage.

To answer a Vocabulary in Context question, look back at the passage and find the underlined word. It will probably be a word that you don't know. Cover the word with your finger. Reread the lines around that word, and think of the word that you would put there. Then look at the answer choices and see which comes closest to the word that you think should go there. If you can't think of the exact word, it's okay to simply note that the word should be a "positive word" or a "negative word."

To answer a Specific Interpretation/Purpose question, look back at the passage and find the lines that discuss the thing you are asked about. Use your passage labels or skim the passage. Reread those lines to see exactly what the passage says. The correct answer will always be very closely based on the information in the passage. For instance, if a passage tells us that John likes to play tennis, we can infer that he will probably play tennis if he is given the chance. Cross off any choices that are not stated in the passage or sound very far off from what the passage says.

3. According to the passage, Greenland was discovered by

   A) Amerigo Vespucci
   B) Bjarni Herjolfsson's father
   C) Bjarni Herjolfsson
   D) Eric the Red

To answer this question, we should look back at the passage and find the line that talks about the discovery of Greenland. If you skim for the word *Greenland*, you'll find it in the second paragraph: "Discovered by an <u>infamous</u> murderer and criminal named Eric the Red, Greenland lay at the limit of the known world." Therefore the answer is D.

4. The word <u>infamous</u> probably means

   A) lazy
   B) strong
   C) wicked
   D) intelligent

Let's reread the line that mentions the word *infamous*: "Discovered by an <u>infamous</u> murderer and criminal named Eric the Red . . . ." Since the word *infamous* describes a *murderer and criminal*, it must be a word that describes someone who is bad. B and D are positive words, so you can eliminate them. C sounds much more like a description of a bad person than A, so the best choice is C.

5. According to the passage, Bjarni Herjolfsson left Norway to

   A) start a new colony
   B) open a trade route to America
   C) visit his relatives
   D) map the North Sea

The end of the first paragraph discusses Herjolfsson's departure. There it states, "Bjarni sailed from Norway to Iceland, heading for the Viking settlement where his father Heriulf resided." The correct answer will use different words, but it should restate this same idea. Can we find anything here about starting a colony? No, so A can be eliminated. Does it mention opening a trade route to America? No, so B can also be eliminated. (It's true that he does eventually reach America, but that isn't the reason why he left.) Does it mention visiting his relatives? Well, it does say that he wanted to find his father. So let's leave C. Does this sentence mention mapping the North Sea? No. C is the answer.

6. Bjarni's reaction upon landing in Iceland can best be described as

   A) disappointed
   B) satisfied
   C) amused
   D) fascinated

Where can we find a description of Bjarni Herjolfsson's arrival in Iceland? At the beginning of the second paragraph. There it states, "When he arrived in Iceland, Bjarni discovered that his father had already sold his land and estates and set out for the latest Viking settlement on the subarctic island called Greenland." Since he had missed his father, he was probably unhappy. Which word best states this idea? A.

7. When the author says, "The crew lost their bearings," this probably means that

A) the ship was damaged beyond repair
B) the sailors did not know which way they were going
C) the sailors were very angry
D) the sailors misplaced their clothes

Let's reread the lines around "the crew lost their bearings": "Since the Vikings traveled without a chart or compass, it was not uncommon for them to lose their way in the unpredictable northern seas. Beset by fog, the crew lost their bearings." Since the story says that the crew would often "lose their way," the best answer is B.

PROCESS OF ELIMINATION

If you're stuck on which answer is correct, remember to use Process of Elimination to cross off answers you know are wrong.

On general questions, you'll usually want to cross off answers that:

- Are not mentioned in the passage.

- Are too detailed. If the passage mentions something in only one line, it is a detail, not a main idea.

- Go against, or say the opposite of, information in the passage.

- Are too big. You can't say much in four or five paragraphs; any answer that says something like, "The passage proves that the theory Einstein spent his entire life creating was right" is probably a wrong answer.

- Are too extreme. If a choice uses absolute terms such as "all," "every," "never," or "always," it's probably a wrong answer.

- Go against common sense.

On specific questions, you should probably cross off answers that:

- Are extreme.

- Go against information in the passage.

- Are not mentioned in the passage.

- Go against common sense.

If you look back at the questions in the sample reading comp passage above, you'll see that following these guidelines eliminates many of the wrong answer choices. Use these guidelines when you take the HSPT!

WHAT KIND OF ANSWERS DO I KEEP?

Correct answers tend to be:

- Restatements or paraphrases of what is said in the passage.

- Traditional and conservative.

- Moderate, using words such as "may," "can," and "often."

HSPT READING COMPREHENSION EXERCISE (ANSWERS ARE ON PAGE 249)

Try the following reading comprehension passage. Don't forget to label your paragraphs!

Although many people associate indoor lighting with modern electrical wiring, practical indoor lighting existed thousands of years before Thomas Edison invented the light bulb. <u>Rudimentary</u> oil lamps, a primitive ancestor of the gaslight, were used in the caves in which prehistoric humans lived.

Approximately 50,000 years ago, cave-dwelling humans fashioned a basic oil-based lamp out of animal fat that was kept inside a stone base as well as a wick made out of a clothlike material. Due to the fact that animal fat smells awful when burned, the lamp gave off a terrible odor.

Thousands of years later, during the Egyptian era (around 1300 B.C.) the structure and design of the lamp changed. Instead of using only stone, the Egyptians used a form of decorated pottery with a papyrus-based wick and vegetable oil instead of the <u>foul</u>-smelling animal fat.

In times of need people burned whatever oil was plentiful. Because vegetable oil and animal fat are both edible, in times of hunger people did not burn lamps; they used the oil for food. But oil lamps brought with them other problems. Wicks for the lamps did not always burn away and had to be changed periodically. Soon the oil lamp gave way to the candle, which became a popular source of light in Rome during the first century B.C.

1. What is this passage mostly about?

   A) how Egyptians lit their homes
   B) why the candle is better than the oil lamp
   C) the history of indoor lighting
   D) why vegetable fat replaced animal fat in oil lamps

2. It can be inferred that the author views the change from oil lamps to candles as

   A) the most important discovery of human history
   B) a mistake made by the Romans
   C) important to the discovery of electricity
   D) a step in the development of indoor lighting

3. The word <u>rudimentary</u> most likely means

   A) expensive
   B) basic
   C) colorful
   D) handy

4. The author mentions Thomas Edison in the passage in order to

   A) explain his discoveries
   B) compare him with other modern inventors
   C) introduce someone that the author will discuss later
   D) show that Edison was not the first to discover indoor lighting

5. The word <u>foul</u> probably means

   A) awful
   B) sweet
   C) fruity
   D) clean

6. People probably stopped burning animal fat in lamps because

   A) vegetable oil was more plentiful
   B) they needed the animal fat for cooking
   C) animal fat smelled bad
   D) burning animal fat was against the law

7. The author's tone can best be described as

   A) angry
   B) unconcerned
   C) instructive
   D) critical

READING VOCABULARY

When you get to the reading vocabulary section, you should have only a few minutes left. As we mentioned earlier, these questions are very much like the synonym questions from chapter 17, and can be solved using the same techniques.

1. To <u>recall</u> an event

   A) plan
   B) leave
   C) remember
   D) attend

Here's how to crack vocabulary questions
If you know the meaning of the word:

Step 1:   Cover the answer choices with your hand. If you read the answer choices first, you might get confused.

Step 2:   State what the word means to you in your own words.

Step 3:   Uncover the answer choices and see which choice most closely matches what you said.

In this case, let's cover up the word *recall*. In your own words, what does it mean? Maybe you came up with something like "remember" or "think about." Now uncover the answer choices and see which best matches your word. Chances are good that you came up with something very close to C.

If you "sort of" know what the word means:

Maybe you have a sense of what the word means but can't quite put your finger on it. Perhaps you can think of a saying that uses the word—even if you're not sure what the word means—and you should still be able to get the right answer or at least come up with a good guess. If either of these is the case, use the "side of the fence" trick. This is when you ask yourself whether the word is a positive word or a negative word. If the word is positive, you can eliminate any words that are not positive. If the word is negative, you can eliminate any words that are not negative.

Take a look at the following example.

2.   A <u>surplus</u> of food

    A) basket

    B) excess

    C) lack

    D) field

You might have a sense that the word *surplus* is positive, especially because of the word *plus*, which you can see inside it. Then you may guess that the word *surplus* means something like "a lot." If so, you can eliminate A and C, and take your best guess from the remaining choices. (The answer is B.)

What if you have no idea what the word means?

If you have no idea what the word means, take your best guess and move on to the next problem. If you've spent your time wisely, you shouldn't have much time left at this point anyway. That's a good thing! It means you spent most of your time on reading comprehension—the more difficult of the two sections.

20
Mathematics

RATIOS AND PROPORTIONS

What Is a Ratio?

A ratio is a way of stating the relationship of two numbers in a reduced form. For instance, if there are 50 boys and 25 girls in a room, we can say that the ratio of boys to girls is 50 to 25. But we can also reduce this ratio just like a fraction: $\frac{50}{25} = \frac{2}{1}$. So we can also say that the ratio of boys to girls is 2 to 1. This is sometimes written as "The ratio of boys to girls is 2:1."

Of course, if we say that the ratio of boys to girls is 2 to 1, this doesn't tell us exactly how many boys and girls there are. The actual number could be 8 boys and 4 girls, or 10 boys and 5 girls, or 200 boys and 100 girls. Each of these can be reduced to the ratio 2 to 1.

But if we know one of the actual values, we can always solve for the other one. For instance, if we know that the ratio of boys to girls is 2 to 1, and there are 200 boys, we know that there must be 100 girls. Most of you can probably do that in your heads. But how do you calculate it?

Solving Ratio and Proportion Problems

The way you solve almost all ratio and proportion questions is by setting up two fractions and cross multiplying.

$$\frac{A}{B} = \frac{C}{D}$$

Whenever you set up two equal fractions, you know that $A \times D$ is equal to $C \times B$. The only thing you have to make sure to do is keep the same thing on top and bottom of each fraction.

In this case, if we know that the ratio of boys to girls is 2 to 1 and that there are 200 boys, we can figure out the number of girls by setting up these fractions.

$$\frac{\text{boys}}{\text{girls}} \frac{2}{1} = \frac{200}{x}$$

Now we can cross multiply: We know that $2x = 1 \times 200$. This means that $x = 100$.
Take a look at the following problem.

1. John has a bowl of red and blue marbles. The ratio of red to blue marbles is 5 to 4. If there are 35 red marbles in the bowl, how many blue marbles are in the bowl?

   A) 16
   B) 20
   C) 28
   D) 39

Here's how to crack it

Let's set up our fractions, with red marbles on top and blue marbles on the bottom. It will look like this.

$$\frac{\text{red}}{\text{blue}} \frac{5}{4} = \frac{35}{x}$$

Now we can cross multiply. We know that $5x = 4 \times 35$. After we multiply, $5x = 140$. We can solve for x by dividing both sides by 5 to get $x = 28$. Therefore there are 28 blue marbles in the bowl, which is C.

AVERAGES

The formula we use to figure out the average is

$$\text{average} = \frac{\text{sum total}}{\text{\# of things}}$$

For instance, if you take 3 tests on which you score 50, 55, and 57, the sum total of your scores is

$50 + 55 + 57$, or 162. Since the number of tests was 3, the average on these tests must be $\frac{162}{3} = 54$.

Try the following problem.

2. During a certain month, David counted the number of apples he ate each week. He ate 2 apples during the first week, 4 apples during the second week, and 2 apples during the third week. The fourth week he ate no apples. On average, how many apples did David eat each week of the month?

   A) 2

   B) $2\frac{1}{2}$

   C) $3\frac{1}{3}$

   D) 7

The total number of apples David ate was $2 + 4 + 2$, or 8. This sum total, over the number of weeks, will give us the average: $\frac{8}{4} = 2$.

PLUGGING IN THE ANSWER CHOICES

Very often you may think that you need to do a lot of complicated math work to set up a problem. This is especially true on those long, wordy problems that give everyone headaches.

You know, however, that one of the answer choices given has to be the correct answer. All you've got to do is figure out which one. Therefore, the easiest way to solve many problems is by simply plugging in each answer choice until you find the one that works. Plugging in just means substituting numbers to figure out the answer quickly.

Take a look at the following problem.

3. If $x(x + 4) = 12$, which of the following could be the value of x?

   A) −1

   B) 0

   C) 1

   D) 2

You might think that you have to do some complicated algebra to solve this problem, but you really don't. Let's just try plugging in each answer choice for the value of x and see which one makes the equation work.

If we plug in –1 for x, does $-1(-1 + 4) = 12$? No. Cross off A. If we plug in 0 for x, does $0(0 + 4) = 12$? No. Cross off B. If we plug in 1 for x, does $1(1 + 4) = 12$? No. Cross off C. If we plug in 2 for x, does $2(2 + 4) = 12$? Yes, so D is the answer.

Let's try one more.

4. David is five years older than his brother Jim, and Jim is twice as old as Ann. If David is 10 years older than Ann, how old is Jim?

A) 20
B) 15
C) 10
D) 8

The question asks how old Jim is, so this is what we'll be plugging in for. Let's start with A. Could Jim be 20? We know that David is five years older than Jim, so if Jim is 20, then David is 25. We also know that Jim is twice as old as Ann, so Ann must be 10. But the last sentence says that David should be 10 years older than Ann, which he's not. Therefore A can't be the answer.

How about B? Could Jim be 15? We know that David is five years older than Jim, so if Jim is 15, then David must be 20. We also know that Jim is twice as old as Ann, so Ann must be $7\frac{1}{2}$. But the last sentence says that David should be 10 years older than Ann, which he's not. Therefore B can't be the answer.

Let's try C. Could Jim be 10? We know that David is five years older than Jim, so if Jim is 10, then David is 15. We also know that Jim is twice as old as Ann, so Ann must be 5. Does this make David 10 years older than Ann? Yes. So C is the answer.

Here's a slightly harder problem. Trying to solve it using algebra is difficult, but by plugging in the answer choices, it becomes very easy.

5. If the average of 4 and x is equal to the average of 5, 4, and x, what is the value of x?

A) 1
B) 2
C) 6
D) 8

Let's start with A, and plug 1 in for x. Does the average of 4 and 1 (which is 2.5) equal the average of 5, 4, and 1 (which is $\frac{10}{3}$)? No, so A can be eliminated. Let's try B. Does the average of 4 and 2 (which is 3) equal the average of 5, 4, and 3 (which is 4)? No. B can also be eliminated. How about C? Does the average of 4 and 6 (which is 5) equal the average of 5, 4, and 6 (which is 5)? Yes. C is the answer.

PLUGGING IN YOUR OWN NUMBERS

The problem with doing algebra is that it's just too easy to make a mistake. Whenever you see a problem with variables (x's) in the answer choices, PLUG IN. Start by picking a number for the variable in the problem (or for more than one variable, if necessary); solve the problem using that real number; then see which answer choice gives you the correct answer.

Have a look at the following problem.

6. If x is a positive integer, then 20 percent of $5x$ equals

    A) x

    B) $2x$

    C) $5x$

    D) $15x$

Let's start by picking a number for x. Let's plug in the nice round number 10. When we plug in 10 for x, we change every x in the whole problem into a 10. Now the problem reads:

6. If 10 is a positive integer, then 20 percent of 5(10) equals

    A) 10

    B) 2(10)

    C) 5(10)

    D) 15(10)

Look how easy the problem becomes! Now we can solve: 20 percent of 50 is 10. Which answer says 10? A does.

Let's try it again.

7. If $0 < x < 1$, then which of the following is true?

    A) $x > 0$

    B) $x > 1$

    C) $x > 2$

    D) $2x > 2$

This time when we pick a number for x, we have to make sure that it is between 0 and 1, because that's what the problem states. So let's try $\frac{1}{2}$. If we make every x in the problem into $\frac{1}{2}$, the answer choices now read:

    A) $\frac{1}{2} > 0$

    B) $\frac{1}{2} > 1$

    C) $\frac{1}{2} > 2$

    D) $1 > 2$

Which one of these is true? A. Plugging In is such a great technique that it makes even the hardest algebra problems easy. *Anytime you can, Plug In!*

GEOMETRY

LINES AND ANGLES

On every line, all the angles must add up to a total of 180 degrees.

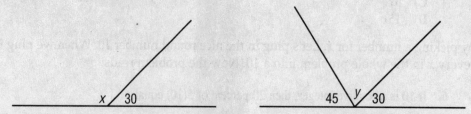

Since x and 30 must add up to 180, we know that x must measure 180 – 30, or 150 degrees. Since 45, y, and 30 must add up to 180, we know that y must measure 180 – 45 – 30, or 105 degrees.

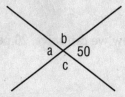

In this case, b and the angle measuring 50 are on a line together. This means that b must measure 130 (180 – 50 = 130). Also, c and the angle measuring 50 are on a line together. This means that c must also measure 130 (180 – 50 = 130). Finally, a must measure 50, because a + b (and we already know that b = 130) must measure 180 (50 + 130 = 180).

This explains why vertical angles (the angles opposite each other when two lines cross) are always equal. Angles b and c are both 130, and angle a (which is opposite the angle 50) is 50.

In a triangle, all the angles must add up to 180 degrees. In a four-sided figure, all the angles must add up to 360 degrees.

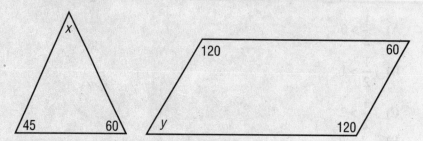

In this triangle, two of the angles are 45 and 60. They make a total of 105 degrees. The sum of the angles needs to equal 180. Therefore angle x must be 180 – 105, or 75 degrees.

In the figure on the right, three of the angles have a total of 300 degrees. Therefore y must be equal to 360 – 300, or 60 degrees.

A triangle is *isosceles* if it has two equal sides. This means that the two opposite angles are also equal.

A triangle is *equilateral* if it has three equal sides. This means that all three angles are equal. Since these angles must equally divide 180 degrees, they must each be 60.

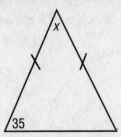

The triangle on the left is isosceles, so the two bottom angles must each be 35 degrees. This makes a total of 70 degrees for the two bottom angles. Since all of the angles must add up to 180, we know that x is equal to 180 − 70, or 110 degrees.

Area, Perimeter, and Circumference

The area of a square or rectangle is length × width.

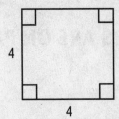 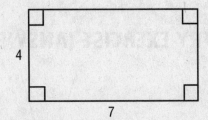

The area of this square is 4 × 4, or 16. The area of the rectangle is 4 × 7, or 28.

The area of a triangle is $\frac{1}{2}$ base × height.

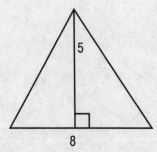 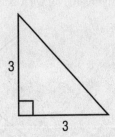

The area of the triangle on the left is $\frac{1}{2} \times 5 \times 8$, or 20.

The area of the triangle on the right is $\frac{1}{2} \times 3 \times 3$, or $4\frac{1}{2}$.

The perimeter of any object is the sum of the lengths of its sides.

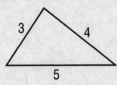 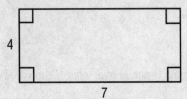

The perimeter of the triangle is 3 + 4 + 5, or 12. The perimeter of the rectangle is 4 + 7 + 4 + 7, or 22 (opposite sides are always equal to each other in a rectangle or a square).

The circumference of a circle with radius r is $2\pi r$. A circle with a radius of 5 has a circumference of 10π. The area of a circle with radius r is π^2. A circle with a radius of 5 has an area of 25π.

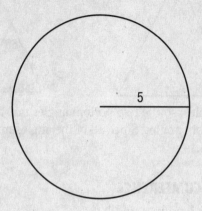

HSPT GEOMETRY EXERCISE (ANSWERS ARE ON PAGE 250)

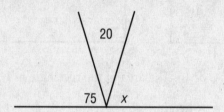

1. In the figure above, what is the value of x?

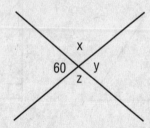

2. In the figure above, what is the value of $y + z$?

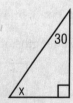

3. In the figure above, what is the value of x?

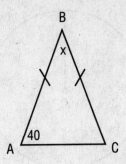

4. If triangle *ABC* is isosceles, what is the value of *x*?

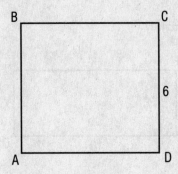

5. What is the area of square *ABCD* above?

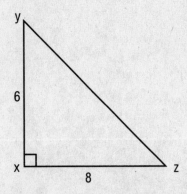

6. What is the area of triangle *XYZ* above?

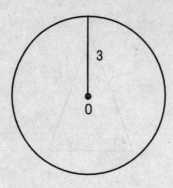

7a. What is the area of the circle above with center *O*?

7b. What is its circumference?

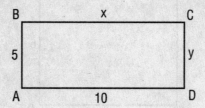

8a. If *ABCD* is a rectangle, *x* = ___ and *y* = ___

8b. What is the perimeter of rectangle *ABCD*?

21
Language

USAGE QUESTIONS

Most of the questions in the language section of the HSPT will ask you to look at four sentences and figure out which one, if any, contains an error. If the sentence contains no error, pick D, "No mistake."

ERRORS

What kind of errors should you look for? The HSPT tests only a few kinds of errors. Learn them, and you'll know what to look for and can greatly increase your score.

SUBJECT/VERB AGREEMENT

What is wrong with the following sentences?

1. The cats in the house watches the bird.

2. A wild dingo from Sydney were caught last year.

To spot subject/verb agreement errors, always find the subject and the verb in the given sentence. To find the subject, ask yourself, "Who or what is acting or being described?" To find the verb, find the action word by asking yourself, What is the subject doing?" Then make sure that the subject and the verb agree. Subjects and verbs have to agree in both number (singular or plural) and person (I, she, we, you). You may have to read around other parts of the sentence to make it clear to yourself.

What is the subject in sentence 1? It's the cats who are watching the bird. Can you say, "The cats **watches** the bird"? No. *Cats*, in this case, is plural—more than one cat—so the verb has to agree. It should be "The cats **watch** the bird."

What is the subject in sentence 2? A *wild dingo* is the thing being described. Can you say, "A wild dingo **were** caught last year"? No; in this case *dingo* is singular, and the verb has to agree with a singular subject. It should be "A wild dingo **was** caught last year."

VERB FORM AND TENSE

What is wrong with the following sentences?

3. Yesterday, John is going to the playground.

4. Patricia has took her hamster to the vet.

Verb tense

The word yesterday in sentence 3 tells us that the verb should be in the past tense. You can see that this sentence has an error because it clearly says that the action happened yesterday, but the verb "is going" is in the present tense. The sentence should read "Yesterday, John **went** to the playground." *Went* is the past tense of the infinitive verb *to go*. To spot tense problems, look for words and phrases that indicate present or past, such as:

today (present)

now (present)

yesterday (past)

last week (past)

in 1956 (past)

once (past)

a long time ago (past)

during the Second World War (past)

Verb form

Sometimes the error will be in the verb form, such as in sentence 4. Recognizing correct verb form is as simple as knowing the proper present, past, and future forms of verbs. The HSPT will ask you not to identify and name verb forms, just to choose the correct version of the sentence. Usually, it should be obvious to you when a verb form is wrong because the sentence just won't make sense. The past tense form of the verb *to take* would be either *took* or *has taken*. You could say, "Patricia **took** her hamster to the vet" or "Patricia **has taken** her hamster to the vet." But *has took* is not a possible form. Make sure that you review proper verb forms as part of your preparation for the HSPT.

ADJECTIVE/ADVERB

What is wrong with the following sentence?

5. Kim ran quick around the track.

What is the word *quick* describing? The way that Kim ran around the track. If a word describes a person or a thing, it should be an adjective like *quick*. But if a word describes an action (verb), it should be an adverb like *quickly*. Don't forget: Most adverbs end in *-ly*.

Remember this rule: Adjectives modify nouns; adverbs modify everything else.

COMPARISON WORDS

What is wrong with the following sentences?

6. He was one of the most greatest authors of his time.
7. She is intelligenter than he is.

Some questions on the HSPT will ask you to determine the right form of a comparison word. In the sentences above, *greatest* and *more intelligent* are the correct forms of the comparison words. For most adjectives that have only one syllable, we make them into comparison words by adding *-er* and *-est* to the end of the word, such as big, bigger, biggest and great, greater, greatest.

For most adjectives with more than one syllable, we make the comparison using the words *more* and *most*, as with intelligent, more intelligent, most intelligent and interesting, more interesting, most interesting.

PRONOUN AGREEMENT AND CASE

What is wrong with the following sentences?
8. The dog ran away, but they came back soon.
9. Murray is a man which loves to play the piano.
10. Olivia gave the assignment to Peter and I.

Pronouns are words such as *I, it, they, me,* and *she* that take the place of nouns. Whenever you see pronouns in a sentence, check to make sure that they agree with the nouns they stand for and that they are in the proper case. Pronoun agreement means that singular pronouns stand in for singular nouns, and plural pronouns stand in for plural nouns. In sentence 8, the subject is "the dog," which is singular, but the pronoun "they" is plural. The sentence should read "The dog ran away, but **it** came back soon."

Another important rule to remember is to use the pronoun *who* for people and *which* or *that* for things. Therefore sentence 9 should read "Murray is a man **who** loves to play the piano."

Pronoun case means that the subject of the sentence (the thing doing the acting) needs a subject pronoun, and the object of a sentence (the thing receiving the action) needs an object pronoun. In the sentence "Mary threw the ball to John," Mary is the subject and John is the object. Below is a chart that tells you how to use a pronoun whether it is the subject or the object.

Subject	Example	Object	Example
I	I left the office.	me	My boss told me to go home.
you	You should get some rest.	you	A good night's sleep would do you some good.
he/she/it	He knew the best route to take.	him/her/it	Jenny refused to tell him the best route to take.
we	We love to visit our grandparents.	us	Our grandparents love us.
they	They live in California.	them	We visited them in California.

In sentence 10, does the word *I* describe someone who is giving the book (a subject) or someone to whom the book was given (an object)? Think about it this way: We say *I* gave it to *him*, but *he* gave it to *me*. In the example sentence, the word I describes someone who received the action, not someone who was doing the action. So the pronoun used should be the object pronoun, and the sentence should read "Olivia gave the assignment to Peter and *me*." If you are confused about the correct answer, try this trick: Take away the word *Peter* and see what is left. You wouldn't say, "Olivia gave the assignment to I," but you would say, "Olivia gave the assignment to me."

> Important note: Whenever a pronoun follows a preposition (such as *to, of, in, at, around, between,* and *from*) the pronouns are *always* in the object case.

> Here are some common pronoun mix-ups. Don't forget them because recognizing them is a simple way to rack up points on the HSPT.

> it's = it is It's raining outside.
>
> its = belongs to it The dog eats its bone.
>
> you're = you are You're a great friend.
>
> your = belongs to you I love your shoes.
>
> who's = who is Who's at the door?
>
> whose = belongs to who Whose car is this?

SENTENCE FRAGMENTS

What is wrong with the following sentences?

11. Told me that I would have to see the dentist.

12. The elephant, after eating dinner, walking around the zoo.

Every sentence has to express a complete thought and have both a subject and a verb. What is the subject in sentence 11? Who or what told me to go to the dentist? There is no subject in this sentence, and therefore it is only a sentence fragment. Sentence fragments are not complete sentences and are never the correct answer on the COOP.

Sentence 12 has a subject—the elephant—but it has no true verb. It is also a fragment so we know it's an error!

PARALLELISM

What is wrong with the following sentences?

13. Lawrence left the house and going to school.

14. Erica wanted to eat lunch, visit her friend, and to play soccer.

Whenever you read a sentence that contains a list of actions or objects, check to make sure that the items in the list are all in the same form. For instance, in sentence 13 there are two actions. The first action is that Lawrence left the house. So the second action must be in the same form; however, *left* and *going* aren't in the same form. The second part of the sentence should read "Lawrence went to school" to make this a parallel sentence.

In sentence 14, there are three items that Erica wanted: *to eat* lunch, *visit* her friend, and *to play* soccer. Are these three items in the same form? No. The first and third items in the list use the infinitive verb forms—*to eat* and *to play*—but the second does not. To be parallel and correct, the sentence should read "Erica wanted to eat lunch, to visit her friend, and to play soccer."

DOUBLE NEGATIVE

What is wrong with the following sentence?

15. Paul has hardly seen no birds today.

In English, you should have only one negative word in the same phrase. This sentence has two, which is called a double negative. All of the following are double negatives, and are always considered incorrect.

can't hardly

can't never

barely none

barely never

won't never

won't hardly

hardly never

hardly none

hasn't got none

CAPITALIZATION AND PUNCTUATION

Always capitalize proper names, including names of the following:

people (Jim)

places (Alaska)

holidays (Independence Day)

months of the year (March)

geographical features (Rocky Mountains)

important words in the titles of books or movies (*All Quiet on the Western Front*)

official titles when they are followed by a proper name (Chief Smith, Aunt Maggie)

names of languages and peoples (French, Cuban)

closings of letters (Sincerely, *but* Sincerely yours,)

PUNCTUATION

Some of the questions will involve punctuation errors. Most of the punctuation problems on the HSPT involve problems with commas.

Remember to always use a comma in the following cases:

between the name of a city and a state (Seattle, Washington)

between the date and the year (April 19, 1999)

between elements in a list (John, Amelia, Robert, and I)

when addressing a person (Penelope, can you come here?)

openings and closings of letters (Sincerely yours,)

A comma should NOT be used between a subject and its verb or between a verb and its object.

INCORRECT: Alexandra, discovered a bone in her backyard.

INCORRECT: David hit, the ball so hard that it broke a window.

HSPT LANGUAGE EXERCISE (ANSWERS ARE ON PAGE 250)

Correct the errors in the following:

1. There is already many people in the auditorium.

2. Since my father's company has so much business, they are very busy.

3. My uncle often help my parents to make dinner.

4. Henry going to school, runs into his friend.

5. The giant mouse ran through the house and escaping from the cat.

6. I met her on March 1 1996.

7. Last year, Ines won the first prize and receives a beautiful trophy.

8. Roger finished his most biggest assignment.

9. Colin cleaned the bowl and gives it to his mother.

10. Rachel read the letter to my brother and I.

SPELLING QUESTIONS

A few questions on the HSPT will ask you to identify which sentence, if any, contains a misspelled word. If none of the words is misspelled, choose D, "No mistake." To approach these questions, read carefully through A, B, and C. Pay close attention to the long or unusual words. If you find an error, pick it. If you can't find an error, pick D.

COMPOSITION QUESTIONS

Other questions in the language section will ask you to find the sentence that is correctly written. For these questions, three of the choices will contain grammatical errors or awkward constructions.

Here's the procedure for attacking composition questions.

Step 1: Read all five sentences and eliminate any choice that breaks a rule of grammar.

Step 2: Reread the choices that are left, and cross off any choices that are awkward or don't make sense.

Step 3: Make your choice. The sentence you are left with may not sound great, but you should always pick the one that is the best of the bunch—the one that makes the most sense. If you can't get it down to only one sentence, that's okay. Cross off what you can, and guess from among the remaining choices.

SENTENCE COMPLETIONS

A few questions in the language section will ask you to complete a sentence by filling in a blank. Some of the questions in this section of the HSPT will test how well you can pick the correct word based on the "direction" of the sentence.

How would you fill in the blanks in the following sentences?

1. I really like you _____ you are very friendly.

2. I really like you _____ you are a very nasty person.

In sentence 1, you probably picked a word like "because." How did you know that this word was the right one to choose? Because the idea after the blank ("are very friendly") kept going in the *same direction* as the idea before the blank ("I really like you"). The sentence started out with a positive idea and continued with a positive idea.

In sentence 2, you probably picked something like "but," "although," or "even though." Why? Because the idea after the blank ("you are a very nasty person") went in the *opposite direction* from the idea before the blank ("I really like you"). The sentence started out with a positive idea and then changed to a negative idea.

Here are lists of same-direction and opposite-direction words:

Same-Direction

and

moreover

in fact

for instance

for example

so

therefore

because

since

Opposite-Direction

however

but

yet

although

though

nevertheless

nonetheless

despite

rather

instead

in contrast

Try the following example:

1. Susie's mother wanted her to be a dancer; _____ Susie felt like becoming a doctor.
   A) because,
   B) however,
   C) in fact,
   D) rather,
   E) in general,

Here's how to crack it

In this case, the idea after the blank ("becoming a doctor") goes in the opposite direction from the idea before the blank ("be a dancer"). Therefore we can eliminate A, C, and E. If you get no further, you have a great guess. The best choice is B.

STRUCTURE QUESTIONS

A few questions in this section will ask you to choose which sentences fit best with other sentences in a paragraph. You may be asked to find:

Where does this sentence belong in the paragraph?
Which sentence does not belong in the paragraph?

To answer these questions, make sure that the ideas are in a logical order from one sentence to the next.

To answer a question that asks you where a sentence belongs in the paragraph, read the sentence and ask yourself what the sentence is about. Then read the paragraph and ask yourself, "Where in the paragraph is this same idea discussed?"

To answer a question that asks you which sentence does not belong, read the paragraph and ask yourself what the paragraph is about. Then reread it, and find the sentence that does not discuss this same idea or suddenly changes the topic.

Take a look at the following examples.

5. Where should the sentence "At first it was rough" be placed in the paragraph?

[1]Paper has a long and interesting history. [2]It was first made in China around 100 B.C. from bits of plants and tree bark. [3]This made it difficult to use for writing. [4]Soon, however, people found ways to make it flat and even. [5]Over the next few hundred years, paper was introduced to the rest of Asia, where it was used to keep government documents and religious inscriptions.

A) after sentence 1
B) after sentence 2
C) after sentence 3
D) after sentence 4

If we read the paragraph, we see that it discusses the history of paper, from early years to later years. The sentence "At first it was rough" belongs in the discussion of the early years of paper. Sentence 3 discusses the properties of early paper, so the new sentence should come right after sentence 2.

6. Which of the following sentences does not belong in the paragraph?

[1]One of the most loved musical styles today is blues. [2]Blues originated in the early 1900s in America. [3]It was born from a combination of African-American work chants and gospel songs. [4]The blues got its name from the introduction of special "blue notes," which are created by "bending" normal notes up or down. [5]These blue notes give the song a certain sad sound that people recognize as part of the blues. [6]While some people like sad music, other people prefer happier songs. [7]In the 1920s, blues began to incorporate elements from jazz, dance music, and show tunes. [8]Today, blues has spread to many different countries and is one of the most popular types of music in the world.

A) sentence 3
B) sentence 4
C) sentence 5
D) sentence 6

If we read the paragraph, we see that it is about the musical style called blues. Each sentence talks about this idea except for sentence 6, which talks about whether people like happy or sad music. This makes D the best choice.

22

Answers to HSPT Exercises

CHAPTER 17

HSPT ANALOGY EXERCISE

A mansion is a very large house.

A leaf is part of a tree.

A desert is full of sand.

An engine allows an automobile to run.

Bread is made by a baker.

A brush is used by a painter.

HSPT VERBAL SKILLS EXERCISE

1. C
2. C
3. B
4. D
5. A
6. B
7. B
8. B
9. A
10. B
11. C

CHAPTER 18

HSPT MATH VOCABULARY EXERCISE

1. $-3, -2, -1, 0, 1, 2, 3, 4$ are all integers. That makes a total of 8.
2. $0, 1, 2, 3, 4$ are all positive integers. That makes a total of 5.
3. $6 + 7 + 8 = 21$
4. $2 \times 4 \times 8 = 64$

HSPT Order of Operations Exercise

1. 13
2. 9 (Do multiplication first!)
3. 5 (Do parentheses, then multiplication.)
4. 45 (Do multiplication first!)
5. 108 (Do parentheses first!)

HSPT Fractions Exercise

1. $\dfrac{1}{5}$ (Divide the top and bottom by 12.)

2. $\dfrac{3}{8} \times \dfrac{2}{3} = \dfrac{9}{24} + \dfrac{16}{24} = \dfrac{25}{24}$

3. $\dfrac{3}{4} \times \dfrac{2}{3} = \dfrac{9}{12} - \dfrac{8}{12} = \dfrac{1}{12}$

4. $\dfrac{3}{5} \cdot \dfrac{3}{2} = \dfrac{9}{10}$

5. $\dfrac{1}{3} \div \dfrac{1}{2} = \dfrac{1}{3} \div \dfrac{2}{1} = \dfrac{2}{3}$

HSPT Decimals Exercise

1. 7.68
2. 2.63
3. 4.5
4. 1.25
5. 5
6. $\dfrac{632}{100}$

HSPT Exponents, Scientific Notation, and Square Roots Exercise

1. $4 \times 4 \times 4 = 64$
2. $2 \times 2 \times 2 \times 2 = 16$
3. 340
4. 52,300
5. This becomes $2 + 4 = 6$.

HSPT Solve for x Exercise

1. $x = 5$
2. $x = 7$
3. $x = \dfrac{1}{4}$
4. $x = 3$

HSPT Percent Translation Exercise

1. $\dfrac{30}{100} \times 60 = 18$

2. $\dfrac{40}{100} \times 200 = 80$

3. $15 = \dfrac{x}{100} \times 60 = 25$

4. $x = \dfrac{25}{100} \times \dfrac{10}{100} \times 200 = 5$

HSPT Computation Exercise

1. The difference of 75 and 30 is 45; $3 \times 45 = 135$.

2. The sum of 50 and 14 is 64; $\dfrac{1}{8} \times 64 = 8$.

3. Half of 30 is 15; $16 + 15 = 31$.

4. $\dfrac{160}{100} \times 40 = 64$.

5. $6^2 = 36$ and $5^2 = 25$; the difference of 36 and 25 is 11; $11 + 2 = 13$.

HSPT Series Exercise

1. 4 (+ 4) 8 (+ 4) 12 (+ 4) 16 (+ 4) 20 (+ 4) **24**
2. 38 (− 6) 32 (− 6) 26 (− 6) 20 (− 6) **14**
3. 6 (× 2) 12 (+ 4) 16 (× 2) 32 (+ 4) 36 (× 2) 72 (+ 4) **76**
4. 10 (− 5) 5 (+ 10) 15 (− 5) 10 (+ 10) 20 (− 5) 15 (+ 10) **25**
5. 7 (× 2) 14 (− 2) 12 (× 2) 24 (− 2) 22 (× 2) 44 (− 2) **42**
6. 8 (× 2) 16 (+ 4) 20 (× 2) 40 (+ 4) **44** (× 2) 88
7. 20 (− 2) 18 (+ 7) 25 (− 2) 23 (+ 7) **30** (− 2) 28

HSPT Comparison Exercise

1. C (a) is $2 \times 4 = 8$. (b) is $18 - 5 = 13$. (c) is $18 - 5 = 13$. Therefore, (b) and (c) are equal and greater than (a).

2. B (a) is $\dfrac{40}{100} \times 60 = 24$. (b) is $\dfrac{60}{100} \times 40 = 24$. (c) is $\dfrac{50}{100} \times 90 = 45$. So (a) is equal to (b) and less than (c).

3. C (a) is 230. (b) is 2,300. (c) is 2,300. So (b) and (c) are equal and greater than (a).

4. A The area of a square is one side squared, so (a) is $6 \times 6 = 36$. The perimeter of a square is the sum of all sides, which are equal, so (b) is $6 + 6 + 6 + 6 = 24$. (c) is $\dfrac{1}{2} \times 8 \times 8$ (one-half times one side squared) $= 32$. Therefore, (a) is greater than (b) and (c).

5. B Since angle a measures 40 degrees and the triangle is isosceles, we know that angle c is also 40 degrees, and therefore angle b must be 100 degrees. So angle a is less than $b + c$.

CHAPTER 19

HSPT Reading Comprehension Exercise

1. C If you summarized the passage well, you probably wrote something like "People have had lights for a long time in different ways." A is too precise, since the Egyptians are discussed in only one paragraph. B and D are just details that are discussed in only one or two lines.

2. D In the final paragraph, the author says that "oil lamps brought with them other problems." Therefore the Romans began to use candles. B and C are not stated in the paragraph, so they can be eliminated. A is extreme because of *most important*.

3. B If we reread the line that mentions the word *rudimentary*, it states, "Rudimentary oil lamps, a primitive ancestor of the gaslight . . ." Therefore the word *rudimentary* must be something like *primitive*. This will eliminate A, C, and D.

4. D If we skim the passage looking for Edison, we can find him mentioned in the first paragraph. There it states that "practical indoor lighting existed thousands of years before Thomas Edison invented the light bulb." Now we need to find the choice that best restates this idea. Does this sentence explain his discoveries or mention other inventors? No, so we can eliminate A and B. Does the author later discuss Edison? No, so C can also be eliminated.

5. A The passage says that "the lamp gave off a terrible odor," and "foul-smelling" is used to describe the odor of the lamp.

6. **C** There is no evidence in the passage to support A, B, or D. The passage does say that the "animal fat smells awful when burned," so C is the best answer.

7. **C** Nothing in the passage sounds angry, so we can eliminate A. B probably isn't right, since someone who was unconcerned wouldn't have written the passage. If that's as far as you get, take a guess between C and D. Critical means that the author disagrees with something, but there's nothing in the passage that shows disagreement.

CHAPTER 20

HSPT GEOMETRY EXERCISE

1. Since these angles must add up to 180 degrees, $x = 85$.

2. x and z must be 120 and y must be 60, so $y + z = 180$.

3. The angles in a triangle must add up to 180. Since we already have angles 90 and 30, the remaining angle must be 60.

4. Since this triangle is isosceles, the two bottom angles measure 40 degrees each. To make a total of 180 degrees, $x = 100$.

5. The area of this square is 6×6, or 36.

6. The area of a triangle is $\frac{1}{2}$base $\times$ height, or $\frac{1}{2} \times 8 \times 6 = 24$.

7a. The area of this circle is $3^2\pi$, or 9π.

7b. The circumference of this circle is $2(3)\pi$, or 6π.

8a. Since this figure is a rectangle, $x = 10$ and $y = 5$.

8b. The perimeter is $10 + 5 + 10 + 5 = 30$.

CHAPTER 21

HSPT LANGUAGE EXERCISE

1. Since "many people" is plural, it needs the plural verb form *are*: "There **are** already many people in the auditorium."

2. Since "my father's company" is singular, the pronoun and verb should be the singular *it is* instead of the plural *they are*: "Since my father's company has so much business, **it is** very busy."

3. "My uncle" is singular, so it needs the singular verb form *helps*: "My uncle often **helps** my parents to make dinner."

4. This is a sentence fragment. A complete sentence would read "On his way to school, Henry ran into his friend."

5. The first verb, "ran," is in the past tense; to maintain parallel form, the second verb, "escaping," should also be in the past tense: "The giant mouse ran through the house and **escaped** from the cat."

6. There should be a comma after the date and before the year: "I met her on March 1, 1996."

7. The first verb, "won" is in the past tense, and the second verb, "receives," is in the present tense. You know the sentence should be in the past tense because of the clue words *Last year*. To maintain parallel form, the verbs should both be in the same tense: "Last year, Ines won the first prize and **received** a beautiful trophy."

8. "Most biggest" is not a valid comparative form. The sentence should simply read "Roger finished his **biggest** assignment."

9. The first verb, "cleaned," is in the past tense, but the second verb, "gives," is in the present tense. To maintain parallel form, these verbs should both be in the same tense: "Colin cleaned the bowl and **gave** it to his mother."

10. Since "my brother and I" are the people being read to, not doing the reading, the pronoun should be objective: "Rachel read the letter to my brother and **me**."

PART IV

HSPT Practice Tests

23

The Princeton Review
HSPT Practice Test 1

HSPT Practice Test 1

Verbal Skills
Questions 1–60, 16 minutes

1. Conquer most nearly means
   A) defeat
   B) fear
   C) dislike
   D) calm

2. Company is to president as army is to
   A) battle
   B) general
   C) soldier
   D) weapon

3. Fortify means the *opposite* of
   A) load
   B) weaken
   C) sail
   D) clean

4. Which word does *not* belong with the others?
   A) sad
   B) lonely
   C) feeling
   D) upset

5. Compel most nearly means
   A) see
   B) force
   C) ask
   D) hope

6. Gigantic is to large as hilarious is to
   A) serious
   B) interesting
   C) insulting
   D) funny

7. Opaque means the *opposite* of
   A) dirty
   B) clear
   C) normal
   D) late

8. Which word does *not* belong with the others?
   A) oregano
   B) parsley
   C) spice
   D) pepper

9. Fragile most nearly means
   A) important
   B) dangerous
   C) clean
   D) delicate

10. John has more marbles than Alice. Alice has fewer marbles than Kenny. John has more marbles than Kenny. If the first two statements are true, the third is
    A) true
    B) false
    C) uncertain

11. Generate most nearly means
    A) imagine
    B) create
    C) project
    D) lose

12. Juanita finished the race before Lucy. Mary finished the race after Lucy. Lucy finished the race before Juanita. If the first two statements are true, the third is
    A) true
    B) false
    C) uncertain

GO ON TO THE NEXT PAGE.

13. Labor most nearly means
   A) glue
   B) animal
   C) work
   D) science

14. Which word does *not* belong with the others?
   A) touch
   B) sight
   C) sense
   D) hearing

15. Abundant means the *opposite* of
   A) meager
   B) honest
   C) foolish
   D) tame

16. Morose most nearly means
   A) content
   B) new
   C) flexible
   D) sad

17. Which word does *not* belong with the others?
   A) feather
   B) bird
   C) beak
   D) wing

18. Robert read his paper before Weston. Abigail read her paper after Tyrone. Robert read his paper before Tyrone. If the first two statements are true, the third is
   A) true
   B) false
   C) uncertain

19. Portrait most nearly means
   A) history
   B) picture
   C) investigation
   D) device

20. Cage is to bird as jail is to
   A) cell
   B) crime
   C) prisoner
   D) warden

21. Strive most nearly means
   A) follow
   B) dive
   C) try hard
   D) divide

22. Which word does *not* belong with the others?
   A) water
   B) ocean
   C) lake
   D) river

23. Sentence is to paragraph as verse is to
   A) rhyme
   B) line
   C) novel
   D) poem

24. Valid most nearly means
   A) possible
   B) forgotten
   C) old-fashioned
   D) true

25. Ruthless means the *opposite* of
   A) protective
   B) merciful
   C) small
   D) healthy

26. Quest most nearly means
   A) search
   B) discovery
   C) plan
   D) talent

27. Which word does *not* belong with the others?
   A) yard
   B) length
   C) mile
   D) foot

28. Colleague most nearly means
   A) cook
   B) coworker
   C) criminal
   D) teacher

GO ON TO THE NEXT PAGE.

29. Chaos means the *opposite* of
    A) act
    B) motion
    C) order
    D) gravity

30. Which word does *not* belong with the others?
    A) sandal
    B) slipper
    C) shoe
    D) glove

31. Vacant most nearly means
    A) future
    B) open
    C) empty
    D) circular

32. Bread is to grain as jam is to
    A) bread
    B) fruit
    C) knife
    D) jar

33. Hat is to cap as shoe is to
    A) sneaker
    B) foot
    C) lace
    D) race

34. Prevalent means the *opposite* of
    A) common
    B) thick
    C) subtle
    D) rare

35. Which word does *not* belong with the others?
    A) tool
    B) hammer
    C) knife
    D) screwdriver

36. Contort most nearly means
    A) polish
    B) touch
    C) sprint
    D) twist

37. Which word does *not* belong with the others?
    A) pear
    B) apple
    C) fruit
    D) orange

38. Reprimand means the *opposite* of
    A) praise
    B) steal
    C) give
    D) forbid

39. Agnes can count faster than Louis and Jeremy. Lisa can count faster than Agnes. Jeremy can count faster than Lisa. If the first two statements are true, the third is
    A) true
    B) false
    C) uncertain

40. Tree is to trunk as flower is to
    A) bee
    B) stem
    C) leaf
    D) pollen

41. Which word does *not* belong with the others?
    A) dog
    B) mammal
    C) cat
    D) rabbit

42. Culpable most nearly means
    A) guilty
    B) careful
    C) honest
    D) skilled

43. Which word does *not* belong with the others?
    A) peanut
    B) cashew
    C) shell
    D) walnut

44. Mile is to distance as pound is to
    A) weight
    B) ounce
    C) food
    D) kilogram

GO ON TO THE NEXT PAGE.

45. Ray, Eric, and Steve have the same number of baseball cards. Carl has fewer baseball cards than Eric. Steve has fewer baseball cards than Carl. If the first two statements are true, the third is
  A) true
  B) false
  C) uncertain

46. Erratic means the *opposite* of
  A) abrupt
  B) stable
  C) jealous
  D) upset

47. Conspicuous most nearly means
  A) optional
  B) new
  C) obvious
  D) expected

48. Mayville has more inhabitants than Samtown but fewer than Lanville. Pinton has fewer inhabitants than Samtown. Lanville has more inhabitants than Pinton. If the first two statements are true, the third is
  A) true
  B) false
  C) uncertain

49. Esteem means the *opposite* of
  A) respect
  B) dislike
  C) debate
  D) certainty

50. Which word does *not* belong with the others?
  A) speak
  B) yell
  C) sound
  D) whisper

51. Indifferent means the *opposite* of
  A) concerned
  B) soft
  C) casual
  D) clever

52. Which word does *not* belong with the others?
  A) flute
  B) violin
  C) orchestra
  D) cello

53. Ollie is older than Quinn and Joseph. Sally is older than Steven and Joseph. Ollie is younger than Sally. If the first two statements are true, the third is
  A) true
  B) false
  C) uncertain

54. Cook is to kitchen as doctor is to
  A) patient
  B) hospital
  C) medicine
  D) needle

55. Which word does *not* belong with the others?
  A) theater
  B) stadium
  C) arena
  D) crowd

GO ON TO THE NEXT PAGE.

56. Howard can sing more songs than Bill but fewer than Enid. Adam can sing more songs than Becky and Enid. Adam can sing fewer songs than Howard. If the first two statements are true, the third is
  A) true
  B) false
  C) uncertain

57. Which word does *not* belong with the others?
  A) book
  B) cover
  C) page
  D) spine

58. Penelope has more cats than Uma but fewer than Michael. Michael has fewer cats than Petra. Penelope has more cats than Petra. If the first two statements are true, the third is
  A) true
  B) false
  C) uncertain

59. Tree is to forest as star is to
  A) sun
  B) sky
  C) planet
  D) constellation

60. Intentional means the *opposite* of
  A) distracted
  B) unhappy
  C) accidental
  D) hungry

GO ON TO THE NEXT PAGE.

Quantitative Skills

Questions 61–112, 30 minutes

61. What number should come next in this series: 4, 12, 20, 28, __?
   A) 32
   B) 34
   C) 36
   D) 38

62. Examine the rectangle below and find the best answer.

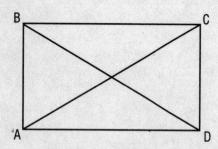

   A) *AC* is bigger than *BD* and bigger than *AB*
   B) *AC* is equal to *BD* and bigger than *AB*
   C) *BC* is bigger than *AB* and bigger than *BD*
   D) *AB* is equal to *CD* and equal to *BD*

63. What number divided by 2 is $\frac{2}{3}$ of 39?
   A) 13
   B) 26
   C) 39
   D) 52

64. Examine (a), (b), and (c) and find the best answer.

   (a) $\frac{1}{4}$ of 84

   (b) $\frac{1}{2}$ of 48

   (c) $\frac{1}{2}$ of 42

   A) a > b > c
   B) a = b = c
   C) b > a = c
   D) b > a > c

65. What number should come next in this series: 3, 6, 12, 24, __?
   A) 27
   B) 30
   C) 36
   D) 48

66. Examine (a), (b), and (c) and find the best answer.

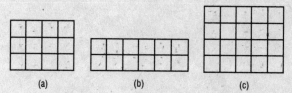

(a)   (b)   (c)

   A) (a) has as many squares as (b) and fewer than (c)
   B) (a) has more squares than (b) and fewer than (c)
   C) (b) and (c) each have more squares than (a)
   D) (a), (b), and (c) each have the same number of squares

GO ON TO THE NEXT PAGE.

67. What number should come next in this series: 4, 8, 12, 16, __?
A) 18
B) 20
C) 22
D) 24

68. Examine (a), (b), and (c) and find the best answer.

(a) 20% of 60

(b) 60% of 20

(c) 200% of 6

A) (a) is greater than (b) or (c)
B) (a), (b), and (c) are equal
C) (a) is equal to (b) and greater than (c)
D) (b) is less than (a) and (c)

69. 20% of what number is 5 times 3?
A) 15
B) 25
C) 50
D) 75

70. What number should come next in this series; 5, 8, 12, 15, 19, __?
A) 21
B) 22
C) 23
D) 24

71. Examine (a), (b), and (c) and find the best answer.

(a) 3^3

(b) 4^2

(c) 5^1

A) $a > b > c$
B) $a = b = c$
C) $b > a = c$
D) $b > a > c$

72. What number should come next in this series: 8, 5, 9, 6, 10, __?
A) 7
B) 8
C) 9
D) 14

73. $\frac{2}{3}$ of what number is $\frac{1}{2}$ of 24?
A) 36
B) 18
C) 12
D) 6

74. What number should come next in this series: 4, 7, 9, 12, 14, 17, __?
A) 18
B) 19
C) 20
D) 21

75. What number is $\frac{3}{4}$ of the product of 3, 4, and 5?
A) 45
B) 60
C) 75
D) 240

76. Examine (a), (b), and (c) and find the best answer.

(a) $\frac{5}{10}$

(b) $\frac{70}{100}$

(c) $\frac{8}{100}$

A) $a > b > c$
B) $a = b = c$
C) $b > a = c$
D) $b > a > c$

77. What number is 200% of the difference between 12 and 3?
A) 3
B) 9
C) 12
D) 18

GO ON TO THE NEXT PAGE.

78. Examine (a), (b), and (c) and find the best answer.

(a) $3(5 \times 9)$

(b) $(3 \times 5) \times 9$

(c) $3 \times 5 \times 9$

A)   (a) is greater than (b) and (c)
B)   (a) is equal to (b) and less than (c)
C)   (b) and (c) are equal and greater than (a)
D)   (a), (b), and (c) are equal

79. What number should fill the blank in this series: 12, 18, 22, 28, __, 38?
A)   28
B)   30
C)   32
D)   34

80. $\frac{5}{100}$ of the product of 5 and 4 is
A)   1
B) $\frac{1}{4}$
C)   4
D)   5

81. Below is a circle with center O. Find the best answer.

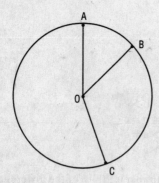

A) $OA > OB > OC$
B) $OA = OB > OC$
C) $OA = OB < OC$
D) $OA = OB = OC$

82. What number divided by 4 is 15% of 90?
A)   42
B)   48
C)   52
D)   54

83. What number should fill the blank in this series: 4, 8, 10, 20, 22, __, 46?
A)   44
B)   42
C)   36
D)   32

84. Examine (a), (b), and (c) and find the best answer

(a) the smallest prime number bigger than 4

(b) the square root of 25

(c) 75% of 8

A)   (a) is greater than (b) and (c)
B)   (a) is equal to (b) and less than (c)
C)   (b) and (c) are equal and greater than (a)
D)   (a), (b), and (c) are equal

85. The sum of 20 and what number is equal to the product of 6 and 8?
A)   22
B)   24
C)   28
D)   32

86. What number should fill the blank in this series:

$2, \frac{1}{2}, 3, \frac{1}{3}, \underline{}, \frac{1}{4}$?

A) $\frac{1}{5}$
B)   3
C)   4
D)   5

GO ON TO THE NEXT PAGE.

87. Below is a square and an equilateral triangle. Find the best answer.

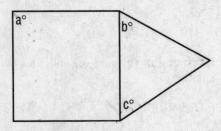

- **A)** a is greater than $b + c$
- **B)** a is less than $b + c$
- **C)** a is equal to $b + c$
- **D)** a, b, and c are all equal

88. What number should come next in this series: 30, 28, 25, 21, __?
- **A)** 18
- **B)** 17
- **C)** 16
- **D)** 15

89. What number is 140% of 40?
- **A)** 16
- **B)** 32
- **C)** 56
- **D)** 64

90. What number should come next in this series: 2, 4, 3, 5, 4, 6, 5, __?
- **A)** 6
- **B)** 7
- **C)** 8
- **D)** 9

91. Examine (a), (b), and (c) and find the best answer.

(a) the area of a square with side 3

(b) the area of a circle with radius 3

(c) the area of an equilateral triangle with side 3

- **A)** $a > b > c$
- **B)** $a = c < b$
- **C)** $c < a < b$
- **D)** $c < a = b$

92. What number is 2 more than the difference of 3^3 and 3^4?
- **A)** 3
- **B)** 5
- **C)** 29
- **D)** 56

93. Examine the figure below and find the best answer.

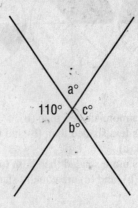

- **A)** $a + c = b + c = a + b$
- **B)** $a + c = b + c > a + b$
- **C)** $a + b > a + c > b + c$
- **D)** $a + b > a + c = b + c$

GO ON TO THE NEXT PAGE.

94. What number should come next in this series:
11, 22, 44, 88, __?
A) 122
B) 124
C) 144
D) 176

95. What number should fill the blank in this series:
15, 30, 35, 50, 55, __, 75?
A) 70
B) 65
C) 60
D) 55

96. 75% of 20% of 200 is
A) 30
B) 40
C) 45
D) 50

97. Examine (a), (b), and (c) and find the best answer.

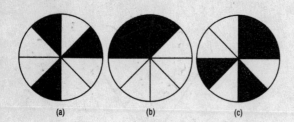

(a)   (b)   (c)

A) (a) is more shaded than (b)
B) (a) is less shaded than (b) and more shaded than (c)
C) (c) is more shaded than both (a) and (b)
D) (a), (b), and (c) are equally shaded

98. $\frac{3}{5}$ of the average of 20, 25, and 45 is

A) 14
B) 18
C) 22
D) 24

99. What number should fill the blank in this series:
20, 30, 45, 65, __, 120?
A) 70
B) 80
C) 90
D) 110

100. Examine (a), (b), and (c) and find the best answer.

(a) 6.5×10^{-3}

(b) 0.0065

(c) 650×10^{-4}

A) (a) is greater than (b) and (c)
B) (a) is equal to (b) and less than (c)
C) (b) and (c) are equal and greater than (a)
D) (a), (b), and (c) are equal

101. What number should come next in this series:
1, 1, 2, 4, 3, 9, 4, __?
A) 12
B) 14
C) 16
D) 18

102. Examine (a), (b), and (c) and find the best answer if $x = 2$.

(a) $2x^2$

(b) $(2x)^2$

(c) $2^2 \times x^2$

A) (a) is greater than (b) and (c)
B) (a) is equal to (c) and less than (b)
C) (b) and (c) are equal and greater than (a)
D) (a), (b), and (c) are equal

103. What is 40% of 20% of 600?
A) 24
B) 48
C) 60
D) 120

GO ON TO THE NEXT PAGE.

104. What number leaves a remainder of 3 when divided by 4?
A) 25
B) 31
C) 33
D) 37

105. What number should come next in this series: 15, 20, 18, 23, 21, 26, 24, __?
A) 22
B) 26
C) 28
D) 29

106. Examine (a), (b), and (c) and find the best answer.

(a) the area of a square with side 2

(b) the area of a square with side 3

(c) the area of half of a square with side 4

A) b > a > c
B) c > a > b
C) c > b > a
D) b > c > a

107. What number is 5 greater than the product of 15 and $\frac{1}{3}$?
A) 5
B) 10
C) 15
D) 20

108. What number should fill the blank in this series: 56, 51, 48, 43, 40, __, 32?
A) 37
B) 36
C) 35
D) 34

109. Examine (a), (b), and (c) and find the best answer.

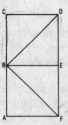

(a) the perimeter of square *BCDE*

(b) the perimeter of triangle *BDF*

(c) the perimeter of rectangle *ACDF*

A) b > a > c
B) c > a > b
C) c > b > a
D) b > c > a

110. What number is $\frac{1}{6}$ of the average of 18, 24, 25, and 29?
A) 4
B) 5
C) 6
D) 7

111. What number should come next in this series: 110, 55, 50, 25, 20, __?
A) 15
B) 10
C) 5
D) 0

112. What number is 16 more than six squared?
A) 22
B) 36
C) 48
D) 52

GO ON TO THE NEXT PAGE.

Reading
Questions 113–174, 25 minutes

Comprehension

I do not remember crossing the Missouri River, or anything about the long day's journey through Nebraska. Probably by that time I had crossed so many rivers that I was dull to them. The only thing very noticeable about Nebraska was that it was still, all day long.

I had been sleeping, curled up in a red plush seat, for a long while when we reached Black Hawk. Jake <u>roused</u> me and took me by the hand. We stumbled down from the train to a wooden siding, where men were running about with lanterns. I couldn't see any town, or even distant lights; we were surrounded by utter darkness. The engine was panting heavily after its long run. In the red glow from the fire-box, a group of people stood huddled together on the platform, encumbered by bundles and boxes.

I knew this must be the immigrant family the conductor had told us about. The woman wore a fringed shawl tied over her head, and she carried a little tin trunk in her arms, hugging it as if it were a baby. There was an old man, tall and stooped. Two half-grown boys and a girl stood holding oilcloth bundles, and a little girl clung to her mother's skirts. Presently a man with a lantern approached them and began to talk, shouting and exclaiming. I pricked up my ears, for it was positively the first time I had ever heard a foreign <u>tongue</u>.

113. When the story begins, the narrator is on a
   A) plane
   B) ship
   C) rooftop
   D) train

114. The narrator finds the rivers in Nebraska "dull" probably because
   A) the narrator has never liked rivers
   B) the narrator has seen too many rivers
   C) the rivers in Missouri were much more interesting
   D) they were all too small to be interesting

115. The word <u>roused</u>, as used in the passage, most nearly means
   A) woke
   B) saw
   C) ran
   D) told

116. The narrator finds Nebraska remarkable for its
   A) cows
   B) interesting scenery
   C) silence
   D) fields of corn

GO ON TO THE NEXT PAGE.

117. The word <u>tongue</u>, as used in the passage, most nearly means
A) song
B) mouth
C) language
D) handle

118. The people described in the second paragraph are carrying "bundles and boxes" probably because they
A) are farmers taking their goods to market
B) are coming back from a shopping trip
C) have recently arrived in this country from elsewhere
D) are paid to move other people's things

119. The narrator "stumbled down from the train" probably because the narrator
A) was still sleepy
B) was not wearing shoes
C) wore a cast on one leg
D) was very hungry

120. Which of the following is true of the family described in the final paragraph?
A) The family has four children—three boys and a girl.
B) The family has four children—two boys and two girls.
C) The family has three children—two boys and a girl.
D) The family has three children—all boys.

GO ON TO THE NEXT PAGE.

Though electricity has only recently been used to drive machines, people have known about electricity for thousands of years. The ancient Greeks discovered that they could make objects cling together by rubbing cloth against amber. This, we now know, is due to static electricity.

Benjamin Franklin was one of the earliest people to investigate this curious phenomenon. His curiosity in electricity was sparked when he began to play with an electricity tube that was given to him by his friend Peter Collinson.

Franklin is widely regarded as the first person to realize that lightning was made of electrically charged air. As a way of testing his theory, he attempted to discover whether lightning would pass through a metal object. To show this, he used a kite to raise a key into the air on a stormy night. From this experiment, Franklin realized that this electricity could be guided to the ground by a metal wire or rod, thereby protecting houses, people, and ships from being hurt.

Many other people in the late 1700s to mid-1800s worked to discover more of the laws and uses of electricity. In 1779 Allesandro Volta, an Italian inventor, created the first battery. For the first time, a controlled and regular stream of electricity could be used. For his discovery, the volt was named after him.

Perhaps the most <u>significant</u> development was made by Michael Faraday. He discovered that when you move a magnet back and forth inside a wire coil, you will generate electricity inside the wire. With this knowledge he was able to build the first electric generator and the first electric motor (which is essentially an electric generator in reverse). Even today, the generators that we use to make electricity in our hydroelectric dams are almost identical to the one he created well over a century ago.

Later, Thomas Edison and Nikola Tesla improved the generator and created transformers, which change the voltage of an electrical current to adapt it to a particular purpose. While Edison <u>advocated</u> direct current (DC), Tesla argued for alternating current (AC), which we use today in our homes.

Without the hard work and intelligence of these people, we never would have developed the use of electricity. Almost our whole modern world—computers, radios, even lights—depends on their discoveries.

121. One of Franklin's discoveries was
  A) how to protect houses from lightning
  B) the battery
  C) the electric generator
  D) a hydroelectric dam

122. This passage is mostly about
  A) what lightning really is
  B) how a battery works
  C) the early scientists who investigated electricity
  D) how much the Greeks knew about electricity

123. With which of the following would the author probably agree?
  A) The electric generator was the most important discovery of all time.
  B) Modern electric generators are not very different from Faraday's generator.
  C) The discovery of electricity was very important to the development of the modern world.
  D) Benjamin Franklin was a better writer than a scientist.

GO ON TO THE NEXT PAGE.

124. According to the passage, which of the following is true?
    A) Thomas Edison was a good friend of Benjamin Franklin's.
    B) The word *volt* is named after Michael Faraday.
    C) Benjamin Franklin was the first person to know about the existence of electricity.
    D) Faraday built the first electric generator.

125. The word significant, as used in the passage, most nearly means
    A) readable
    B) important
    C) well known
    D) accidental

126. According to the passage, Edison and Tesla disagreed about
    A) whether hydroelectric dams should be built
    B) whether to use direct or alternating current
    C) how a transformer should be designed
    D) how to create electricity

127. According to the passage, what device can change the voltage of an electric current?
    A) a generator
    B) a transformer
    C) an electric motor
    D) a battery

128. The word advocated, as used in the passage, most nearly means
    A) disagreed
    B) promoted
    C) imagined
    D) threw away

GO ON TO THE NEXT PAGE.

After Charles Lindbergh made history with his flight across the Atlantic Ocean, New York publisher George Putnam wanted to have a woman make the same flight. He found Amelia Earhart.

At first, Putnam didn't trust her to fly the plane. Earhart made the transatlantic flight as a passenger with two male <u>colleagues</u> at the controls. However, Amelia decided that she wanted to be the pilot. She began to improve her flight skills, breaking record after record in speed and number of miles flown by a woman.

Finally in 1932, she decided that she wanted to make a solo transatlantic flight. She wanted to do it not only for herself, but to show that <u>aviation</u> was not exclusive to men. When she touched down in Ireland, she became an instant hero. She was showered with awards and attention from the international press.

Amelia began flying greater and greater distances. She flew across America, and then across the Pacific Ocean. Finally, she decided that she wanted to fly around the world at its widest point: the equator. This would be a journey longer than anyone had ever made.

On May 20, 1937, she took off from Oakland, California, with her navigator, Fred Noonan, in an attempt to fly around the globe. At that time, airplanes could not go very far on a tank of fuel. Moreover, her small Lockheed Electra 10E could not carry enough fuel to fly more than about 6,000 miles. Therefore she had to make several small flights, stopping every few thousand miles in order to refuel.

After flying more than half the distance around the world, Amelia's plane was lost. Ten ships searched for more than two weeks, but no trace of the plane could be found. To this day, nobody is sure what became of Amelia Earhart.

129. According to the passage, who was the first person to make a transatlantic flight?
   A) Fred Noonan
   B) Charles Lindbergh
   C) George Putnam
   D) Amelia Earhart

130. The word <u>colleagues</u>, as used in the passage, most nearly means
   A) coworkers
   B) brothers
   C) students
   D) mechanics

131. What would be the best title for this passage?
   A) "How to Make a Transatlantic Flight"
   B) "The Amazing Story of Amelia Earhart"
   C) "Modern American Airplanes"
   D) "The Life of George Putnam"

132. The word <u>aviation</u>, as used in the passage, most nearly means
   A) birdwatching
   B) the flying of airplanes
   C) airplane repair
   D) going on vacation

GO ON TO THE NEXT PAGE.

133. You would probably find this article in
- **A)** an encyclopedia
- **B)** a science textbook
- **C)** a book on European history
- **D)** a book on the Lockheed Electra 10E

134. Which of the following can be inferred from the passage?
- **A)** The Lockheed Electra 10E was the best airplane available in 1937.
- **B)** Charles Lindbergh taught Earhart how to fly.
- **C)** Amelia was never afraid of flying.
- **D)** The equator represents the largest path around the earth.

135. With which of the following would the author probably agree?
- **A)** The U.S. government should have looked harder for Earhart's plane.
- **B)** Nobody is certain what happened to Earhart's plane.
- **C)** Earhart could have flown around the world without stopping.
- **D)** Earhart's plane must have run out of fuel and crashed into the Pacific Ocean.

136. Fred Noonan was Earhart's
- **A)** teacher
- **B)** sponsor
- **C)** navigator
- **D)** mechanic

GO ON TO THE NEXT PAGE.

Louis Pasteur, born in 1822, is perhaps best known for having discovered the role of germs in disease. Before Pasteur, nobody was certain what caused most illnesses. Nobody thought that small creatures, invisible to the naked eye, could be the cause of so many dangerous diseases.

Pasteur, however, after spending many hours looking through a microscope, discovered that germs could reproduce very rapidly and be very dangerous to humans. This led him to conclude that doctors—who, up until that time, did not always wash their hands or their instruments—were spreading disease and that they needed to <u>sterilize</u> their equipment and scrub their hands. People began for the first time to use antiseptics, and this helped to greatly reduce the number of infections in hospitals.

Pasteur also discovered that heat could kill bacteria. He discovered this one day while experimenting with chickens. He realized that a certain bacteria, called anthrax, could live in sheep but could not live in chickens. The reason for this, he discovered, was that chickens had a body temperature of 44 degrees Celsius, or more than 110 degrees Fahrenheit. Today, we heat our dairy products to kill the germs, a process that we call pasteurization.

Finally, and most important, Pasteur discovered the principle of vaccination. Pasteur realized that animals could make defenses against diseases such as anthrax. The problem was to find a way to help their bodies make these defenses without making them sick. He realized that he could kill the anthrax germs by injecting them into chickens, and then take those dead germs and inject them into sheep. Since the germ was dead, it would not make the sheep sick; but it still allowed the animal to make <u>antibodies</u> to protect it if it ever came into contact with live anthrax.

Today, people all over the world get vaccines and are free from dangerous diseases such as polio, thanks to Louis Pasteur.

137. This passage is mostly about
   A) Louis Pasteur's childhood
   B) the important discoveries of Louis Pasteur
   C) how to make a vaccine
   D) why it is important to wash your hands

138. It can be inferred from the passage that an antiseptic is
   A) something that kills germs
   B) a machine used to heat milk
   C) a kind of bacteria
   D) a kind of microscope

139. Pasteur's advice for doctors was that they should
   A) read more books
   B) wash their hands and equipment
   C) begin to use anesthetics
   D) be nicer to their patients

140. It can be inferred from the passage that sheep
   A) have a body temperature of less than 44 degrees Celsius
   B) are not as smart as chickens
   C) could pass diseases on to other kinds of animals
   D) often became ill with polio

GO ON TO THE NEXT PAGE.

141. The word <u>sterilize</u>, as used in the passage, most nearly means
   A) rebuild
   B) sell
   C) check for safety
   D) kill the germs

142. According to the facts in the passage, which of these might be pasteurized?
   A) beef
   B) cheese
   C) broccoli
   D) apples

143. With which of the following would the author probably agree?
   A) 44 degrees Celsius is hot enough to kill any germ.
   B) Receiving a vaccine is usually very painful.
   C) Polio was the most dangerous disease of all time.
   D) Pasteur made many important contributions to good health

144. The word <u>antibodies</u>, as used in the passage, most nearly means
   A) holes
   B) defenses
   C) wool
   D) shepherds

GO ON TO THE NEXT PAGE.

The cocoa plant, from which chocolate is made, is native to Central and South America. Many of the native cultures—most notably the Aztecs, but even the ancient Mayans—cultivated and ate the fruit of the cocoa plant. In certain cultures, cocoa beans were even used as a form of money. The Aztecs made cocoa beans into a hot drink with no sugar at all. In fact, the Aztecs used chili peppers to make it spicy. It was bitter and strong, and they called it xocoatl.

When Spanish explorers arrived in South America, they discovered the cocoa bean and brought it back to Europe in huge quantities. This was how chocolate was introduced to Europeans. At the beginning, the Europeans drank it in the Aztec <u>fashion</u>—hot, spicy, and unsweetened.

It wasn't until the seventeenth century that Europeans began to add sugar instead of chili peppers to their cocoa, and chocolate became a sweet drink. At first, when cocoa was rare, chocolate was considered a delicacy; as trade with the Americas became more regular, chocolate became accessible to almost everyone.

The last step in the evolution of chocolate was its <u>transformation</u> from a drink to a solid bar. In the 1820s, a process was developed to press out some of the fat (the "butter") in the cocoa bean. The resulting powder could be mixed with sugar, recombined with the cocoa butter, and formed into solid bars. By the 1850s, what we know today as chocolate was finally available.

145. This story is mostly about
    A) the evolution of chocolate
    B) the importance of cocoa beans to the Aztecs
    C) how to make xocoatl
    D) when chocolate arrived in Europe

146. The word <u>fashion</u>, as used in the passage, most nearly means
    A) clothes
    B) way
    C) house
    D) cup

147. The people who brought chocolate to Europe were the
    A) Mayans
    B) Aztec
    C) Spanish
    D) Dutch

148. It can be inferred from the passage that
    A) cocoa plants have never been grown in Europe
    B) the Aztecs did not have sugar
    C) Europeans began to add sugar to their chocolate in the fifteenth century
    D) one ingredient in solid chocolate is cocoa butter

149. The author says that when it first arrived in Europe, chocolate was a "delicacy" because it was
    A) very sweet
    B) rare
    C) difficult to make
    D) inexpensive

GO ON TO THE NEXT PAGE.

150. According to the passage, which of the following is true?
- A) Cocoa beans have been used as a form of money.
- B) The Aztecs put sugar in their chocolate drink.
- C) The first Europeans to discover the cocoa bean were the Germans.
- D) The cocoa plant was originally grown in Asia.

151. Which of the following can be inferred from the passage?
- A) Most Europeans didn't like chocolate until it was sweetened with sugar.
- B) Chocolate was the most important discovery of European explorers in the Americas.
- C) When chocolate first arrived in Europe, it was not available to everyone.
- D) The Aztecs were the first people to drink chocolate.

152. The word <u>transformation</u>, as used in the passage, most nearly means
- A) discussion
- B) melting
- C) change
- D) cooking

GO ON TO THE NEXT PAGE.

Vocabulary

153. a <u>malleable</u> substance
    A) slimy
    B) soft
    C) interesting
    D) bumpy

154. an <u>impartial</u> jury
    A) fair
    B) whole
    C) new
    D) thankful

155. a <u>meritorious</u> act
    A) quick
    B) silent
    C) unknown
    D) noble

156. to <u>abdicate</u> the throne
    A) seize
    B) give up
    C) envy
    D) control

157. a large <u>receptacle</u>
    A) picture
    B) table
    C) container
    D) tool

158. an <u>inquisitive</u> mind
    A) curious
    B) normal
    C) distracted
    D) entertained

159. a <u>cynical</u> attitude
    A) silly
    B) remarkable
    C) distrustful
    D) loyal

160. the <u>dominant</u> party
    A) youngest
    B) largest
    C) intelligent
    D) hopeful

161. a <u>tactful</u> remark
    A) probable
    B) crude
    C) steady
    D) polite

162. a <u>thorough</u> investigation
    A) complete
    B) late
    C) official
    D) thoughtless

163. an unintended <u>consequence</u>
    A) interruption
    B) result
    C) discovery
    D) section

164. a <u>mediocre</u> performance
    A) excellent
    B) public
    C) lengthy
    D) average

165. an <u>elaborate</u> project
    A) original
    B) complex
    C) expensive
    D) ordinary

166. a recently discovered <u>paradox</u>
    A) treasure
    B) puzzle
    C) witness
    D) map

GO ON TO THE NEXT PAGE.

167. the <u>pinnacle</u> of his career
  A) peak
  B) end
  C) study
  D) talent

168. to <u>guarantee</u> a victory
  A) dream
  B) avoid
  C) desire
  D) promise

169. a <u>grave</u> situation
  A) serious
  B) honorable
  C) poor
  D) customary

170. to <u>imply</u> something else
  A) add
  B) reply
  C) suggest
  D) see

171. a <u>sedate</u> individual
  A) famous
  B) calm
  C) picky
  D) dry

172. to require great <u>exertion</u>
  A) audience
  B) preparation
  C) effort
  D) money

173. a <u>mobile</u> home
  A) popular
  B) small
  C) movable
  D) country

174. an <u>equitable</u> settlement
  A) closed
  B) fair
  C) proud
  D) lost

GO ON TO THE NEXT PAGE.

Mathematics
Questions 175–238, 45 minutes

Mathematical Concepts

175. Which can be divided by 8 with no remainder?
 A) 38
 B) 56
 C) 65
 D) 81

176. Which of the following is the largest?

 A) $\dfrac{2}{3}$

 B) $\dfrac{1}{4}$

 C) $\dfrac{1}{3}$

 D) $\dfrac{2}{5}$

177. If you add two even whole numbers, the result will be
 A) odd
 B) prime
 C) even
 D) odd and positive

178. How many distinct prime factors does the number 18 have?
 A) 1
 B) 2
 C) 3
 D) 4

179. The radius of a circle with a circumference of 16π is
 A) 4π
 B) 4
 C) 8
 D) 16

180. Which of the following is the least common multiple of 3 and 9?
 A) 3
 B) 9
 C) 18
 D) 27

181. What is $3.096 + 2.85$ rounded to the nearest tenth?
 A) 5.95
 B) 5.94
 C) 5.946
 D) 5.9

182. What is the greatest integer less than -2.4?
 A) -3
 B) -2.5
 C) -2
 D) -1

183. Which of the following is equal to 3.21×10^2?
 A) 0.0321
 B) 0.321
 C) 32.1
 D) 321

GO ON TO THE NEXT PAGE.

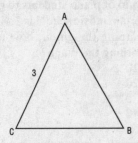

184. What is the perimeter of equilateral triangle *ABC*?
A) 3
B) 4.5
C) 6
D) 9

185. Which of the following is closest in value to –4?
A) –3.8
B) –4.01
C) –4.078
D) –4.101

186. The ratio of 3.5 to 2 is the same as the ratio of
A) 14 to 8
B) 7 to 6
C) 350 to 20
D) 6 to 4

187. Two positive integers have a sum of 18 and a product of 72. Which of the following could be one of the two numbers?
A) 6
B) 8
C) 10
D) 14

188. At Davis Junior High the ratio of students to teachers in each classroom is 18:1. What fractional part of the people in the classroom are teachers?
A) $\frac{1}{19}$
B) $\frac{1}{18}$
C) $\frac{18}{19}$
D) $\frac{18}{1}$

189. If $-5.2 < x < 3.4$, how many possible integer values for x are there?
A) 6
B) 7
C) 8
D) 9

190. What is the perimeter of a square with area 36?
A) 12
B) 18
C) 24
D) 36

191. $3^3 =$
A) 9^1
B) 9^2
C) 27^1
D) 27^2

192. Which of the following is a pair of reciprocals?
A) $(\frac{1}{3}, \frac{9}{3})$
B) $(1, \frac{1}{2})$
C) $(\frac{1}{3}, -\frac{1}{3})$
D) $(3, \frac{3}{3})$

GO ON TO THE NEXT PAGE.

193. Which of the following is equal to 0.16?

A) $\dfrac{4}{25}$

B) $\dfrac{16}{10}$

C) $\dfrac{8}{5}$

D) $\dfrac{4}{10}$

194. Which of the following is equal to $2\sqrt{2^3}$?

A) 2^4

B) $2\sqrt{3}$

C) $4\sqrt{2}$

D) 2

195. If the area of a triangle is 30 and its height is 10, what is its base?

A) 3
B) 5
C) 6
D) 9

196. The ratio of piano students to guitar students at a certain music school is 2:4. If 80 students are learning the guitar, how many students are learning the piano?

A) 10
B) 20
C) 30
D) 40

197. How many 1-inch cubes can fit into a cube with side 3?

A) 3
B) 6
C) 9
D) 27

198. In Amy's bag are three cans of cola and one can of lemon-lime soda. If Amy randomly takes one can at a time out of her bag, what is the greatest number of cans she must take out of her bag to make sure that she gets a can of cola?

A) 1
B) 2
C) 3
D) 4

GO ON TO THE NEXT PAGE.

Problem Solving

199. $\dfrac{5}{0.25} =$

A) 0.2
B) 2
C) 20
D) 200

200. Mary went shopping one day. She spent $8 on a hat, $12 on a dress, and $2 on a scarf. If she had $30 to spend, how much money did she have left at the end of the day?

A) 8
B) 20
C) 22
D) 52

201. If $5x + 3 = 21$, then $x =$

A) $\dfrac{18}{5}$
B) $\dfrac{5}{18}$
C) $\dfrac{24}{5}$
D) $\dfrac{5}{24}$

202. What percent of 96 is 8?

A) $1\dfrac{1}{2}$
B) $8\dfrac{1}{3}$
C) $8\dfrac{3}{8}$
D) 12

203. $7\dfrac{2}{5} - 3\dfrac{2}{3} =$

A) $4\dfrac{11}{15}$
B) $4\dfrac{4}{15}$
C) $3\dfrac{4}{15}$
D) $3\dfrac{11}{15}$

204. Annie buys 1 pack of gum every day of the week, except for Saturday, when she buys 2 packs of gum. If a pack of gum costs 75 cents, how much does Annie spend on gum every week?

A) $5.75
B) $6.00
C) $6.25
D) $2.25

205. On a certain map, 1 mile is represented as 2.5 inches. How long is a road that has a length of 12.5 inches on the map?

A) 0.2 miles
B) 5 miles
C) 7.5 miles
D) 10 miles

GO ON TO THE NEXT PAGE.

206. During a special sale, a dress originally priced at $80 was marked down by 30%. What was the price of the dress during the sale?
 A) $79
 B) $67
 C) $56
 D) $50

207. $\dfrac{16}{5} \times \dfrac{15}{8} =$
 A) 6
 B) 8
 C) 9
 D) 11

208. If $x^2 + 4 = 20$ then x could be
 A) 3
 B) 4
 C) 5
 D) 6

209. $5.2 \times 2.1 =$
 A) 10.92
 B) 10.22
 C) 7.3
 D) 3.1

210. Molly scored 86, 87, 93, and x on her four history tests. If her average for the four tests was 91, what is the value of x?
 A) 91
 B) 93
 C) 96
 D) 98

211. 25% of 80 is equal to 10% of what number?
 A) 200
 B) 2,000
 C) 400
 D) 4,000

212. Which of the following is equal to $\dfrac{\frac{1}{3}}{\frac{3}{7}}$?

 A) $\dfrac{1}{7}$

 B) $\dfrac{7}{3}$

 C) $\dfrac{7}{9}$

 D) $\dfrac{9}{7}$

213. At a birthday party there were 3 boxes of doughnuts. Each box contained 14 doughnuts. If the 12 party guests ate 3 doughnuts each, how many doughnuts were left over at the end of the party?
 A) 4
 B) 6
 C) 8
 D) 10

214. How many minutes will it take for an airplane traveling 400 miles per hour to travel 6,000 miles?
 A) 15
 B) 90
 C) 900
 D) 1200

215. $4 - (5 - 2) + 3 \times 5 =$
 A) 12
 B) 16
 C) 20
 D) 23

GO ON TO THE NEXT PAGE.

216. Albert is twice as old as Bert, and Bert is 7 years younger than Carl. If Albert is 12 years old, how old will Carl be in 8 years?
A) 21
B) 18
C) 13
D) 6

217. If $4^x = 16^3$ then $x =$
A) 4
B) 5
C) 6
D) 8

218. If the ratio of tomatoes to cucumbers in David's garden is 2:6, and there are 72 cucumbers in the garden, how many tomatoes are there?
A) 6
B) 12
C) 18
D) 24

219. $\dfrac{6\frac{1}{4}}{12\frac{1}{2}} =$

A) $\dfrac{3}{4}$

B) $\dfrac{2}{3}$

C) $\dfrac{1}{2}$

D) $1\dfrac{1}{3}$

220. If $5x + 5 = 3x - 9$, then $x =$
A) −7
B) −5
C) 5
D) 7

221. Tabatha decided to save some money to buy a plant. If the plant costs $20, and Tabatha saves $1.25 per day, how many days will she have to save in order to have enough money to buy the plant?
A) 16
B) 18
C) 22
D) 24

222. Alex has three times as many cards as David. If the average number of cards that Alex and David have is 20, how many cards does Alex have?
A) 30
B) 25
C) 20
D) 10

223. If a square has a perimeter of 40 feet, what is its area?
A) 16 ft²
B) 64 ft²
C) 100 ft²
D) 124 ft²

224. If $-5x - 1 < 9$, which of the following is true?
A) $x < -2$

B) $x > -2$

C) $x < -\dfrac{1}{2}$

D) $x > -\dfrac{1}{2}$

GO ON TO THE NEXT PAGE.

225. If a bus leaves city A at 9:45 A.M. and arrives in city B at 4:05 P.M., how long did it take the bus to travel from city A to city B?
   A) 5 hours 40 minutes
   B) 6 hours 20 minutes
   C) 6 hours 40 minutes
   D) 7 hours 20 minutes

226. If the average of 3, 8, and x is equal to the average of 7 and x, what is the value of x?

   A) 1
   B) 2
   C) 3
   D) 4

227. Kim put 40 blue beads and 20 red beads on a necklace. Approximately what percent of the beads on the necklace were red?
   A) 25%
   B) 30%
   C) 33%
   D) 40%

228. How many times greater is $2\frac{1}{4}$ than $\frac{3}{4}$?

   A) 3
   B) 5
   C) 6
   D) 8

229. If $\frac{1}{4x} + 3 = 6$ then $x =$

   A) 12

   B) 6

   C) $\frac{1}{12}$

   D) $\frac{1}{6}$

230. The price of a toy is reduced by $15. If the new price of the toy is 80% of the original price, what was the original price of the toy?
   A) $30
   B) $45
   C) $75
   D) $80

231. $\dfrac{.08 + .08 + .08 + .08}{4} =$
   A) 0.8
   B) 0.16
   C) 0.02
   D) 0.2

232. If Leslie can run 2 miles in 35 minutes, how long will it take her to run 16 miles at the same rate?
   A) 3 hours 50 minutes
   B) 4 hours 40 minutes
   C) 5 hours 50 minutes
   D) 6 hours 20 minutes

233. $2\sqrt{12} \times 2\sqrt{3} =$
   A) 12

   B) $2\sqrt{12}$

   C) $4\sqrt{12}$

   D) 24

234. $(55 - 62) \times 4 - 2^3 =$
   A) −36
   B) −28
   C) 28
   D) 36

GO ON TO THE NEXT PAGE.

235. Jason gets 35 cents for every weed he pulls from his neighbor's yard. He wants to earn enough money to buy a game that costs $52.50. How many weeds must he pull in order to earn enough money to buy the game?

A)   80
B)   100
C)   120
D)   150

236. At Davis High, 150 students take biology and 120 take physics. Of these students, 30 take both biology and physics. How many students take biology but do not take physics?

A)   20
B)   30
C)   120
D)   130

237. If $2(2x + 2) = 16$, then $x =$

A)   2
B)   3
C)   4
D)   5

238. Which of the following is *not* the product of two distinct prime numbers?

A)   3
B)   6
C)   10
D)   15

GO ON TO THE NEXT PAGE.

Language

Questions 239–298, 25 minutes

Usage

For questions 239–278, check the sentences for errors of usage, capitalization, or punctuation. If there is no error, choose D.

239.
- A) Supermarkets try to make its food look as appetizing as possible.
- B) The Tower of London is the city's most popular tourist attraction.
- C) Many people enjoy listening to quiet music while they work.
- D) No mistake.

240.
- A) There is three kinds of rooms at the Main Street Hotel.
- B) Today's cars are much more powerful than cars of the past.
- C) It is always important to read the directions very carefully.
- D) No mistake.

241.
- A) Lisa bought a silk dress from a store at the mall.
- B) Jason left the cake in the oven and burned it.
- C) Most seashells are made from calcium.
- D) No mistake.

242.
- A) I know some words that my friends don't know.
- B) Camels can travel for days without stopping to drink.
- C) My three favorite vegetables are carrots spinach and onions.
- D) No mistake.

243.
- A) Most of the food we eat is grown in foreign countries.
- B) If you paint indoors, make sure that your room is well ventilated.
- C) Last year I saw an exhibition of modern american art at the museum.
- D) No mistake.

244.
- A) I jumped when I heard a loud knock on the door.
- B) "That's interesting," he said "I never knew that."
- C) There is more than one correct answer to Luke's question.
- D) No mistake.

245.
- A) Jeff visited a cheese factory and learned how cheese is made.
- B) I forgot to invite my brother's best friend to the party.
- C) Though Mark is not a doctor, he knows a great deal about medicine.
- D) No mistake.

246.
- A) Many people do not know that snakes are reptiles.
- B) He gave my brother and I a book.
- C) Max went to the museum last week with his mother.
- D) No mistake.

GO ON TO THE NEXT PAGE.

247.

A) Frogs lay their eggs in the water.
B) Julie had a hard time reading her sisters handwriting.
C) Franklin D. Roosevelt was an expert politician.
D) No mistake.

248.

A) Everyone should read Shakespeare's plays.
B) The dog licked it's paw after stepping on a sharp rock.
C) Since I didn't have enough money, I couldn't buy the book.
D) No mistake.

249.

A) Martina is a naturally optimistic person.
B) David said, "I hope we find her soon."
C) My brother has a large amount of baseball cards.
D) No mistake.

250.

A) Some animals sleep all winter.
B) My father took some great pictures of me.
C) Amy saw the cat and shows it to her sister.
D) No mistake.

251.

A) Peter is always late for school.
B) My Doctor recommends that I eat more fruit.
C) Carpentry and cabinetmaking are very different skills.
D) No mistake.

252.

A) David greatly enjoyed the new opera that he saw last night.
B) Isn't it beautiful asked Laurie when she saw her sister's new pet.
C) Pavlov won a Nobel Prize for his work with dogs.
D) No mistake.

253.

A) I always wash my hands before eating.
B) Some people mistakenly believe that he knows how to fly an airplane.
C) After winning the race, the runner began to cry.
D) No mistake.

254.

A) My father gave the car to my brother and I.
B) We never thought that they would arrive on time.
C) When it rains, the roads can become very slippery and dangerous.
D) No mistake.

255.

A) Unless you finish your spinach, you won't be allowed to have cake.
B) Troy played the most brilliantly game of his life last night.
C) Tom held his breath and hoped that his brother would score a goal.
D) No mistake.

256.

A) Even after losing, David refused to give up hope.
B) Manny warmly greeted his guests at the door.
C) "Penelope," Jason replied, "I don't think you're ready."
D) No mistake.

257.

A) They weren't sure of the address, so they asked for directions.
B) Paul is a man which loves to play baseball in the park.
C) Abigail thanked her teacher at the end of the school year.
D) No mistake.

GO ON TO THE NEXT PAGE.

258.
A) Everyone thinks that they have the right answer.
B) When Ines arrived at school, she did not know which classes to take.
C) Jan suddenly became very pale.
D) No mistake.

259.
A) Jackson was born in a log cabin in North Carolina.
B) The audience was obviously very pleased with the performance.
C) The birds in the park by the lake sings beautifully.
D) No mistake.

260.
A) Any citizen over 18 years old can vote in the election.
B) It is always important to read every page of the book.
C) It is easier to learn to walk than is dancing.
D) No mistake.

261.
A) I am very worried at his failing health.
B) The easiest way to move heavy cargo is by ship.
C) I would much rather take the bus to work than drive.
D) No mistake.

262.
A) You need to try a mango to know whether you like it.
B) The jugglers attracted a large crowd.
C) Kim realized that she had forgotten to bring her lunch and her homework.
D) No mistake.

263.
A) After beginning her career as a schoolteacher, Ida Tarbell became a writer.
B) Airplanes require frequent inspections to Ensure that they are safe.
C) Early ice skates were made of wood and leather.
D) No mistake.

264.
A) This puzzle is one of the most complicated ever made.
B) The fruit I ate yesterday was much better than today.
C) Jack keeps his trophies on a shelf in the basement.
D) No mistake.

265.
A) While hiking in the forest we ate lunch near a small creek.
B) The most greatest book I have ever read was written by Ernest Hemingway.
C) The mayor of the town is very concerned about pollution.
D) No mistake.

266.
A) Matt washed the dishes while Alex dried them.
B) Tomorrow, Richard and his sister have gone to the amusement park.
C) Woodrow, my pet hamster, escaped from his cage last night.
D) No mistake.

GO ON TO THE NEXT PAGE.

267.

A) I was very impressed to see him lift that heavy weight.

B) Nathan always carries a leather wallet in his back pocket.

C) I hardly never drink coffee before noon.

D) No mistake.

268.

A) It has been so long since I've seen them that I've forgotten what they look like.

B) Owen thought that his brother was not very nicely toward his mother.

C) I need to buy some new strings for my guitar.

D) No mistake.

269.

A) When I see him again, I'll give him the message.

B) I seen that book on the shelf just behind the counter.

C) Tammy plays the violin but she prefers the flute.

D) No mistake.

270.

A) Building a treehouse can be a very educational experience.

B) While chasing a squirrel, my cat bumped into the wall.

C) My parents told me that I am mature enough to have my own bank account.

D) No mistake.

271.

A) Anis goes to Brattleborough every summer to study physics.

B) How many languages does Mr. Ferral speak?

C) I think that Ms. Walton is the more intelligent of all my teachers.

D) No mistake.

272.

A) Barry was so inspired by the book that he decided to become a cook.

B) The Constitution of the United States was signed in September 1787.

C) The human body stores excess energy in the form of fat.

D) No mistake.

273.

A) My mother said she think that I should drink more milk.

B) My friend Jim found a snake hiding in the grass behind his house.

C) Anna returned her books to the library yesterday.

D) No mistake.

274.

A) Max did not respond to David's letter.

B) "Can you bring me a chair" asked my sister.

C) The river is on the other side of the hill.

D) No mistake.

275.

A) Most people do not think of fish as dangerous, but the barracuda is an exception.

B) Each of the guests at the party was a professor.

C) Walter was excited to hear that his mother had gotten a promotion.

D) No mistake.

276.

A) David will arrive at the airport sometime next week.

B) Vivian told me that she had not never gone so far in the woods alone.

C) Everyone at the party received a note from the father of the bride.

D) No mistake.

GO ON TO THE NEXT PAGE.

277.

   A) The marbles are in a jar on the top shelf of the closet.

   B) Most of the people at the party thinks that he is 15 years old.

   C) Sarah thought her father's job was very dull.

   D) No mistake.

278.

   A) Yesterday my best friend David says he wants to be a policeman someday.

   B) Harriet Tubman made nineteen trips to the South and guided more than 300 slaves to freedom.

   C) Few people know that Massachusetts has the country's biggest crop of cranberries.

   D) No mistake.

Spelling

For questions 279–288, look for errors in spelling.

279.

   A) Martin was very happy with the toy he purchased.

   B) Early automobiles had headlights made of brass.

   C) He complemented her on her pretty dress.

   D) No mistake.

280.

   A) Some films are serious while others are merely for entertainment.

   B) Lawrence walked for eight days in the dessert without finding any water.

   C) Mr. Carter tried to improve the working conditions in his factory.

   D) No mistake.

281.

   A) Jennifer was a vigorous and effective public speaker.

   B) There was very little difference between their two positions.

   C) Most nations switched from sail to steam power at the turn of the century.

   D) No mistake.

282.

   A) Patrick thinks that he made the wrong descision the other day.

   B) It is never easy to choose between two people who are so similar.

   C) John has been a student of political science for over five years.

   D) No mistake.

283.

   A) Lonny likes to read magazines on the weekends.

   B) Everyone can benefit from improvements in transportation.

   C) The people cheered when the war was finally over.

   D) No mistake.

284.

   A) Last week Sally's father took her to the aquarium.

   B) My essay was supposed to be fifty sentenses long.

   C) Lindsay was the best musician of the group.

   D) No mistake.

285.

   A) Tina was worried that she could not pay off her debts.

   B) The sun was shinning brightly and the birds were singing.

   C) David's parents sat down and waited for the concert to begin.

   D) No mistake.

GO ON TO THE NEXT PAGE.

286.
- **A)** Modern farmers make good use of agricultural technology.
- **B)** Our history teacher sent David to the principle's office.
- **C)** There are several advantages to this method.
- **D)** No mistake.

287.
- **A)** Carol accomplished much less than she promised.
- **B)** Many disasters are caused by poor management.
- **C)** Both candidates agreed on most of the important political issues.
- **D)** No mistake.

288.
- **A)** Mr. Bowles helped to put these historical events into perspective for us.
- **B)** Amelia is an ambitious woman who wants to become a lawyer someday.
- **C)** The British goverment was unhappy with his performance.
- **D)** No mistake.

Composition

289. Choose the sentence that is correct and most clearly written.
- **A)** Yesterday five miles Alex ran around the track.
- **B)** Around the track, yesterday Alex ran five miles.
- **C)** Five miles was how far Alex ran around the track yesterday.
- **D)** Alex ran five miles around the track yesterday.

290. Choose the sentence that is correct and most clearly written.
- **A)** 21 years old was the age when Jonathan decided that he wanted to become a linguist.
- **B)** Jonathan decided, at the age of 21 years old, that a linguist was what he wanted to become.
- **C)** Jonathan decided to become a linguist when he was 21 years old.
- **D)** When he was 21 years old, Jonathan decided that a linguist was what to be.

291. Choose the sentence that is correct and most clearly written.
- **A)** To read the works of Shakespeare was what Dr. Thornton recommended to his students.
- **B)** The works of Shakespeare was what Dr. Thornton recommended to his students to read.
- **C)** Dr. Thornton suggested that his students read the works of Shakespeare.
- **D)** The works of Shakespeare, suggested by Dr. Thornton, were what his students should read.

GO ON TO THE NEXT PAGE.

292. Where should the following sentence be placed in the paragraph below?

Her career as an activist began when she was a schoolteacher.

⏺ Susan B. Anthony, born in 1820, was one of the strongest advocates for women's rights in America. ⏺ She was filled with horror when she realized that the male schoolteachers were being paid much more for performing the same job. ⏺ Shortly after that she began to fight for equality and for women's suffrage, or the right to vote. ⏺ She was never deterred by her many traditionalist opponents. ⏺ Before she died in 1906, Susan B. Anthony addressed the women's suffrage convention. ⏺ She urged them to fight on and not to surrender. ⏺ Just over ten years later, women were finally given the right to vote.

A) after sentence 1
B) after sentence 2
C) after sentence 3
D) after sentence 4

293. Where should the following sentence be placed in the paragraph below?

Nonetheless, they are powerful animals and some of the fastest birds in the air.

⏺ Hummingbirds are most commonly found in South America, but can be found in other parts of the Western Hemisphere. ⏺ They are extremely small in size, as small as 3 inches in length. ⏺ They can reach speeds of up to 60 miles per hour, and can beat their wings up to 75 times every second. ⏺ They expend so much energy that they have to constantly eat. ⏺ At night, when they cannot feed, they fall into a deep sleep similar to hibernation.

A) after sentence 1
B) after sentence 2
C) after sentence 3
D) after sentence 4

294. Choose the word or words that best fills the blank.

Many dogs have natural hunting instincts; _____ retrievers enjoy fetching and carrying things in their mouths.
A) in contrast,
B) for example,
C) because,
D) likewise,

295. Choose the word or words that best fills the blank.

I was not able to go to the concert last week _____ I could not get tickets.
A) therefore
B) nevertheless
C) moreover
D) because

296. Choose the word or words that best fills the blank.

Picking apples off the tree too early is not good for the tree; _____ the apples won't taste very good either.
A) however,
B) for example,
C) furthermore,
D) but,

GO ON TO THE NEXT PAGE.

297. Which sentence does *not* belong in the following paragraph?

⬚ My paternal grandfather worked for many years as a photographer's assistant. ⬚ In the evenings, he gave private dance lessons to actors. ⬚ Since he didn't have a lot of money, the apartment his family lived in was very small. ⬚ But he earned enough to send my father to college. ⬚ There were not many colleges in rural America in the 1950s. ⬚ It was very important to my grandfather to see that his son had a good education.

A) sentence 2
B) sentence 3
C) sentence 4
D) sentence 5

298. Which sentence does *not* belong in the following paragraph?

⬚ A few years ago, I was looking through some old photographs that my parents kept in the attic. ⬚ I uncovered pictures of my family as they stood in line at Ellis Island and looked at the Statue of Liberty. ⬚ The Statue of Liberty was a gift from the French government. ⬚ My grandparents spent a few days in a shelter that overlooked the Hudson River. ⬚ However, they did not stay in New York for long. ⬚ Thankfully their cousins in Chicago gave them jobs and so they moved to the Midwest to begin their new lives. ⬚ This is the story of how my family arrived in America.

A) sentence 2
B) sentence 3
C) sentence 4
D) sentence 5

GO ON TO THE NEXT PAGE.

24

Answers and
Explanations to
HSPT Practice Test 1

VERBAL SKILLS

1. **A**

2. **B**   The U.S. as a country is led by a president; the army as a whole is led by generals.

3. **B**   To fortify means to strengthen, so the opposite is weaken.

4. **C**   Sad, lonely, and upset are all types of feelings.

5. **B**

6. **D**   Gigantic means very large; hilarious means very funny.

7. **B**   Opaque means hard to see or understand; the opposite is clear.

8. **C**   Oregano, parsley, and pepper are all kinds of spices.

9. **D**

10. **C**   We can diagram this as follows: $J > A$, $K > A$. We know that John and Kenny each have more than Alice, but we don't know whether John has more than Kenny.

11. **B**

12. **B**   We can diagram this as follows: $J > L$, $L > M$. We know that Juanita finished before Lucy, so Lucy did not finish the race before Juanita.

13. **C**

14. **C**   Touch, sight, and hearing are all types of senses.

15. **A**   Abundant means plentiful; the opposite is meager.

16. **D**

17. **B**   Feathers, beak, and wings are all parts of a bird.

18. **C**   We can diagram this as follows: $R > W$, $T > A$. We have no idea how Robert and Weston relate to Abigail and Tyrone, so we can't know whether Robert or Tyrone read first.

19. **B**

20. **C**   A bird is kept in a cage; a prisoner is kept in a jail.

21. **C**

22. **A**   Oceans, lakes, and rivers are all bodies of water.

23. **D**   A paragraph is made up of sentences; a poem is made up of verses.

24. **D**

25. **B**   Ruthless means without mercy; the opposite is merciful

26. **A**

27. **B**   Yard, mile, and foot are all measures of length.

28. **B**

29. **C**   Chaos means disorder; the opposite is order.

30. **D**   Sandal, slipper, and shoe are all worn on the foot; a glove is worn on the hand.

31. **C**

32. **B** Bread is made from grain; jam is made from fruit.

33. **A** A hat and a cap are both worn on the head; a shoe and a sneaker are both worn on the foot.

34. **D** Prevalent means common; the opposite is rare.

35. **A** Hammer, knife, and screwdriver are all kinds of tools.

36. **D**

37. **C** Pear, apple, and orange are all kinds of fruit.

38. **A** Reprimand means to scold; the opposite is to praise.

39. **B** We can diagram this as follows: $A >$ Louise, Lisa $> A > J$. Since Lisa counts faster than Agnes, and Agnes can count faster than Jeremy, we know that Jeremy does not count faster than Lisa.

40. **B** A trunk is the base of a tree; a stem is the base of a flower.

41. **B** Dog, cat, and rabbit are all kinds of mammals.

42. **A**

43. **C** Peanuts, cashews, and walnuts all have shells.

44. **A** Mile is a measure of distance; pound is a measure of weight.

45. **B** We can diagram this as follows: $R\ E\ S > C$. Since Eric has the same number of cards as Steve, they both have more than Carl. Therefore it is false, that Steve has fewer cards than Carl.

46. **B** Erratic means unstable; the opposite is stable.

47. **C**

48. **A** We can diagram this as follows: $L > M > S,\ S > P$. Since Lanville has more inhabitants than Samtown, and Samtown has more than Pinton, we know that Lanville has more inhabitants than Pinton.

49. **B** Esteem means admiration or respect; the opposite is dislike.

50. **C** Speak, yell, and whisper all describe ways of making sounds.

51. **A** Indifferent means unconcerned; the opposite is concerned.

52. **C** Flute, violin, and cello are all instruments in an orchestra.

53. **C** We can diagram this as follows: $O > Q,\ O > J$, Sally $>$ Stephen, Sally $> J$. All we know about Ollie and Sally is that they are each older than Joseph. But we don't know whether Ollie or Sally is older.

54. **B** A cook works in a kitchen; a doctor works in a hospital.

55. **D** Theater, stadium, and arena are all places where crowds gather.

56. **B** We can diagram this as follows: $E > H >$ Bill, $A >$ Becky $> E$. Since Adam can sing more songs than Enid, and Enid can sing more songs than Howard, we know that Adam cannot sing fewer songs than Howard.

57. **A**   Cover, page, and spine are all parts of a book.

58. **B**   We can diagram this as follows: M > Penelope > U, Petra > M. Since Petra has more cats than Michael, and Michael has more than Penelope, we know that Penelope does not have more cats than Petra.

59. **D**   A group of trees is a forest; a group of stars is a constellation.

60. **C**   Intentional means done on purpose; the opposite is accidental.

QUANTITATIVE SKILLS

61. **C**   The series goes 4 (+ 8) 12 (+ 8) 20 (+ 8) 28 (+ 8) **36**.

62. **B**   In a rectangle, the diagonals are always equal, and they are the longest lines.

63. **D**   Divide 39 by 3 to get 13. That's one-third of 39, so $\frac{2}{3}$ of 39 = 26. Divide each answer choice by 2 to see which one gives you 26.

64. **C** $\frac{1}{4}$ of 84 = 21. $\frac{1}{2}$ of 48 = 24. $\frac{1}{2}$ of 42 = 21. Therefore (a) and (c) are identical and smaller than (b).

65. **D**   The series goes 3 ($\times$ 2) 6 ($\times$ 2) 12 ($\times$ 2) 24 ($\times$ 2) **48**.

66. **A**   If we count the squares, we find that (a) has 12 squares, (b) has 12 squares, and (c) has 20 squares.

67. **B**   The series goes 4 (+ 4) 8 (+ 4) 12 (+ 4) 16 (+ 4) **20**.

68. **B**   20% of 60 is the same as $\frac{20}{100} \times 60$, or 12. 60% of 20 is the same as $\frac{60}{100} \times 20$, or 12. 200% of 6 is the same as $\frac{200}{100} \times 6$, or 12.

69. **D** $5 \times 3 = 15$. Try taking 20% of each of the choices to see which gives you 15. When you get to D, you'll see that 20% of 75 = $\frac{20}{100} \times 75$.

70. **B**   The series goes 5 (+ 3) 8 (+ 4) 12 (+ 3) 15 (+ 4) 19 (+ 3) **22**.

71. **A** $3^3 = 3 \times 3 \times 3 = 27$. $4^2 = 4 \times 4 = 16$. $5^1 = 5 \times 1 = 5$.

72. **A**   The series goes 8 (− 3) 5 (+ 4) 9 (− 3) 6 (+ 4) 10 (− 3) **7**.

73. **B** $\frac{1}{2}$ of 24 = 12. Try taking $\frac{2}{3}$ of each answer choice to see which equals 12.

74. **B**   The series goes 4 (+ 3) 7 (+ 2) 9 (+ 3) 12 (+ 2) 14 (+ 3) 17 (+ 2) **19**.

75. **A**   The product of 3, 4, and 5 is 60. $\frac{3}{4} \times 60 = 45$.

76. D $\frac{5}{10} = 0.5$. $\frac{70}{100} = 0.7$. $\frac{8}{100} = 0.08$.

77. D The difference between 12 and 3 is 9 . 200% of 9 = $\frac{200}{100} \times 9 = 18$.

78. D Each of (a), (b), and (c) multiplied out equals 135.

79. C The series goes 12 (+ 6) 18 (+ 4) 22 (+ 6) 28 (+ 4) **32** (+ 6) 38.

80. A The product of 5 and 4 is 20. $\frac{5}{100} \times 20 = \frac{5}{5} = 1$.

81. D Since O is the center of the circle, OA, OB, and OC are all radii. All radii of a circle have the same length.

82. D 15% of 90 is the same as $\frac{15}{100} \times 90 = 13.5$. Try each answer choice to see which number divided by 4 is 13.5.

83. A The series goes 4 ($\times$ 2) 8 (+ 2) 10 ($\times$ 2) 20 (+ 2) 22 ($\times$ 2) **44** (+ 2) 46.

84. B The smallest prime number bigger than 4 is 5. The square root of 25 is 5. 75% of 8 is $\frac{75}{100} \times 8 = 6$.

85. C The product of 6 and 8 is 48. Add 20 to each of the choices to see which number gives you 48.

86. C Each number in the series is followed by its reciprocal.

87. B Each of the angles in a square is 90 degrees, and each of the angles in an equilateral triangle is 60. Therefore a = 90, b = 60, and c = 60.

88. C The series goes 30 (– 2) 28 (– 3) 25 (– 4) 21 (– 5) **16**.

89. C Translate 140% of 40 as $\frac{140}{100} \times 40 = 56$.

90. B The series goes 2 (+ 2) 4 (– 1) 3 (+ 2) 5 (– 1) 4 (+ 2) 6 (– 1) 5 (+ 2) **7**.

91. C The area of a square with side 3 is 3 $\times$ 3 = 9. The area of a circle with radius 3 is 9π. You may not know how to solve for the area of an equilateral triangle with side 3, but you know that its area is smaller than that of a square with side 3.

92. D $3^3 = 3 \times 3 \times 3 = 27$. $3^4 = 3 \times 3 \times 3 \times 3 = 81$. The difference between 27 and 81 is 54. Two more than this is 56.

93. B Since angle a is on the same line with the angle 110, we know that a must be 70. Angle c must also be 110, since it is across from 110; angle b must be 70, since it is across from angle a. Therefore $a + c$ and $b + c$ are each 180, and are bigger than $a + c$, which is 70.

94. **D**   The series goes 11 ($\times$ 2) 22 ($\times$ 2) 44 ($\times$ 2) 88 ($\times$ 2) **176**.

95. **A**   The series goes 15 (+ 15) 30 (+ 5) 35 (+ 15) 50 (+ 5) 55 (+ 15) **70** (+ 5) 75.

96. **A**   Don't make this one too complicated; just translate this as $\dfrac{75}{100} \times \dfrac{20}{100} \times 200$. Once you cancel out all the zeros, you get $\dfrac{75}{10} \times 2 \times 2 = 30$.

97. **C**   (a) and (b) each have three parts shaded, while (c) has four parts shaded.

98. **B**   Use the average circle to find the average of 20, 25, and 45. The sum of these numbers is 90. Divide the sum by the number of items: $90 \div 3 = 30$. $\dfrac{3}{5}$ of 30 is 18.

99. **C**   The series goes 20 (+ 10) 30 (+ 15) 45 (+ 20) 65 (+ 25) **90** (+ 30) 120.

100. **B**   To figure out 6.5×10^{-3}, move the decimal 3 places to the left, and get 0.0065. Likewise, to solve 650×10^{-4}, move the decimal 4 places to the left, and get 0.065. Since (c) has a 6 in the hundredths place, it is the largest.

101. **C**   The series goes $1(^2) = 1$, $2(^2) = 4$, $3(^2) = 9$, $4(^2) = $ **16**.

102. **C**   If $x = 2$, then (a) = 8, (b) = 16, and (c) = 16.

103. **B**   Translate this question as $\dfrac{40}{100} \times \dfrac{20}{100} \times 600$. If you cancel all the zeros, you get $4 \times 2 \times 6$, or 48.

104. **B**   Plug in each answer choice. 25 divided by 4 is 6 with a remainder of 1, so cross off A. 31 divided by 4 is 7 with a remainder of 3.

105. **D**   The series goes 15 (+ 5) 20 (– 2) 18 (+ 5) 23 (– 2) 21 (+ 5) 26 (– 2) 24 (+ 5) **29**.

106. **D**   The area of any rectangle is equal to its length $\times$ width. Since a square has equal sides, we use the same number for each. (a) is therefore 4, (b) is 9, and (c) is 4×4 = 16, but half of that is 8.

107. **B**   The product of 15 and $\dfrac{1}{3}$ is 5, and 5 more is 10.

108. **C**   The series goes 56 (– 5) 51 (– 3) 48 (– 5) 43 (– 3) 40 (– 5) **35** (– 3) 32.

109. **C**   One diagonal of a square is always longer than one side of a square. But a diagonal is always shorter than two sides of a square. (Try measuring this if you want to prove it to yourself.) Since BD and BF are longer than CD and CB, we know that (b) is larger than (a). Since BD and BF are less than the sum of $BC + CD$ and $BA + AF$ we know that (c) is larger than (b).

110. **A**   First we need to find the average of 18, 24, 25, and 29. To do this, we add them to get 96, and then divide by 4 to get 24. $\dfrac{1}{6}$ of 24 is 4.

111. **B**   The series goes 110 ($\div$ 2) 55 (– 5) 50 ($\div$ 2) 25 (– 5) 20 ($\div$ 2) **10**.

112. **D**   Six squared is $6 \times 6 = 36$. 16 more is 52.

READING

COMPREHENSION

113. **B** The first paragraph says, "I had crossed so many rivers." Therefore the narrator must be on a ship.

114. **B** The first paragraph says, "I had crossed so many rivers that I was dull to them." The best paraphrase of this idea is B.

115. **A** Just before the word *roused*, we see that the narrator "had been sleeping."

116. **C** At the end of the first paragraph, the narrator says that Nebraska is remarkable because "it was still, all day long."

117. **C** In the sentences before the word *tongue*, the narrator hears people talking, shouting, and exclaiming.

118. **C** According to the last paragraph, the people were immigrants.

119. **A** Just before mentioning that he "stumbled down from the train," the narrator "had been sleeping."

120. **C** The last paragraph says that they had "two half-grown boys and a girl."

121. **A** The third paragraph says that he discovered something to help protect "houses, people, and ships."

122. **C** A, B, and D are too narrow to be the main idea. The passage discusses Franklin, Volta, Faraday, and Edison. This makes C the best choice.

123. **C** A is extreme, and there is no evidence to support B or D in the passage. The author does say in the last sentence, however, that electricity is important to the modern world.

124. **D** According to the fifth paragraph, Faraday invented the generator.

125. **B** The fifth paragraph says that Faraday's discovery helped create the first electric motor, and that today's generators are almost identical to his.

126. **B** According to the sixth paragraph, they disagreed about whether to use direct or alternating current.

127. **B** The sixth paragraph states that the transformer can "change the voltage of an electrical current."

128. **B** In the sixth paragraph, the word *advocated* is used with the same meaning as argued for.

129. **B** The first sentence says that Lindbergh was the first one to make a transatlantic flight.

130. **A** The second paragraph says that Earhart was in a plane with two people "at the controls."

131. **B** The passage mostly talks about Amelia Earhart.

132. **B** The third paragraph says that Earhart wanted to fly "to show that aviation was not exclusive to men."

133. A   This story is mostly about a person, Amelia Earhart.

134. D   According to the fourth paragraph, the "widest point" of the world is the equator.

135. B   The final sentence of the story says that "nobody is sure what became of Amelia Earhart."

136. C   The fifth paragraph says that Fred Noonan was "her navigator."

137. B   A, C, and D are only details of the story.

138. A   The second paragraph says that Pasteur encouraged people to use antiseptics, which reduced infection caused by germs.

139. B   The second paragraph says that Pasteur wanted doctors to "wash their hands [and] their instruments."

140. A   The third paragraph says that anthrax could live in sheep but not in chickens, whose body temperature is above 44 degrees Celsius. Therefore, the body temperature of sheep must be less than 44 degrees Celsius.

141. D   In the second paragraph, the word *sterilize* is used to describe a cleaning process to eliminate germs.

142. B   The third paragraph says that pasteurization refers to the process of heating "dairy products." The only choice that is a dairy product is cheese.

143. D   The final sentence of the passage says that Pasteur helped to free people from diseases.

144. B   In the fourth paragraph, the word *antibodies* is used to refer to something that can protect the body from disease.

145. A   Choices B, C, and D are details of the story. The main idea discusses chocolate from the time it was used by the Aztecs through its use in Europe.

146. B   The word *fashion* is used to describe the flavor ("hot, spicy, and unsweetened") of the Aztec drink.

147. C   According to the second paragraph, it was the Spanish who brought chocolate to Europe.

148. D   A is extreme, so it can be eliminated. There is no evidence in the passage to support choices B or C. However, the final paragraph says that cocoa butter is part of solid chocolate.

149. B   The third paragraph says, "At first, when cocoa was rare, chocolate was considered a delicacy."

150. A   The first paragraph says that "cocoa beans were even used as a form of money."

151. C   The third paragraph says that later, "chocolate became accessible to almost everyone." Therefore, at first, it must not have been available to everyone.

152. C   The final paragraph discusses how chocolate was changed from a drink to solid form.

Vocabulary

153. B
154. A
155. D
156. B
157. C
158. A
159. C
160. B
161. D
162. A
163. B
164. D
165. B
166. B
167. A
168. D
169. A
170. C
171. B
172. C
173. C
174. B

MATHEMATICS

MATHEMATICAL CONCEPTS

175. B Try dividing each answer choice by 8. All of the choices except 56 leave a remainder.

176. A Use the Bowtie to see which fraction is largest. You can also Ballpark—only A and D are more than $\frac{1}{2}$.

177. C Try adding any two even whole numbers. 2 + 2 = 4, which is an even number.

178. B First, factor 18, which can be written as 1 × 18, 2 × 9, nad 3 × 6. Of these, only 2 and 3 are prime.

179. C The circumference of a circle is equal to 2πr. Since the circumference is equal to 16π, we know that 16π = 2πr.

180. B Plug in the answer choices one at a time. Is 3 a multiple of 3 and 9? No. Is 9 a multiple of 3 and 9? Yes.

181. D 3.096 + 2.85 = 5.946, but don't forget to round.

182. A Draw a number line and find –2.4 on it. Now move to the left (less than –2.4), and find the largest integer.

183. D 10^2 means that you move the decimal two places to the right.

184. D The perimeter of a triangle is the sum of all sides: 3 + 3 + 3 = 9.

185. B You can either plot these points on a number line or find the difference between each and –4. –4.01 is only 0.01 away from –4.

186. A One easy way to test ratios is to try either reducing or expanding each number by the same power. For instance, if we double 3.5 and 2, we get 7 and 4. Now we see that B and D won't work. If we double again, we get 14 and 8.

187. A Plug in the answers one at a time. If one of the numbers is 6, then the other must be 12, so that their sum is 18. Is their product also 72? Yes.

188. A The fractional part is always the part over the whole. Since there is one teacher, but a total of 19 people, the fractional part that is teachers is $\frac{1}{19}$.

189. D Draw a number line and count the integer numbers between –5.2 and 3.4. You have –5, –4, –3, –2, –1, 0, 1, 2 and 3.

190. C If a square has area 36, each of its sides is 6. So its perimeter is 6 + 6 + 6 + 6 = 24.

191. C $3^3 = 3 \times 3 \times 3 = 27$. $9^1 = 9$, so cross off A. $9^2 = 9 \times 9 = 81$, so cross off B. $27^1 = 27$.

192. A Since reciprocals are numbers that when multiplied together become 1, try multiplying together the numbers in each choice: $\frac{1}{3} \times \frac{9}{3} = 1$.

193. A 0.16 is the same as $\frac{16}{100}$, which can be reduced to $\frac{4}{25}$.

194. C We can change this expression to $2\sqrt{4 \times 2}$ and take the square root of 4 out from under the root sign.

195. A The formula for the area of a triangle is area = base × height. We know the area is 30 and the height is 10, so we can plug these values into the equation: 30 = base × 10.

196. D We can multiply 4 by 20 to get 80. This means that there must be 2 × 20 = 40 piano students.

197. D The volume of a cube with side 3 is 3 × 3 × 3 = 27. The volume of a cube with side 1 is 1 × 1 × 1 = 1. Therefore we can fit 27 of the smaller cubes into the larger cube.

198. **B**   To make *sure* she gets a can of cola, she will have to remove all of the lemon-lime soda first. This means if on the first try she pulls out a can of lemon-lime soda, she will be certain to pull out a can of cola on the next try.

PROBLEM SOLVING

199. **C**   This is the same as $\dfrac{5}{\frac{1}{4}}$. To divide fractions, we flip and multiply: $5 \times \dfrac{4}{1} = 20$.

200. **A**   Mary spent $8 + $12 + $2 = $22. Since she started with $30, she had $8 left at the end of the day.

201. **A**   First subtract 3 from both sides of the equation, which becomes $5x = 18$. Now divide each side by 5.

202. **B**   Translate this as $\dfrac{x}{100} \times 96 = 8$. Then solve for x.

203. **D**   First, turn these into ordinary fractions. To solve the first fraction, multiply 5 times 7 and add two to get the numerator (37) and keep the same denominator (5). To solve the second fraction, multiply 3 times 3 and add 2 to get the numerator (11) and keep the same denominator (2). Then the problem becomes $\dfrac{37}{5} - \dfrac{11}{3}$.

Now use the Bowtie to subtract them: $\dfrac{111}{15} - \dfrac{55}{15} = \dfrac{56}{15} = 3\dfrac{11}{15}$.

204. **B**   If she buys 1 pack of gum every day except Saturday, that makes 6 packs of gum. If we add the 2 she buys on Saturday, we get a total of 8 packs for the week. Now we multiply by 75 cents to find out the total cost for the week.

205. **B**   We can set up this problem as a ratio. If 1 mile = 2.5 inches, we want to know how many miles is shown by 12.5 inches: $\dfrac{1}{25} = \dfrac{x}{12.5}$. Cross multiply, and we get 5.

206. **C**   First, take 30% of $80: $\dfrac{30}{100} \times 80 = 24$. So the dress will be marked down by $24. $80 − $24 = $56.

207. **A**   It will be easier if we reduce before we multiply. If we cross-reduce, the problem becomes $2 \times 3 = 6$.

208. **B**   If we subtract 4 from each side of the equation, we get $x^2 = 16$. Now try plugging in the answer choices. Which choice squared equals 16? B does.

209. **A**   To multiply decimals, multiply the numbers without decimals: $52 \times 21 = 1092$. Now we put back the two decimal places.

210. **D**   Since her average on 4 tests was 91, her total score on those four tests must have been $4 \times 91 = 364$. The sum of the other three tests is $86 + 87 + 93 = 266$. The last test must be $364 − 266 = 98$. You can also plug in the answer choices to get the same answer.

211. A Translate this as $\frac{25}{100} \times 80 = \frac{10}{100}x$. Now solve for x.

212. C To divide fractions, flip and multiply: $\frac{1}{3} \div \frac{3}{7} = \frac{1}{3} \times \frac{7}{3} = \frac{7}{9}$.

213. B If 3 boxes contained 14 doughnuts each, that makes $3 \times 14 = 42$ total doughnuts. If 12 guests ate 3 doughnuts each, there were $12 \times 3 = 36$ doughnuts eaten. $42 - 36 = 6$.

214. C If the airplane goes 400 miles per hour, we divide 6,000 total miles by 400 to find out how many hours it will take. This makes 15 hours to complete the trip. But the answer asks for the number of minutes! Since 1 hour = 60 minutes, we need to multiply 15 by 60 to get the number of minutes..

215. B Remember order of operations! First do the parentheses $(5 - 2) = 3$. Then multiply $3 \times 5 = 15$. Now it reads $4 - 3 + 15$, which equals 16

216. A If Albert is 12, and he is twice as old as Bert, then Bert is 6. We also know that Bert is 7 years younger than Carl, so Carl is 13. In 8 years, then, Carl will be 21.

217. C Try plugging in the answer choices. Could x be 4? Does $4^4 = 16^3$? The easy way to find out is to write it out longhand: $4^4 = 4 \times 4 \times 4 \times 4$. $16^3 = 16 \times 16 \times 16$, which is the same as $4 \times 4 \times 4 \times 4 \times 4 \times 4$. Therefore A can't be right. But we've made an interesting discovery. We know that $16^3 = 4 \times 4 \times 4 \times 4 \times 4 \times 4$. Therefore we need a total of six 4s on the left side of the equation. This means the answer is C.

218. D We can set up a proportion: $\frac{2}{6} = \frac{x}{72}$. Cross multiply to find that $x = 24$.

219. C First let's convert these to normal fractions. This gives us $\dfrac{\frac{25}{4}}{\frac{25}{2}}$. To divide these fractions, we need to flip the second one and multiply: $\frac{25}{4} \div \frac{25}{2} = \frac{25}{4} \times \frac{2}{25} = \frac{1}{2}$.

220. A To solve for x, begin by getting the x's on one side of the equation. To do this, subtract $3x$ from each side, and we get $2x + 5 = -9$. Now subtract 5 from each side, which gives us $2x = -14$. Now divide each side by 2.

221. A To find out how many days she will need to save $20, we divide $\frac{\$20}{\$1.25}$, which gives us 16.

222. A The easiest way to solve this is by plugging in the answer choices. Let's try A. If Alex has 30 cards, and he has three times as many as David, then David has 10 cards. Do their cards average 20? Yes.

223. C If the perimeter of a square is 40 feet, its sides are 10 (the perimeter of a square equals four times the length of one side). To find the area, square the length (s^2) of the sides: $10^2 = 10 \times 10 = 100$.

224. B Let's try solving for x. If we add 1 to each side, we get $-5x < 10$. Now divide each side by -5. Remember that when dividing by a negative number, you have to change the direction of the inequality sign, changing the < into a > sign. So we get $x > -2$.

225. B This question should be answerable if you work carefully. From 9:45 to 10:05 is 20 minutes. From 10:05 to 4:05 is 6 hours.

226. A The easiest way to solve this is by plugging in the answer choices. Let's try A first. Could x be 1? Is the average of 3, 8, and 1 equal to the average of 7 and 1? Yes.

227. C There are a total of 60 beads on the necklace, and 20 of them are red. Therefore the percentage of red beads on the necklace is $\frac{20}{60} = 33\%$.

228. A To see how many times greater one number is than another, you divide: $\dfrac{2\frac{1}{4}}{\frac{3}{4}}$. If we change the fractions into normal fraction form, we get $\dfrac{\frac{9}{4}}{\frac{3}{4}}$. To divide, flip and multiply: $\frac{9}{4} \times \frac{4}{3} = 3$.

229. C First move the numbers to the other side of the equation by subtracting 3 from each side. This gives us $\frac{1}{4x} = 3$. To get the x on top, we can invert both sides of the equation, which gives us $4x = \frac{1}{3}$. Now divide each side by 4.

230. C Since \$15 is equal to 20% off the original price, we can translate: 15 is 20% of what number? $15 = \frac{20}{100}x$. If we solve for x, we get $x = 75$. You can also plug in the answer choices to get the same answer.

231. A Add the decimals on top to get $\frac{3.2}{4}$. To divide, let's move the decimals one place to the right, which gives us $\frac{32}{40}$. Divide this, and we get 0.8.

232. B Let's set up a proportion: $\frac{2\ miles}{35\ minutes} = \frac{16\ miles}{x\ minutes}$. Cross multiply to get 280 minutes, which is the same as 4 hours and 40 minutes.

233. D If we multiply these together, we get $4\sqrt{36}$. Since $\sqrt{36} = 6$, this becomes $4 \times 6 = 24$.

234. A Remember order of operations. We do parentheses and exponents first, to get $-7 \times 4 - 8$. Now we do multiplication to get $-28 - 8 = -36$.

235. **D**   To see how many 35-cent weeds he needs to pull, we can divide $\dfrac{\$52.50}{.35}$. To make this easier to divide, move the decimal point two places to the right:

$$\frac{5250}{35} = 150.$$

236. **C**   We know that 150 students take biology, but 30 of them take physics as well. So we need to subtract 30 from 150 to see how many take biology without taking physics.

237. **B**   Try plugging in the answer choices. Let's start with A. Could x be 2? Does $2(2(2) + 2) = 16$? No. Try B. Could x be 3? Does $2(2(3) + 2) = 16$? Yes.

238. **A** $6 = 2 \times 3$, $10 = 5 \times 2$, and $15 = 5 \times 3$. Only 3 is not the product of two distinct prime numbers. (Remember that 1 is not prime!)

LANGUAGE

USAGE

239. **A**   "Supermarkets" is plural, so the pronoun should be the plural pronoun *their*.

240. **A**   Since "three kinds" is plural, the sentence needs to begin "There are."

241. **D**

242. **C**   Items in a list should be separated by commas.

243. **C**   Adjectives that refer to nationalities should be capitalized.

244. **B**   A comma should be placed after the word *said* and before the quotation.

245. **D**

246. **B**   Since the book was given to me, "I" should be "me."

247. **B**   The word *sister's* is possessive and needs an apostrophe.

248. **B**   The word *it's* is not possessive and should be spelled *its*.

249. **C**   Since baseball cards are countable, the sentence should say "number of baseball cards."

250. **C**   The sentence begins in the past tense with the verb *saw*. It should continue in the past tense with the verb *showed*.

251. **B**   The word *doctor* is not a proper name and should not be capitalized.

252. **B**   The sentence begins with a direct quotation, which requires quotation marks.

253. **D**

254. **A**   Since the car was given to me, "I" should be "me."

255. **B**   The word *brilliant* describes the game, which is a noun. Therefore it should be the adjective *brilliant* and not the adverb *brilliantly*.

256. **D**

257. **B**   Do not use *which* when referring to people. Use *who* instead.

258. **A**   "Everyone" is singular, so it needs the singular: "he or she has the right answer."

259. **C**   "The birds" is plural, so it needs the plural verb *sing*.

260. **C**   To maintain parallel form, the sentence should read, "It is easier to learn to walk than to dance."

261. **A**   The correct idiom is *worried about*.

262. **D**

263. **B̶B**

264. **B**   This sentence has a comparison problem. It compares fruit and today. It ought to compare the "fruit I ate yesterday" and the "fruit I ate today."

265. **B**   "Most greatest" is an invalid comparative form. It should be simply "greatest."

266. **B**   Since the sentence discusses tomorrow, it should use the future tense *will go*.

267. **C**   "Hardly never" is a double negative.

268. **B**   Since the word *nice* describes the brother, it should be the adjective form *nice* and not the adverb *nicely*.

269. **B**   Since "seen" is an invalid verb form, the sentence should read either "I saw" or "I have seen."

270. **D**

271. **C**   Since Ms. Walton is being compared to all the other teachers, you should use the form "most intelligent."

272. **D**

273. **A**   "She think" is a problem of subject/verb agreement. It should read "she thinks."

274. **B**   A direct question should end with a question mark.

275. **D**

276. **B**   "Not never" is a double negative.

277. **B**   "Most of the people" is plural, and requires the plural verb form "think."

278. **A**   "Yesterday" requires the past tense "said."

SPELLING

279. **C**   The word *complimented* is misspelled.

280. **B**   The word *desert* is misspelled.

281. **D**

282. **A**   The word *decision* is misspelled.

283. **D**

284. **B**   The word *sentences* is misspelled.

285. **B**   The word *shining* is misspelled.

286. **B**   The word *principal's* is misspelled.

287. **D**

288. **C**   The word *government* is misspelled.

COMPOSITION

289. **D**   A, B, and C separate "five miles" and "around the track," which should be together.

290. **C**   A, B, and D are wordy and awkward.

291. **C**   A, B, and D are wordy and awkward.

292. **A**   The sentence we need to place introduces the idea of her working as a school-teacher.

293. **B**   The sentence we need to place introduces a contrast by saying that they are powerful animals. Therefore it should follow a sentence that implies they are not powerful.

294. **B**   Since the second phrase continues the idea of the first, we need a same-direction word such as B or C. C, however, is not logical in this context.

295. **D**   Since the second phrase continues the idea of the first, we need a same-direction word such as A or D. It is the second phrase that explains the first, so D is the best choice.

296. **C**   The second phrase continues the idea of the first, so we need a same-direction word such as B or C. Since the second phrase gives additional information and not an example, C is best.

297. **D**   The rest of the paragraph is about the narrator's grandfather.

298. **B**   While the rest of the paragraph is about the arrival of a family in America, sentence 3 is only about the Statue of Liberty.

25

The Princeton Review HSPT Practice Test 2

Verbal Skills
Questions 1–60, 16 minutes

1. Diligent most nearly means
   A) stable
   B) lost
   C) hardworking
   D) original

2. Severe means the *opposite* of
   A) buried
   B) informative
   C) historic
   D) mild

3. Candle is to wax as tire is to
   A) road
   B) car
   C) rubber
   D) tread

4. Which word does *not* belong with the others?
   A) spoon
   B) food
   C) knife
   D) fork

5. Horse is to stable as chicken is to
   A) farm
   B) coop
   C) sty
   D) rooster

6. Which word does *not* belong with the others?
   A) winter
   B) season
   C) fall
   D) summer

7. Prohibit most nearly means
   A) punish
   B) disallow
   C) locate
   D) paint

8. Which word does *not* belong with the others?
   A) shirt
   B) dress
   C) clothes
   D) shorts

9. Famished is to hungry as arid is to
   A) dry
   B) desert
   C) water
   D) heat

10. Biased means the *opposite* of
    A) original
    B) neutral
    C) merciful
    D) closed

11. Suitcase is to clothes as briefcase is to
    A) papers
    B) business
    C) leather
    D) handle

12. Hinder means the *opposite* of
    A) help
    B) gather
    C) decrease
    D) blame

13. Content most nearly means
    A) able to be heard
    B) satisfied
    C) precise
    D) courteous

14. Rachel finished the test before Alice. Barry finished the test after Richard. Rachel finished the test before Richard. If the first two statements are true, the third is
    A) true
    B) false
    C) uncertain

GO ON TO THE NEXT PAGE.

15. Container is to lid as house is to
    A) door
    B) people
    C) roof
    D) window

16. Credible most nearly means
    A) edible
    B) lazy
    C) believable
    D) drinkable

17. Sincere means the *opposite* of
    A) final
    B) dishonest
    C) common
    D) complete

18. Ines stood ahead of Marcus in line. Larry stood after Marcus in line. Larry stood before Ines in line. If the first two statements are true, the third is
    A) true
    B) false
    C) uncertain

19. Contaminate most nearly means
    A) infect
    B) produce
    C) learn
    D) suggest

20. Bink had more balloons than David. David had fewer balloons than Alex and Carol. Alex had more balloons than Bink. If the first two statements are true, the third is
    A) true
    B) false
    C) uncertain

21. Which word does *not* belong with the others?
    A) sail
    B) mast
    C) rudder
    D) ship

22. Fortunate most nearly means
    A) proud
    B) hopeful
    C) late
    D) lucky

23. Zoologist is to animal as biologist is to
    A) rock
    B) plant
    C) ocean
    D) book

24. Which word does *not* belong with the others?
    A) fruit
    B) apple
    C) peach
    D) pear

25. John is taller than Bart and Evelyn. Mark is taller than John. Mark is taller than Evelyn. If the first two statements are true, the third is
    A) true
    B) false
    C) uncertain

26. Which word does *not* belong with the others?
    A) water
    B) liquid
    C) oil
    D) vinegar

27. Frank most nearly means
    A) clean
    B) honest
    C) light
    D) annoying

28. Famine is to food as drought is to
    A) water
    B) sound
    C) bread
    D) room

29. Olivia ate more apples than Jennifer. Jennifer ate fewer apples than Nancy. Nancy ate more apples than Olivia. If the first two statements are true, the third is
    A) true
    B) false
    C) uncertain

GO ON TO THE NEXT PAGE.

30. Which word does *not* belong with the others?
   A) tree
   B) trunk
   C) branch
   D) leaf

31. Immune means the *opposite* of
   A) shared
   B) complex
   C) vulnerable
   D) learned

32. Which word does *not* belong with the others?
   A) tea
   B) coffee
   C) water
   D) cereal

33. Elude most nearly means
   A) escape
   B) show
   C) remain
   D) shout

34. Frank has seen more films than Jonathan and Nicholas. Jonathan has seen the same number of films as Manny. Manny has seen fewer films than Frank. If the first two statements are true, the third is
   A) true
   B) false
   C) uncertain

35. Which word does *not* belong with the others?
   A) sole
   B) shoe
   C) lace
   D) heel

36. Mimic most nearly means
   A) talk
   B) study
   C) imitate
   D) search

37. Counterfeit means the *opposite* of
   A) genuine
   B) amusing
   C) young
   D) loose

38. Felix walked farther than Danielle but not as far as Kate. Amanda walked farther than Kate. Amanda walked farther than Felix. If the first two statements are true, the third is
   A) true
   B) false
   C) uncertain

39. Barbaric means the *opposite* of
   A) equal
   B) popular
   C) civilized
   D) embarrassed

40. Which word does *not* belong with the others?
   A) dog
   B) fish
   C) hamster
   D) pet

41. Conventional means the *opposite* of
   A) usual
   B) boring
   C) strange
   D) rough

42. Inspect most nearly means
   A) practice
   B) jump
   C) stretch
   D) examine

43. Varied means the *opposite* of
   A) similar
   B) finished
   C) ironic
   D) simple

44. Which word does *not* belong with the others?
   A) milk
   B) goat
   C) cow
   D) horse

45. Maple is to tree as apple is to
   A) fruit
   B) leaf
   C) green
   D) seed

GO ON TO THE NEXT PAGE.

46. Diminish most nearly means
  A) announce
  B) please
  C) discover
  D) reduce

47. Mindy read fewer books than Mike, but more than Walter. Rochelle read fewer books than Mike. Mindy read more books than Rochelle. If the first two statements are true, the third is
  A) true
  B) false
  C) uncertain

48. Which word does *not* belong with the others?
  A) movie
  B) book
  C) fiction
  D) play

49. Unbiased most nearly means
  A) weak
  B) neutral
  C) helpful
  D) realistic

50. Criticize means the *opposite* of
  A) stare
  B) praise
  C) read
  D) catch

51. Which word does *not* belong with the others?
  A) mop
  B) floor
  C) broom
  D) vacuum

52. Bird is to wing as fish is to
  A) water
  B) fin
  C) salmon
  D) gill

53. Permanent most nearly means
  A) active
  B) proud
  C) unchanging
  D) difficult

54. Sergio has more badges than Terence, but fewer than Wendy. Zack has fewer badges than Terence. Wendy has fewer badges than Zack. If the first two statements are true, the third is
  A) true
  B) false
  C) uncertain

55. Serene most nearly means
  A) peaceful
  B) tired
  C) clever
  D) thoughtful

56. Enlarge means the *opposite* of
  A) greet
  B) enjoy
  C) reduce
  D) expand

57. Which word does *not* belong with the others?
  A) wind
  B) rain
  C) snow
  D) coat

58. Hour is to day as month is to
  A) year
  B) time
  C) week
  D) calendar

59. Which word does *not* belong with the others?
  A) brick
  B) stone
  C) house
  D) wood

60. Authentic most nearly means
  A) valuable
  B) genuine
  C) sharp
  D) gradual

GO ON TO THE NEXT PAGE.

Quantitative Skills
Questions 61–112, 30 minutes

61. What number should come next in this series: 2, 4, 8, 16, __?
A) 18
B) 24
C) 32
D) 36

62. Examine (a), (b), and (c) and find the best answer.

    (a)   (b)   (c)

A) (a) is more shaded than (b)
B) (a) is less shaded than (b) and more shaded than (c)
C) (b) and (c) are both more shaded than (a)
D) (a), (b), and (c) are equally shaded

63. What number should come next in this series: 6, 15, 24, 33, __?
A) 42
B) 40
C) 38
D) 36

64. 25% of what number is 3 times 5?
A) 15
B) 25
C) 50
D) 60

65. What number should come next in this series: 1, 3, 9, 27, __?
A) 24
B) 36
C) 66
D) 81

66. Examine (a), (b), and (c) and find the best answer.

(a) 40% of 80

(b) 50% of 64

(c) 150% of 16

A) (a) is greater than (b) or (c)
B) (a), (b), and (c) are equal
C) (a) is equal to (b) and larger than (c)
D) (b) is less than (a) and (c)

67. What number divided by 3 is $\frac{1}{4}$ of 24?
A) 18
B) 14
C) 12
D) 6

68. What number should come next in this series: 100, 99, 97, 94, __?
A) 90
B) 89
C) 88
D) 86

69. Examine (a), (b), and (c) and find the best answer.

(a) $\frac{1}{4}$ of 96

(b) 2×48

(c) $\frac{1}{2}$ of 192

A) $a > b > c$
B) $a = b = c$
C) $b = c > a$
D) $b > a > c$

GO ON TO THE NEXT PAGE.

70. What number should come next in this series: 5, 8, 13, 16, 21, __?
    A) 22
    B) 23
    C) 24
    D) 26

71. Examine (a), (b), and (c) and find the best answer.

    (a) 32^1

    (b) 2^5

    (c) 3^3

    A) $a > b > c$
    B) $a = b > c$
    C) $b > a = c$
    D) $b > a > c$

72. What number should come next in this series: 10, 7, 8, 5, 6, __?
    A) 2
    B) 3
    C) 5
    D) 9

73. $\frac{4}{5}$ of what number is 10% of 40?
    A) 3
    B) 4
    C) 5
    D) 8

74. What number should come next in this series: 6, 9, 13, 16, 20, __?
    A) 21
    B) 22
    C) 23
    D) 24

75. Examine (a), (b), and (c) and find the best answer.

    (a) 0.008

    (b) 0.0088

    (c) 0.08

    A) $a > b > c$
    B) $c > a > b$
    C) $c > b > a$
    D) $b > a > c$

76. What number should fill the blank in this series: 2, 6, 12, 16, 22, __?
    A) 26
    B) 28
    C) 32
    D) 34

77. What number is $\frac{1}{4}$ of the difference between 80 and 64?
    A) 4
    B) 8
    C) 12
    D) 16

78. Examine (a), (b), and (c) and find the best answer.

    (a) $3(4 + 9)$

    (b) $12 + 27$

    (c) $34 + 9$

    A) (a) is greater than (b) and (c)
    B) (a) is equal to (b) and less than (c)
    C) (b) and (c) are equal and greater than (a)
    D) (a), (b), and (c) are equal

79. What number is 18 more than $\frac{1}{5}$ of 15?
    A) 18
    B) 21
    C) 23
    D) 25

GO ON TO THE NEXT PAGE.

80. Look at the rectangles below. Find the best answer.

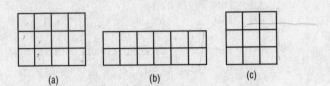

(a)   (b)   (c)

A)   the perimeter of (a) < the perimeter of (b) < the perimeter of (c)

B)   the perimeter of (c) < the perimeter of (a) < the perimeter of (b)

C)   the perimeter of (a) < the perimeter of (c) < the perimeter of (b)

D)   the perimeter of (a) = the perimeter of (c) < the perimeter of (b)

81. What number is 10% of 20% of 300?
A)   6
B)   9
C)   60
D)   90

82. What number should come next in this series: 8, 9, 16, 17, 24, 25, ___?
A)   31
B)   32
C)   33
D)   34

83. Examine (a), (b), and (c) and find the best answer.

(a) 3.02×10^3

(b) 32×10^2

(c) 302×10^1

A)   (a) is greater than (b) and (c)
B)   (b) is larger than (a), which is larger than (c)
C)   (b) and (c) are equal and greater than (a)
D)   (a), (b), and (c) are equal

84. What number leaves a remainder of 2 when divided by 7?
A)   24
B)   51
C)   60
D)   64

85. The figure below is a circle with center O. Find the best answer.

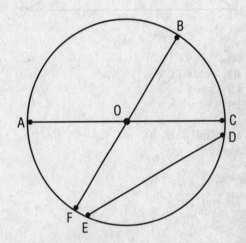

A) AC is equal to FB and larger than ED
B) AC is larger than FB and ED
C) AC is equal to FB and smaller than ED
D) AC, FB, and ED are equal

86. What number should fill the blank in this series: 1, 7, 3, 21, ___, 35?
A)   4
B)   5
C)   7
D)   28

GO ON TO THE NEXT PAGE.

87. Look at the rectangle below. Find the best answer.

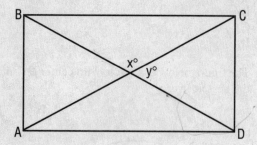

A) $x < y < 90$
B) $x > 90 > y$
C) $x + y = 90$
D) $90 > x > y$

88. Examine (a), (b), and (c) and find the best answer.

(a) $\dfrac{7}{100} + \dfrac{6}{10} + 3$

(b) $\dfrac{3}{100} + \dfrac{7}{10} + 6$

(c) $\dfrac{6}{100} + \dfrac{3}{10} + 7$

A) (a) is greater than (b) and (c)
B) (a) is greater than (b) and less than (c)
C) (c) is greater than (b), which is greater than (a)
D) (a), (b), and (c) are equal

89. What number should come next in this series: 2, 4, 6, 12, 14, 28, __?
A) 30
B) 32
C) 48
D) 56

90. What number is 9 times more than 20% of 60?
A) 21
B) 63
C) 108
D) 180

91. What number should fill the blank in this series: 9, 7, 5, 9, 7, __, 9?
A) 5
B) 7
C) 9
D) 11

92. What is 17 more than twice the difference between 15 and 17?
A) 19
B) 20
C) 21
D) 22

93. What number should come next in this series: 9, 20, 31, 42, __?
A) 52
B) 53
C) 61
D) 84

94. Look at the square below. Find the best answer.

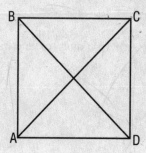

A) $AC = BC > AD$
B) $AC > AB > BD$
C) $AC > AB = BC$
D) $AC = BD = BC$

GO ON TO THE NEXT PAGE.

95. What number should come next in this series: 7, 14, 13, 26, 25, __?
- **A)** 32
- **B)** 37
- **C)** 42
- **D)** 50

96. The sum of 8 and what number is equal to $\frac{1}{11}$ of 121?
- **A)** 2
- **B)** 3
- **C)** 5
- **D)** 7

97. Examine (a), (b), and (c) and find the best answer.

(a) the perimeter of a square with side 4

(b) the area of a square with side 4

(c) the area of half of a square with side 8

- **A)** $b > a > c$
- **B)** $c > a > b$
- **C)** $c > b = a$
- **D)** $b = c > a$

98. What number should fill the blank in this series: 2, 4, 6, 4, 6, 8, __, 8, 10?
- **A)** 2
- **B)** 4
- **C)** 6
- **D)** 10

99. Examine the figure below and find the best answer.

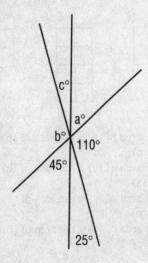

- **A)** $b > a > c$
- **B)** $c > a > b$
- **C)** $c > b > a$
- **D)** $b > c > a$

100. What is the difference between 23 and the average of 42, 45, and 39?
- **A)** 17
- **B)** 19
- **C)** 21
- **D)** 23

101. What number is ¼ of the product of 8 and 18?
- **A)** 6
- **B)** 12
- **C)** 18
- **D)** 36

GO ON TO THE NEXT PAGE.

102. Examine (a), (b), and (c) and find the best answer.

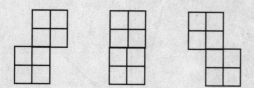

A) the area of (a) > the area of (b) = the area of (c)
B) the area of (b) > the area of (c) = the area of (a)
C) the area of (c) < the area of (a) = the area of (b)
D) the area of (a) = the area of (b) = the area of (c)

103. What number should come next in this series: 88, 85, 83, 80, 78, __?
A) 77
B) 76
C) 75
D) 74

104. Examine (a), (b), and (c) and find the best answer.

(a) −(8 − 10)

(b) 8 − 10

(c) −8 − 10

A) (a) is bigger than (b), which is bigger than (c)
B) (b) is bigger than (c), which is bigger than (a)
C) (a) and (b) are equal and bigger than (c)
D) (a) and (c) are equal and bigger than (b)

105. What number should fill the blank in this series: 49, 7, 81, __, 121, 11?
A) 8
B) 9
C) 10
D) 79

106. What number is 50% greater than the product of 6 and 3?
A) 9
B) 14
C) 18
D) 27

107. What is the difference between 10% of 50 and 20% of 100?
A) 5
B) 10
C) 15
D) 20

108. What number should fill the blank in this series: 6, 8, 7, 9, __, 10, 9, 11?
A) 7
B) 8
C) 9
D) 11

109. What is 4 less than $\frac{5}{3}$ of 9?
A) 5
B) 9
C) 11
D) 13

110. What number is 18 more than half the sum of 4, 9, and 11?
A) 12
B) 20
C) 30
D) 34

111. What number is 2 more than the average of 10, 15, and 8?
A) 9
B) 11
C) 13
D) 15

112. What number should come next in this series: 41, 11, 52, 22, 63, __?
A) 27
B) 33
C) 37
D) 44

GO ON TO THE NEXT PAGE.

Reading

Questions 113–174, 25 minutes

Comprehension

This was our last watch fire of the year, and there were reasons why I should remember it better than any of the others. Next week the other boys were to file back to their old places in Sandtown High School, but I was to go up to the divide to teach my first country school in the Norwegian district. I was already homesick at the thought of <u>quitting</u> the boys with whom I had always played, of leaving the river and going up into a windy plain that was all windmills and cornfields and big pastures, where there was nothing willful or unmanageable in the landscape, no new island, and no chance of unfamiliar birds—such as often followed the watercourses.

Other boys came and went and used the river for fishing or skating, but we six were sworn to the spirit of the stream, and we were friends mainly because of the river. There were the two Hassler boys, Fritz and Otto, sons of the little German tailor. They were the youngest of us—ragged boys of ten and twelve, with sunburned hair, weather-strained faces, and pale blue eyes. Otto, the elder, was the best mathematician in school and clever at his books, but he always dropped out in the spring term as if the river could not get on without him. He and Fritz caught the fat, horned catfish and sold them about the town, and they lived so much in the water that they were as brown and sandy as the river itself.

There was Percy Pound, a fat, freckled boy with chubby cheeks, who took half a dozen boys' story-papers and was always being kept in for reading detective stories behind his desk. There was Tip Smith, destined by his freckles and red hair to be the buffoon in all our games, though he walked like a timid little old man and had a funny, cracked laugh. Tip worked hard in his father's grocery store every afternoon, and swept it out before school in the morning.

113. The word <u>quitting</u>, as used in the passage, most nearly means
    A) leaving
    B) cheating
    C) playing with
    D) feeding

114. According to the story, the narrator belonged to a group that gathered
    A) in the narrator's backyard
    B) in the gym after school
    C) near the river
    D) at Percy Pound's house

115. It can be inferred from the passage that the narrator is
    A) younger than 10 years old
    B) between 10 and 20 years old
    C) between 20 and 30 years old
    D) more than 30 years old

116. This story mostly describes
    A) the narrator's friends
    B) the narrator's teachers
    C) Otto Hassler
    D) the parents of the students at Sandtown High

117. Why will the narrator remember this watch fire better than others?
    A) It is the narrator's birthday.
    B) The narrator is going away soon.
    C) The narrator has just been born.
    D) The narrator has recently gotten a new job.

GO ON TO THE NEXT PAGE.

118. It can be inferred from the passage that the narrator has recently become
    A) a parent
    B) a police officer
    C) a teacher
    D) a journalist

119. According to the passage, who caught and sold catfish?
    A) Otto and Tip
    B) Otto and Fritz
    C) Fritz and the narrator
    D) Fritz and Percy

120. Tip's father was
    A) a tailor
    B) a grocer
    C) a teacher
    D) a fish merchant

GO ON TO THE NEXT PAGE.

The electric eel is one of the most curious animals on the planet. It is found in the marshes of the Amazon Basin, and can grow up to almost eight feet in length—as long as some crocodiles. As the name implies, the electric eel has the ability to <u>generate</u> a strong electric field.

The electric eel uses this special ability in several ways. Mild electrical impulses can help the eel to sense different objects around it and to navigate the waters in which it lives. The eel can send out mild electrical signals, in much the same way as a bat uses sound waves, in order to find its way around.

When it comes time to feed, the eel relies on its electrical system for hunting. Because small animals have a different electrical "signature" than do plants or rocks, the electric eel effectively has a kind of radar that allows it to find fish. When the eel finds its prey, it delivers a strong electric <u>current</u> that can instantly kill smaller animals such as fish. The force of the charge is often strong enough to kill or stun even larger animals. A human could survive one or two shocks, but would probably not survive several. Eels, however, do not hunt humans, and will only shock humans in self-defense.

How does the eel avoid hurting itself? The eel has evolved with a kind of insulation that protects its nervous system. This insulation acts as a <u>buffer</u> against the electricity that it generates.

There may be one more way in which the electric eel uses electricity. Some scientists believe that eels can communicate among themselves using electrical signals akin to the clicks and whistles of other animals such as dolphins. At this point, however, this theory has not yet been proven.

121. The word <u>generate</u>, as used in the passage, most nearly means
    A) examine
    B) create
    C) protect
    D) catch

122. The author of this passage is probably
    A) a marine biologist
    B) an electrician
    C) a history teacher
    D) a fisherman

123. The word <u>current</u>, as used in the passage, most nearly means
    A) modern
    B) charge
    C) vision
    D) river

124. Which of the following can be inferred from the passage?
    A) Bats use electricity to help them see in the dark.
    B) Electric eels are more like crocodiles than like fish.
    C) Without electricity, electric eels would have a hard time feeding.
    D) Electric eels kill many people each year.

125. The word <u>buffer</u>, as used in the passage, most nearly means
    A) cleaner
    B) protection
    C) poison
    D) source

GO ON TO THE NEXT PAGE.

126. Which of the following does the author probably believe?
A) Electric eels are the most dangerous creatures on earth.
B) Electric eels have as many teeth as do crocodiles.
C) We are not yet certain whether electric eels use electricity to communicate.
D) Bats can also generate electric fields.

127. The author uses each of the following animals to help describe the electric eel except
A) the bat
B) the dolphin
C) the crocodile
D) the horse

128. It can be inferred from the passage that the electricity is dangerous because it
A) damages the nervous system
B) interferes with breathing
C) deprives animals of food
D) causes animals to bleed

129. You could probably find this article in
A) a dictionary
B) a guide to an aquarium
C) a chemistry textbook
D) a photography magazine

GO ON TO THE NEXT PAGE.

Ivan Pavlov was a Russian physiologist born in 1849. Instead of becoming a doctor, he chose to work in a medical laboratory, where he worked on the function of the nervous system. It is said that his salary was so <u>meager</u> that he and his family had to live in an unheated apartment in St. Petersburg. Nonetheless, Pavlov was so dedicated to his work that he remained at the laboratory almost all his life.

Pavlov was best known for his research on <u>conditioned</u> reflexes. While some reflexes are <u>innate</u>, such as the knee-jerk response when a doctor strikes with a mallet just below the kneecap, Pavlov showed that other reflexes can be acquired through experience or training. To demonstrate this, Pavlov performed a series of experiments on dogs. For several days in a row, one of Pavlov's assistants rang a bell just before feeding his dogs. The dogs learned to associate the bell with food. Pavlov discovered that afterward, when he rang the bell, the dogs would begin to salivate in anticipation of a meal. Pavlov argued that humans, just like dogs, have many conditioned reflexes.

Following Pavlov's idea, a school of psychology called behaviorism arose. Behaviorists such as B.F. Skinner believed that almost all animal (including human) behavior could be explained in terms of conditioning. Though behaviorism cannot plausibly explain all of human behavior, it has deepened our understanding of the way in which we react to events in the world. For his work, Pavlov received the Nobel Prize in 1904.

130. The word <u>meager</u>, as used in the passage, most nearly means
   A) funny
   B) small
   C) late
   D) critical

131. It can be inferred from Pavlov's experiment that conditioned reflexes
   A) can only be learned when hungry
   B) depend on repeated experiences
   C) can be found mostly in dogs
   D) are stronger than innate reflexes

132. According to the passage, the knee-jerk response is
   A) conditioned
   B) innate
   C) partially conditioned and partially innate
   D) neither conditioned nor innate

133. The word <u>innate</u>, as used in the passage, most nearly means
   A) violent
   B) inborn
   C) puzzling
   D) large

134. The author mentions B.F. Skinner as someone who
   A) disagreed with Pavlov's findings
   B) gave Pavlov the Nobel Prize
   C) believed in Pavlov's work and continued it
   D) was one of Pavlov's students

135. According to what the author says in the passage, the author would probably agree that behaviorism
   A) can explain all of human behavior
   B) is an interesting but limited way of explaining behavior.
   C) was criticized by Pavlov
   D) was wrong and should be forgotten about

136. The word <u>conditioned</u>, as used in the passage, most nearly means
   A) electrical
   B) unknown
   C) mild
   D) learned

GO ON TO THE NEXT PAGE.

She was extraordinarily <u>credulous</u>—would believe anything on earth anyone told her—because, although she had plenty of humor, she herself never would deviate from the absolute truth a moment, even in jest. I do not think she would have told an untruth to save her life. Well, of course we used to play on her to tease her. Frank would tell her the most unbelievable and impossible lies: such as that he thought he saw a mouse yesterday on the back of the sofa she was lying on (this would make her bounce up like a ball), or that he believed he heard—he was not sure—that Mr. Scroggs (the man who had rented her old home) had cut down all the old trees in the yard and pulled down the house because he wanted the bricks to make brick ovens. This would worry her excessively (she loved every brick in the old house, and often said she would rather live in the kitchen there than in a palace anywhere else), and she would get into such a state of depression that Frank would finally have to tell her that he was just "fooling her."

She used to make him do a good deal of waiting on her in return, and he was the one she used to get to dress old Fashion's back when it was raw and to put drops in her eyes. He got quite expert at it. She said it was a penalty for his worrying her so.

She was the great musician of the connection. This is in itself no mean praise, for it was the fashion for every musical gift among the girls to be <u>cultivated</u>, and every girl played or sang more or less, some of them very well. But Cousin Fanny was not only this. She had a way of playing that used to make the old piano sound different from itself, and her voice was almost the sweetest I ever heard except one or two on the stage.

137. We can infer from the passage that the reason Fanny would "bounce up like a ball" is that
   A) she is very energetic
   B) she is afraid of mice
   C) she likes to play games
   D) her couch had very powerful springs

138. The word <u>credulous</u>, as used in the passage, most nearly means
   A) dependable
   B) trusting
   C) intelligent
   D) lazy

139. According to the passage, Fanny's musical talents include
   A) the piano and the violin
   B) her voice and the piano
   C) the violin and the flute
   D) her voice and the violin

140. The word <u>cultivated</u>, as used in the passage, most nearly means
   A) beautiful
   B) planted
   C) encouraged
   D) lonely

141. Which of the following can be inferred from the passage?
   A) Fanny lived in a palace.
   B) Mr. Scroggs's first name is Frank.
   C) Frank liked to tease Fanny.
   D) Fanny was often worried about her children.

GO ON TO THE NEXT PAGE.

Julius Caesar was perhaps the most important politician's leader of all time. It was his military and political genius that created the Roman Empire, a civilization so large and powerful that no other Western government could be considered its equal until the 1700s. Caesar's historical influence was so great that the German and Russian words for emperor (Kaiser and Czar) are derived from his name.

Caesar belonged to a family of many senators and other politicians. In spite of this, Caesar did not simply act in the interests of his family. Early in his life, Caesar not only championed the Roman people but also fought against abuse and <u>corruption</u> in the senate.

For ten years, between 58 and 49 B.C., Caesar led a series of <u>campaigns</u> known as the Gallic Wars. His armies conquered the Gauls in France, and he marched as far north as England. Thanks to Caesar's military skill, almost all of Europe was under Roman control. These battles showed Caesar to be one of the greatest military strategists of all time.

Around 50 B.C. Caesar's popularity and strength began to frighten Pompey, who used to be his friend and colleague. Pompey tried to convince the senate to disband Caesar's army. In response, Caesar marched his army into Rome, defeated Pompey, and declared himself dictator.

Caesar was famously killed on the Ides of March (March 15) by a band of conspirators including Brutus, whom Ceasar had considered a friend.

142. The author gives us the German and Russian words for emperor to demonstrate
    A) the similarities between the German and Russian languages
    B) how words can change over time
    C) the importance of Julius Caesar in Western history
    D) that Julius Caesar spoke German and Russian

143. The author would probably agree that the Roman Empire
    A) was one of the most powerful civilizations of the ancient world
    B) was not as important as modern historians think it is
    C) ended in the 1700s
    D) was led by Pompey

144. It is somewhat surprising that Caesar was a champion of the people because he
    A) did not like the Roman people
    B) was too busy fighting
    C) came from a family of senators and politicians
    D) was not a very nice person

145. The word <u>campaign</u>, as used in the passage, most nearly means
    A) war
    B) story
    C) study
    D) game

146. According to the passage, Pompey became afraid of Caesar because Caesar
    A) had a famous father
    B) was rich
    C) was powerful and popular
    D) had a very big army

147. Which of the following is true based on the passage?
    A) Caesar fought Pompey in the Gallic Wars.
    B) The Gallic Wars took place in 58 to 49 B.C.
    C) Caesar never left the city of Rome.
    D) Caesar died in the month of May.

GO ON TO THE NEXT PAGE.

Mary Shelley was born in 1797. Her parents, Mary Wollstonecraft and William Godwin, were both writers; Wollstonecraft's *Vindication of the Rights of Woman* made her one of the most important early feminist thinkers. Shelley was surrounded as a child by some of the greatest literary figures of her day, including Samuel Coleridge and Charles Lamb. Her parents introduced her to these people because they believed that every child had the potential to develop a great intellect.

Shelley wrote her best-known work, *Frankenstein*, at the age of 19. She wrote it while staying at Lake Geneva with a group of young poets that included Lord Byron and Percy Shelley, whom she would later marry.

Frankenstein is not merely a horror story, but a brilliant work of art. The dark, gloomy imagery in *Frankenstein* was probably in part a reflection of the calamities taking place in Mary Shelley's life, which included several suicides in her extended family. Certain feminist ideas inherited from her mother are also included, as is a romantic mistrust of modern technology.

Shelley's bad luck continued. Her first child died shortly after birth. Later, Percy drowned when Mary was just 24 years old. She continued to write, and lived among other artists and literary figures for the rest of her life.

148. With which of the following would the author probably agree?
A) Mary Shelley was too young to be a writer.
B) Mary Shelley was the best writer of the nineteenth century.
C) *Frankenstein* is one of the great works of modern literature.
D) Shelley would never have written *Frankenstein* had it not been for Coleridge.

149. According to the passage, which one of the following influenced the way Shelley wrote *Frankenstein*?
A) the birth of her first child
B) her mother's feminist ideas
C) the works of John Milton
D) a bad dream she had as a child

150. What is this passage mostly about?
A) the relationship between Mary Shelley and Lord Byron
B) a gathering of poets at Lake Geneva
C) Mary Shelley's life and work
D) why *Frankenstein* is so scary

151. In approximately what year did Shelley write Frankenstein?
A) 1805
B) 1811
C) 1816
D) 1820

152. The word calamities, as used in the passage, most nearly means
A) feelings
B) tragedies
C) suggestions
D) questions

GO ON TO THE NEXT PAGE.

Vocabulary

153. an important <u>era</u>
A) place
B) time
C) story
D) person

154. a <u>concise</u> explanation
A) pleasant
B) famous
C) short
D) proud

155. to show great <u>compassion</u>
A) strength
B) interest
C) dislike
D) sympathy

156. a dangerous <u>felon</u>
A) criminal
B) sport
C) vacation
D) shark

157. a <u>mythical</u> creature
A) farm
B) surprising
C) imaginary
D) muscular

158. a <u>weary</u> traveler
A) busy
B) difficult
C) famous
D) tired

159. an <u>unorthodox</u> approach
A) happy
B) violent
C) unusual
D) marvelous

160. to <u>conceal</u> the truth
A) sing
B) study
C) hide
D) display

161. to <u>tremble</u> with joy
A) shake
B) skip
C) sit
D) pounce

162. a dangerous <u>epidemic</u>
A) idea
B) flight
C) disease
D) package

163. a museum <u>exhibition</u>
A) visitor
B) display
C) building
D) box

164. to <u>reinforce</u> a building
A) decorate
B) examine
C) strengthen
D) project

165. a <u>crucial</u> part
A) important
B) difficult
C) magnetic
D) wasted

166. a <u>tedious</u> speech
A) loud
B) boring
C) received
D) sparse

167. to <u>endorse</u> a candidate
A) write
B) criticize
C) plead
D) support

168. the <u>arduous</u> task
A) school
B) finished
C) difficult
D) adult

GO ON TO THE NEXT PAGE.

169. a <u>qualified</u> person
   A) sick
   B) capable
   C) interesting
   D) older

170. to <u>decline</u> an invitation
   A) refuse
   B) send
   C) paint
   D) dream

171. a <u>potent</u> chemical
   A) strong
   B) common
   C) illegal
   D) mixed

172. to <u>perturb</u> someone
   A) please
   B) bother
   C) introduce
   D) hire

173. rapid <u>respiration</u>
   A) running
   B) selling
   C) breathing
   D) change

174. a moving <u>oration</u>
   A) injury
   B) decision
   C) meal
   D) speech

GO ON TO THE NEXT PAGE.

Mathematics
Questions 175–238, 45 minutes

Mathematical Concepts

175. Which of the following is greatest?
    A) 0.1042
    B) 0.1105
    C) 0.0288
    D) 0.0931

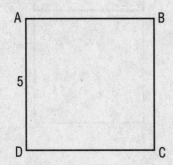

176. What is the area of square *ABCD*?
    A) 5
    B) 20
    C) 25
    D) 50

177. What is the least positive integer divisible by 3, 4, and 5?
    A) 30
    B) 40
    C) 50
    D) 60

178. The decimal representation of $5 + 60 + \dfrac{5}{100}$ is
    A) 65.05
    B) 65.5
    C) 56.05
    D) 56.5

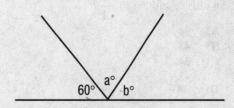

179. What is the sum of $a + b$?
    A) 60
    B) 100
    C) 120
    D) 160

180. The product of 0.28 and 100 is approximately
    A) 0.3
    B) 2.8
    C) 2
    D) 30

181. What is the greatest prime factor of 45?
    A) 2
    B) 3
    C) 5
    D) 9

182. A store normally sells a certain dress for $160. During a special sale, the store reduces the price of the dress to $120. By what percent is the price of the dress being reduced for the sale?
    A) 20%
    B) 25%
    C) 30%
    D) 40%

GO ON TO THE NEXT PAGE.

183. $10^3 \times 10^5 =$
     A) 10^8
     B) 10^{15}
     C) 100^8
     D) 100^{15}

184. All of the following are multiples of 8 except
     A) 24
     B) 96
     C) 178
     D) 192

185. What is the volume of a box with length 6, width 8, and height $\frac{1}{2}$?
     A) 96
     B) 48
     C) 24
     D) $14\frac{1}{2}$

186. If the ratio of boys to girls in a class is 3:4 and there are 124 girls in the class, how many boys are there in the class?
     A) 33
     B) 93
     C) 103
     D) 109

187. $(4^2)^3 =$
     A) 4^5
     B) 4^6
     C) 5^4
     D) 3^{16}

188. In the number 365, the product of the digits is how much greater than the sum of the digits?
     A) 76
     B) 54
     C) 36
     D) 14

189. What is 2.847 rounded to the nearest tenth?
     A) 2.84
     B) 2.9
     C) 2.8
     D) 2.85

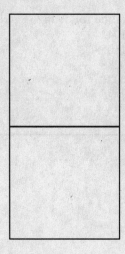

190. Each of the squares in the figure above has an area of 16. What is the perimeter of the figure?
     A) 16
     B) 24
     C) 28
     D) 32

191. If one of the angles inside a triangle measures 85 degrees, what could the other two angles measure?
     A) 45 degrees and 55 degrees
     B) 45 degrees and 50 degrees
     C) 35 degrees and 50 degrees
     D) 50 degrees and 60 degrees

192. $\sqrt{2^2} =$
     A) 1
     B) 2
     C) 4
     D) 16

GO ON TO THE NEXT PAGE.

193. Juan has 5 blue marbles, 9 green marbles, and 3 red marbles. What fractional part of his marbles is blue?

A) $\dfrac{5}{9}$

B) $\dfrac{5}{17}$

C) $\dfrac{17}{5}$

D) $\dfrac{9}{5}$

194. Which of the following is true?

A) $2\sqrt{2} + 3\sqrt{3} = 5\sqrt{5}$ s

B) $2\sqrt{2} \times 3\sqrt{3} = 5\sqrt{5}$

C) $2\sqrt{2} + 3\sqrt{2} = 5\sqrt{2}$

D) $2\sqrt{2} \times 3\sqrt{2} = 6\sqrt{2}$

195. What is the smallest common multiple of 6 and 4?

A) 4
B) 6
C) 12
D) 24

196. Which of the following leaves a remainder of 4 when divided by 6?

A) 18
B) 22
C) 26
D) 32

197. If you multiply a negative even number by a positive odd number, the result will be

A) negative and even
B) negative and odd
C) positive and even
D) positive and odd

198. How many prime numbers are there between 0 and 10?

A) 3
B) 4
C) 5
D) 6

GO ON TO THE NEXT PAGE.

Problem Solving

199. $\dfrac{5}{15} + \dfrac{6}{13} =$

   A) $\dfrac{11}{28}$

   B) $\dfrac{31}{39}$

   C) $\dfrac{6}{39}$

   D) $\dfrac{13}{15}$

200. Maxine scored 42, 45, and 46 on her first three history tests. What score would she need on her fourth test to raise her average score to 48?
   A) 50
   B) 55
   C) 59
   D) 62

201. 20% of 40% of 500 is
   A) 20
   B) 30
   C) 40
   D) 60

202. $6 - 3(2 - 4) + 5 =$

   A) 9
   B) 11
   C) 17
   D) 19

203. $\dfrac{20}{.02} =$

   A) 0.1
   B) 10
   C) 100
   D) 1,000

204. The price of a $25 comic book is decreased by 5%. What is the new price of the comic book?
   A) $23.75
   B) $22.75
   C) $20.25
   D) $20.00

205. On a certain map, 8 miles is represented by 1 inch. If two cities are 3.5 inches apart on the map, what is the distance between these two cities?
   A) 8 miles
   B) 16 miles
   C) 24 miles
   D) 28 miles

206. Which of the following is equal to 0.24?

   A) $\dfrac{12}{5}$

   B) $\dfrac{24}{10}$

   C) $\dfrac{12}{50}$

   D) $\dfrac{4}{10}$

207. Alice's Emporium discounts the price of a shirt by 20%, and then discounts it again by an additional 10%. The final price represents what percent decrease from the original price of the shirt?
   A) 15%
   B) 18%
   C) 28%
   D) 30%

GO ON TO THE NEXT PAGE.

208. Two positive integers have a ratio of 6:9. If the smaller of the two numbers is 18, what is the average of the two numbers?
   A)   15
   B)   22.5
   C)   24
   D)   27

209. $11 + 5 \times 6 + 3 - (2 - 5) =$

   A)   47
   B)   41
   C)   96
   D)   102

210. A swimming pool has dimensions 4 feet by 10 feet by 12 feet. If the pool can be filled at a rate of 8 cubic feet per minute, how many minutes will it take to fill the pool?
   A)   20
   B)   24
   C)   48
   D)   60

211. At Joe's Burger Shop, two hamburgers and an order of french fries cost $3.55. If three hamburgers cost $4.05, what is the price of an order of french fries?
   A) $0.50
   B) $0.65
   C) $0.85
   D) $1.15

212. In a certain classroom the ratio of boys to girls is 3:5. If there are 32 students in the class, how many girls are in the class?
   A)   12
   B)   14
   C)   16
   D)   20

213. The area of a circle with radius 8 is how much greater than its circumference?
   A) 8π
   B) 16π
   C) 24π
   D) 48π

214. $4^4 =$
   A) 16^2
   B) 32^1
   C) 32^2
   D) 64^2

215. If two-thirds of the 660 students at Middleburg Junior High attend the school dance, how many students do *not* attend?
   A)   220
   B)   240
   C)   400
   D)   440

216. Which of the following is equal to $2\sqrt{2} \times 3\sqrt{2}$?

   A) 2^4
   B) $5\sqrt{2}$
   C) $6\sqrt{2}$
   D)   12

217. $18 + \dfrac{3}{4} + \dfrac{3}{6} + \dfrac{1}{4} =$
   A)   19
   B) $19\dfrac{1}{2}$
   C)   20
   D) $20\dfrac{1}{6}$

218. If $3x + 5 = 23$, then $x =$
   A)   3
   B)   4
   C)   5
   D)   6

219. $\dfrac{1}{2} \div \dfrac{1}{10} =$

   A)   5
   B) $\dfrac{1}{5}$
   C) $\dfrac{1}{20}$
   D)   20

GO ON TO THE NEXT PAGE.

220. If $xy + 18 = 36$ and $x = 2$ then $y =$
A)   6
B)   7
C)   8
D)   9

221. What is the area of a rectangle with length 15 feet and width 24 feet?
A)   240 ft^2
B)   280 ft^2
C)   320 ft^2
D)   360 ft^2

222. $\left(7 \times \dfrac{1}{100}\right) + \left(2 \times \dfrac{1}{10}\right) +$
$\left(6 \times \dfrac{1}{1000}\right) + 4 =$
A)   4.267
B)   4.276
C)   4.726
D)   5.627

223. A pound of onions costs \$3.25 at the supermarket. What is the maximum number of pounds of onions that Larry can buy with \$13?
A)   4
B)   5
C)   6
D)   7

224. $5.5 \div 0.2$
A)   11
B)   13.5
C)   23.5
D)   27.5

225. Four years ago, Alex was half as old as he is now. How old is Alex now?
A)   4
B)   5
C)   6
D)   8

226. $5\dfrac{1}{2} \times 2\dfrac{1}{3} =$
A) $10\dfrac{1}{6}$
B) $11\dfrac{5}{6}$
C) $7\dfrac{1}{5}$
D) $5\dfrac{1}{3}$

227. If one gallon of paint can cover $2\dfrac{1}{2}$ square feet, how many gallons of paint will be needed to cover a rectangular wall that measures 20 feet by 12 feet?
A)   48
B)   64
C)   72
D)   96

228. If $2x^2 + y = 55$ and $y = 5$, what could x be?
A)   3
B)   5
C)   6
D)   7

229. $4\sqrt{18} \times 3\sqrt{2} =$
A)   72
B) $12\sqrt{18}$
C) $4\sqrt{32}$
D)   36

230. How many seconds are there in 4 hours?
A)   240
B)   2400
C)   3,600
D)   14,400

GO ON TO THE NEXT PAGE.

231. In a group of 100 children, there are 24 more girls than boys. How many girls are in the group?
A) 62
B) 50
C) 38
D) 24

232. If $-4x - 3 < x + 2$, what is the range of possible values of x?
A) $x < -1$
B) $x < 1$
C) $x > -1$
D) $x > 1$

233. How many multiples of 5 and 6 are there between 1 and 100?
A) 3
B) 5
C) 7
D) 9

234. The figure above is a circle with center O. What is the value of x?
A) 30
B) 45
C) 60
D) 90

235. Emil can shape two cookies every minute. How long will it take him to shape 150 cookies?
A) 1 hour 15 minutes
B) 1 hour 25 minutes
C) 3 hours 15 minutes
D) 5 hours

236. Carl is twice as old as his brother Jim, who is five years older than Liz. If Carl is 15 years older than Liz, how old is Jim?
A) 20
B) 15
C) 10
D) 8

237. The diameter of a circle with a circumference of 8π is
A) 2
B) 8
C) 16
D) 64

238. Alex buys a gallon of soda for $8.50, and wants to split the cost among 5 people. How much will each person pay?
A) $1.70
B) $1.65
C) $1.50
D) $0.65

GO ON TO THE NEXT PAGE.

Language
Questions 239–298, 25 minutes

Usage

For questions 239–278, check the sentences for errors of usage, capitalization, or punctuation. If there is no error, choose D.

239.
- A) David studied french for many years but could not speak it very well.
- B) Ophelia was a great singer as well as a gifted poet.
- C) Some of the world's greatest chess players are under 30 years old.
- D) No mistake.

240.
- A) If I had a telescope, I would be able to see that planet.
- B) Steve ran very quick around the track.
- C) We are all going to sing a song after dinner.
- D) No mistake.

241.
- A) The first typewriters were huge machines that were difficult to operate.
- B) I went home to help clean my fathers' room.
- C) We followed the river for three miles before eating lunch.
- D) No mistake.

242.
- A) My uncle lived in Houston while he was in college.
- B) Belgium was neutral for years, but then they decided to join the war.
- C) There are few things more enjoyable than a walk through the park.
- D) No mistake.

243.
- A) Last year we spent our vacation near lake michigan.
- B) Alicia's teacher is very well educated.
- C) How many times have you seen Martin's father?
- D) No mistake.

244.
- A) We were all so scared that nobody said a word.
- B) "I don't know how you can eat that," said Ms. Carroll.
- C) Each of us has at least three hundred baseball cards.
- D) No mistake.

245.
- A) My mother found a cat behind the grocery store.
- B) I broke my arm on new year's eve.
- C) How many times have you been to the coast of California?
- D) No mistake.

246.
- A) Mary was an imaginative child who read many books.
- B) My teacher asked me if I knew who's backpack was left on the bus.
- C) Cathryn spent her summer working with chimpanzees.
- D) No mistake.

247.
- A) Jane sat at the front of the boat and tried to catch a fish.
- B) My brother and I are going fishing this weekend.
- C) Many great battles of the American Revolution took place around Boston Massachusetts.
- D) No mistake.

GO ON TO THE NEXT PAGE.

248.

   A) The blueberries in Kai's backyard are always delicious.

   B) I have never seen so many people at once.

   C) My book report is due on monday.

   D) No mistake.

249.

   A) The eruption of a volcano is a violent and frightening event.

   B) Since the end of the school year, I have had little to do.

   C) Do you think I should bring flowers to the party?

   D) No mistake.

250.

   A) Nitrogen and oxygen are the most common gases in our atmosphere.

   B) The book was so popular that the author became famous.

   C) Sally asked "Have you seen the new park?"

   D) No mistake.

251.

   A) Annie's letter was dated Saturday July 5.

   B) We were very impressed by his playing.

   C) Manny's brother left for college last week.

   D) No mistake.

252.

   A) Jane's cat ran away two weeks ago, but they finally came back.

   B) Mrs. Hendon greeted her daughter and nephew when they arrived.

   C) The Pulizer Prize is named after the newspaper reporter Joseph Pulitzer.

   D) No mistake.

253.

   A) Dorothea Dix helped to change the way that ill prisoners were treated.

   B) The story was written by my friend and I.

   C) Graphs are useful tools to help organize and display information.

   D) No mistake.

254.

   A) Marion and I have not seen each other for months.

   B) How many times have you seen this movie?

   C) My father and I went to see chief Stanley at the firehouse.

   D) No mistake.

255.

   A) Alison had already took her bath by the time I arrived.

   B) There will be enough wind to fly a kite today.

   C) Almost every culture has its own special kind of music.

   D) No mistake.

256.

   A) Paul went to the park after dinner to play with his friends.

   B) Everyone appreciated Julia's hard work.

   C) Us and them went to the store together.

   D) No mistake.

257.

   A) The driver was the only witness to the crime.

   B) Paula serving dinner on the patio.

   C) Archeology is the study of early civilizations.

   D) No mistake.

GO ON TO THE NEXT PAGE.

258.

   A) Many of Picasso's paintings were based on photographs of his friends.
   B) Rachel's family are very happy for her.
   C) I like white paper better than blue paper.
   D) No mistake.

259.

   A) The cat was searching for it's water dish.
   B) Patricia wants to work for herself.
   C) Laura has seen more films than Jackie has.
   D) No mistake.

260.

   A) Each of my friends have a toy car.
   B) Sarah was fascinated by the pictures.
   C) Jason knows the names of almost all the instruments in an orchestra.
   D) No mistake.

261.

   A) Sarah is probably very hungry.
   B) Her is not ready to finish the job.
   C) Martin's mother gave him two days to clean his room.
   D) No mistake.

262.

   A) I saw several stars in the sky, but my sister saw hardly none.
   B) Charles goes to the pool to practice every day after school.
   C) Some believe that the helicopter was first drawn by Leonardo da Vinci.
   D) No mistake.

263.

   A) Libby begged her parents to let her go to the concert on a weeknight.
   B) Alice and her parents are going to visit their friends at the beach.
   C) Kathy grabbed her books and ran out the door.
   D) No mistake.

264.

   A) This box contains less cookies than the other box.
   B) In my very first game I hit three home runs.
   C) David left his notebook on the kitchen counter.
   D) No mistake.

265.

   A) Lidia's mother had a frown on her face.
   B) The new librarian is very friendly.
   C) Michael has as many pictures than his brother.
   D) No mistake.

266.

   A) Peter's cookies are better than Steve.
   B) She has no reason to be afraid.
   C) Lisa's brother won the first race of the day.
   D) No mistake.

267.

   A) Unlike animals, plants can make their own food.
   B) Mr. Jones is an intelligent and caring teacher.
   C) My mother divided the sandwich between my sister and I.
   D) No mistake.

268.

   A) Paper makes up almost half of the garbage in America.
   B) My brother is more heavier than I am.
   C) I would rather see a movie than go to the opera.
   D) No mistake.

269.

   A) It is impossible to travel faster than the speed of light.
   B) I was invited to his party, but I caught the flu and could not attend.
   C) Frank is not only a great writer, but he can also draw cartoons.
   D) No mistake.

GO ON TO THE NEXT PAGE.

270.
- A) Most bees live in hives, but some live alone.
- B) The members of our team sold candy to raise money for a trip.
- C) That collar belongs to my friends dog, Spot.
- D) No mistake.

271.
- A) Alex and I played in the park after school the other day.
- B) The punch served at Anna's party was delicious.
- C) The planet Pluto is named after a Greek god.
- D) No mistake.

272.
- A) Women played a very important role in the American Revolution.
- B) Computers are now found in almost every home in the United States.
- C) The first westerner to discover Hawaii was Captain James Cook.
- D) No mistake.

273.
- A) My teacher looked at my homework very close and found several mistakes.
- B) Penny looked out the window and saw a rainbow.
- C) Martin was so worried that he couldn't sleep.
- D) No mistake.

274.
- A) There were less houses in my neighborhood than I remembered.
- B) The ship was so badly damaged by the iceberg that it had to return to port.
- C) Katrina gave a presentation to the class on the origins of ballet.
- D) No mistake.

275.
- A) The most greatest singer of the twentieth century was Frank Sinatra.
- B) William the Conqueror invaded England in 1066.
- C) After hurting his knee, David began to groan.
- D) No mistake.

276.
- A) Neither gunpowder nor the compass was invented in Europe.
- B) Janet would believe almost anything that anyone told her.
- C) Missy fell off her horse, but she was not injured.
- D) No mistake.

277.
- A) The computer is one of our most important educational tools.
- B) The giant mouse ran through the house and escaping from the cat.
- C) Did you know that Julie is an experienced guide and mountaineer?
- D) No mistake.

278.
- A) Our parents often helps us with our math homework.
- B) Wallace has always wanted to visit Paris, but he has never had the time.
- C) Rick goes to the library every day after school to study.
- D) No mistake.

GO ON TO THE NEXT PAGE.

Spelling

For questions 279–288, look for errors in spelling.

279.
- A) Everyone should have a good dictionary and thesaurus in the house.
- B) He admited that he had never seen the play.
- C) After years of neglect, the building finally collapsed.
- D) No mistake.

280.
- A) Terry considered joining a traveling circus.
- B) Drew usually exaggerates a bit when he tells a story.
- C) He was seldom late to a party.
- D) No mistake.

281.
- A) Many great discoveries happen entirely by accident.
- B) If we don't show up on time, they're going to be very angry.
- C) Winning the scholarship was a great oportunity for John.
- D) No mistake.

282.
- A) His messy handwriting made his letter nearly illegible.
- B) I think he was sincerely sorry for what he did.
- C) We have a rehearsal for the play almost every night.
- D) No mistake.

283.
- A) His teacher was surprised and very impressed by his artistic ability.
- B) Mr. Worthington thought that Kathy looked upset.
- C) I tried to learn to sew, but I wasn't very good at it.
- D) No mistake.

284.
- A) The play was so long that it required two intermissions.
- B) Uma prefered to sit on the couch.
- C) Each tribe has a cloth with a distinctive pattern.
- D) No mistake.

285.
- A) My sister practises the piano two hours a day.
- B) John told me that he wants to be an astronaut.
- C) His article was misleading, even if true.
- D) No mistake.

286.
- A) The sheriff's deputy caught the thief later that night.
- B) Paul was surprized to hear that he had won the award.
- C) Agnes was very fond of her stuffed bear, named Edward.
- D) No mistake.

287.
- A) Justin was confused by the strange behavior of his pet frog.
- B) Many people enjoy the challenge of an outdoor adventure.
- C) Linus Pauling received the Nobel Prize for his many scientific accomplishments.
- D) No mistake.

288.
- A) Ms. Davis teaches mathmatics and physics.
- B) Cecil did not intend to insult his friend.
- C) George was not sure how his friends would react to his talent.
- D) No mistake.

GO ON TO THE NEXT PAGE.

Composition

289. Choose the sentence that is correct and most clearly written.
    A) Martin decided on the blue suit after several days.
    B) The blue suit was decided upon by Martin after several days.
    C) After several days, the blue suit was decided upon by Martin.
    D) The blue suit, after several days, was what Martin decided on.

290. Choose the sentence that is correct and most clearly written.
    A) Importantly, occasions such as birthdays should not be forgotten.
    B) Occasions, such as birthdays, which are important, should not be forgotten.
    C) Birthdays are important occasions which should not be forgotten.
    D) Occasions should not be forgotten when they are as important as birthdays.

291. Choose the sentence that is correct and most clearly written.
    A) Spinach is my favorite food it goes well with almost anything.
    B) Spinach is my favorite food; it goes well with almost anything.
    C) Spinach is my favorite food and spinach goes well with almost anything.
    D) Spinach is my favorite food to go well with almost anything.

292. Where should the following sentence be placed in the paragraph below?

She was responsible for promoting sanitary surgical methods, a pure water supply, and other hygienic measures.

① Born in Italy and raised in England, Florence Nightingale is recognized universally as the person who established the principles of modern nursing. ② In 1854, Nightingale assembled a team of women to care for British soldiers during the Crimean War. ③ During her nearly two years of service, Nightingale stressed cleanliness and good medical care. ④ These measures led to a drop in the mortality rate from 60% to 2%, saving countless British lives. ⑤ When she returned from the war, she founded the Nightingale School to train the next generation of professional nurses.
    A) after sentence 2
    B) after sentence 3
    C) after sentence 4
    D) after sentence 5

293. Where should the following sentence be placed in the paragraph below?

The ash spread over hundreds of square miles, making the sky look black as night.

① In 1980 Mount Saint Helens, in the state of Washington, became a volcano. ② It exploded for the first time in thousands of years. ③ The explosion was felt as far north as Seattle and as far south as Los Angeles. ④ The mountain threw tons of ash into the air before it stopped exploding a few days later. ⑤ There was, however, no lava. ⑥ Most geologists believe that Mount Saint Helens will not explode again for many thousands of years to come. ⑦ But they admit that another explosion might occur at any time.
    A) after sentence 2
    B) after sentence 3
    C) after sentence 4
    D) after sentence 5

GO ON TO THE NEXT PAGE.

294. Choose the word or words that best fills the blank.

Jason thought that he found a lump of gold, _____ it turned out to be a painted rock.
A) because
B) moreover
C) but
D) or

295. Choose the word or words that best fills the blank.

Most people feel that it is worthwhile to buy a better product, _____ it might cost a little more.
A) therefore
B) even though
C) in fact
D) despite

296. Choose the word or words that best fills the blank.

Brushing your teeth every day is important to prevent cavities; _____ it helps your gums stay healthy and prevents bad breath.
A) moreover,
B) nonetheless,
C) yet,
D) in contrast,

297. Which sentence does *not* belong in the following paragraph?

▯ Many people think that rabbits are rodents, like rats and mice. ▢ In fact, rabbits are not rodents at all. ▣ Rodents scare many people because they have sharp teeth and claws. ▤ Rabbits, along with hares, belong to a class of animals called lagomorphs. ▥ Lagomorph is a Greek word that means "rabbit-shaped."
A) sentence 2
B) sentence 3
C) sentence 4
D) sentence 5

298. Which sentence does *not* belong in the following paragraph?

▯ Of all the animals on earth, the one most suited to its environment is probably the camel. ▢ Camels live in the desert, where water is scarce and breathing is difficult due to the sand in the air. ▣ To cope with these conditions, camels can store several days' worth of water in their humps. ▤ There are no higher animals on earth that can live without water. ▥ Camels also have extra-long eyelashes and hairs that cover their noses to keep the sand out. ▦ Furthermore, their large feet help them walk on the sand, which is difficult terrain for most other pack animals.
A) sentence 2
B) sentence 3
C) sentence 4
D) sentence 5

26

Answers and Explanations to HSPT Practice Test 2

VERBAL SKILLS

1. **C**   Diligent means hard-working.

2. **D**   Severe means serious; the opposite is mild.

3. **C**   A candle is made of wax; a tire is made of rubber.

4. **B**   Spoon, knife, and fork are utensils used to eat food.

5. **B**   A horse lives in a stable; a chicken lives in a coop.

6. **B**   Winter, fall, and summer are seasons of the year.

7. **B**   Prohibit means to disallow.

8. **C**   Shirt, dress, and shorts are all articles of clothing.

9. **A**   Famished means very hungry; arid means very dry.

10. **B**   Biased means taking a position; the opposite is neutral.

11. **A**   A suitcase holds clothes; a briefcase holds papers.

12. **A**   Hinder means to hold back; the opposite is help.

13. **B**   Content means happy or satisfied.

14. **C**   We can diagram this as follows: Rachel > Alice, Richard > Barry. Since we don't know how Rachel and Alice relate to Richard and Barry, we don't know whether Rachel or Richard finished first.

15. **C**   The top of a container is a lid; the top of a house is a roof.

16. **C**   Credible means believable.

17. **B**   Sincere means honest; the opposite is dishonest.

18. **B**   We can diagram this as follows: $I > M > L$. Since Ines is before Marcus, who is before Larry, we know that Larry is not before Ines.

19. **A**   To contaminate means to infect.

20. **C**   We can diagram this as follows: $B > D$, $A > D$, $C > D$. All we know is that Alex and Bink had more balloons than David, but we don't know whether Alex or Bink had more.

21. **D**   Sail, mast, and rudder are all parts of a ship.

22. **D**   Fortunate means lucky.

23. **B**   A zoologist studies animals; a biologist studies plants.

24. **A**   Apple, peach, and pear are all kinds of fruit.

25. **A**   We can diagram this as follows: $J > B$, $M > J > E$. Since Mark is taller than John, who is taller than Evelyn, we know that Mark is taller than Evelyn.

26. **B**   Water, oil, and vinegar are all kinds of liquid.

27. **B**   Frank means honest.

28. **A**   Famine means the lack of food; drought means the lack of water.

29. **C** We can diagram this as follows: $O > J, N > J$. All we know is that Olivia and Nancy each ate more than Jennifer, but we don't know whether Olivia or Nancy ate more.

30. **A** Trunk, branch, and leaf are all parts of a tree.

31. **C** Immune means not vulnerable to disease; the opposite is vulnerable.

32. **D** Tea, coffee, and water are all things you drink; you eat cereal.

33. **A** Elude means to get away or escape.

34. **A** We can diagram this as follows: $F > J = M, F > N$. Since Frank has seen more than Jonathan, who has seen the same number as Manny, we know that Manny has seen fewer films than Frank.

35. **B** Sole, lace, and heel are all parts of a shoe.

36. **C** To mimic means to imitate.

37. **A** Counterfeit means fake or false; the opposite is genuine.

38. **A** We can diagram this as follows: $K > F > D, A > K$. Since Amanda walked farther than Kate, who walked farther than Felix, we know that Amanda walked farther than Felix.

39. **C** Barbaric means rude or uncivilized; the opposite is civilized.

40. **D** Dog, fish, and hamster are all kinds of pets.

41. **C** Conventional means normal; the opposite is strange.

42. **D** To inspect means to examine closely.

43. **A** Varied means different; the opposite is similar.

44. **A** Goat, cow, and horse are all animals that give milk.

45. **A** Maple is a type of tree; an apple is a type of fruit.

46. **D** To diminish means to reduce.

47. **C** We can diagram this as follows: Mike > Mindy > W, Mike > R. All we know is that both Mindy and Rochelle read fewer books than Mike. We don't know which of the two read more.

48. **C** Movie, book, and play are all kinds of works that can be fictional.

49. **B** Unbiased means without bias, or neutral.

50. **B** Criticize is the opposite of praise.

51. **B** Mop, broom, and vacuum are all tools to clean the floor.

52. **B** A bird guides itself with its wings; a fish guides itself with its fins.

53. **C** Permanent means unchanging.

54. **B** We can diagram this as follows: $W > S > T > Z$. Since Wendy has more badges than Terence, who has more than Zack, we know that Wendy does not have fewer than Zack.

55. **A** Serere means calm or peaceful.

56. **C** Enlarge means to grow; the opposite is shrink or reduce.

57. **D** Wind, rain, and snow are all reasons to wear a coat.

58. **A** An hour is a part of the day; a month is a part of the year.

59. **C** Brick, stone, and wood are all materials used to make a house.

60. **B** Authentic means real or genuine.

QUANTITATIVE SKILLS

61. **C** The series goes 2 ($\times$ 2) 4 ($\times$ 2) 8 ($\times$ 2) 16 ($\times$ 2) **32**.

62. **D** Each of the figures has two parts out of four shaded.

63. **A** The series goes 6 (+ 9) 15 (+ 9) 24 (+ 9) 33 (+ 9) **42**.

64. **D** $3 \times 5 = 15$. Now try each choice to see which one, if you take 25% of it, gives you 15. $25\% \times 60 = 15$.

65. **D** The series goes 1 ($\times$ 3) 3 ($\times$ 3) 9 ($\times$ 3) 27 ($\times$ 3) **81**.

66. **C** Translate each of these: $\frac{40}{100}$ 80 = 32. $\frac{50}{100}$ 64 = 32. $\frac{150}{100}$ 16 = 24.

67. **A** $\frac{1}{4}$ of 24 is 6. What number divided by 3 is 6? 18.

68. **A** The series goes 100 (– 1) 99 (– 2) 97 (– 3) 94 (– 4) **90**.

69. **C** Let's calculate each of the choices: $\frac{1}{4} \times 96 = 24$. $2 \times 48 = 96$. $\frac{1}{2} \times 192 = 96$.

70. **C** The series goes 5 (+ 3) 8 (+ 5) 13 (+ 3) 16 (+ 5) 21 (+ 3) **24**.

71. **B** Let's calculate each of the choices: $32^1 = 32$. $2^5 = 32$. $3^3 = 27$.

72. **B** The series goes 10 (– 3) 7 (+ 1) 8 (– 3) 5 (+ 1) 6 (– 3) **3**.

73. **C** 10% of 40 is the same as $\frac{10}{100} \times 40 = 4$. Now we need to figure out $\frac{4}{5}$ of which number is 4. Try taking $\frac{4}{5}$ of each of the choices until you find the one that makes 4.

74. **C** The series goes 6 (+ 3) 9 (+ 4) 13 (+ 3) 16 (+ 4) 20 (+ 3) **23**.

75. **C** Since (c) has an 8 in the hundredths place, it is the largest number. (b) has an extra digit, and is greater than (a).

76. **A** The series goes 2 (+ 4) 6 (+ 6) 12 (+ 4) 16 (+ 6) 22 (+ 4) **26**.

77. **A** The difference between 80 and 64 is 16. $\frac{1}{4}$ of 16 = 4.

78. **B** Let's calculate these choices: $3(4 + 9) = 39$. $12 + 27 = 39$. $34 + 9 = 43$.

79. **B** $\frac{1}{5}$ of 15 is 3. 18 more than 3 is 21.

80. **B** The perimeter of (a) is 14, the perimeter of (b) is 16, and the perimeter of C is 12.

81. **A** Translate this as $\frac{10}{100} \times \frac{20}{100} \times 300 = 6$.

82. **B** The series goes 8 (+ 1) 9 (+ 7) 16 (+ 1) 17 (+ 7) 24 (+ 1) 25 (+ 7) **32**.

83. **B** Let's calculate these choices. For (a) we move the decimal three places to the right to get 3,020. For (b) we move the decimal two places to the right to get 3,200. (c) is 302.

84. **B** Try dividing each number by 7. $51 \div 7 = 7$ with a remainder of 2.

85. **A** Since *AC* and *FB* are both diameters, they are equal; *ED* is shorter than both of them.

86. **B** The series goes 1 ($\times$ 7) 7 | 3 ($\times$ 7) 21 | **5** ($\times$ 7) 35.

87. **B** *x* is larger than *y*. Since their sum is 180, *x* must be larger than 90, and *y* must be less than 90.

88. **C** (a) = 3.67, (b) = 6.73, and (c) = 7.36.

89. **A** The series goes 2 ($\times$ 2) 4 (+ 2) 6 ($\times$ 2) 12 (+ 2) 14 ($\times$ 2) 28 (+ 2) **30**.

90. **C** Translate 20% of 60: $\frac{20}{100} \times 60 = 12$. What number is 9 times 12? 108.

91. **A** The series goes 9 (– 2) 7 (– 2) 5 (+ 4) 9 (– 2) 7 (– 2) **5** (+ 4) 9.

92. **C** Twice the difference between 15 and 17 is 4. 17 more than 4 is 21.

93. **B** The series goes 9 (+ 11) 20 (+ 11) 31 (+ 11) 42 (+ 11) **53**.

94. **C** Since this is a square, all the sides are equal and smaller than the diagonals.

95. **D** The series goes 7 ($\times$ 2) 14 (– 1) 13 ($\times$ 2) 26 (– 1) 25 ($\times$ 2) **50**.

96. **B** $\frac{1}{11}$ of 121 = 11. To make 11, you need to add 8 and 3.

97. **C** (a) = 16, (b) = 16, and (c) = 32.

98. **C** The series goes 2 (+ 2) 4 (+ 2) 6 (– 2) 4 (+ 2) 6 (+ 2) 8 (– 2) **6** (+ 2) 8 (+ 2) 10.

99. **A** Since they are vertical angles, (a) = 45, (b) = 110, and (c) = 25.

100. **B** The average of 42, 45, and 39 is 42. The difference between 23 and 42 is 19.

101. **D** The product of 8 and 18 is 144. $\frac{1}{4}$ of 144 = 36.

102. **C** (a) has an area of 8; (b) has an area of 8; (c) has an area of 7.

103. C   The series should go 88 (– 3) 85 (– 2) 83 (– 3) 80 (– 2) 78 (– 3) **75**.

104. A   (a) = 2, (b) = –2, and (c) = –18.

105. B   The series goes 49 ($\sqrt{\ }$) 7 | 81 ($\sqrt{\ }$) **9** | 121 ($\sqrt{\ }$) 11.

106. D   The product of 6 and 3 is 18. 50% more than 18 is 27.

107. C   10% of 50 = 5; 20% of 100 = 20. The difference between 5 and 20 is 15.

108. B   The series goes 6 (+ 2) 8 (– 1) 7 (+ 2) 9 (– 1) **8** (+ 2) 10 (– 1) 9 (+ 2) 11.

109. C $\frac{5}{3}$ of 9 = 15. 4 less than 15 is 11.

110. C   Half the sum of 4, 9, and 11 is 12. 18 more than 12 is 30.

111. C   The average of 10, 15, and 8 is 11. 2 more than 11 is 13.

112. B   The series goes 41 (– 30) 11 (+ 41) 52 (– 30) 22 (+ 41) 63 (– 30) **33**.

READING

COMPREHENSION

113. A   The passage uses quitting in contrast to playing with her friends. It must therefore mean something like no longer playing with.

114. C   According to the passage, they gathered near the river.

115. B   The first paragraph states that the narrator is going to take a job while the friends go back to high school. The narrator is probably around 18 years old.

116. A   Each paragraph of the passage describes the various friends of the narrator.

117. B   According to the first paragraph, the narrator will "remember it better" because the narrator is about to leave.

118. C   The first paragraph says that the author was going "to teach my first country school."

119. B   The second paragraph says that Otto and Fritz "caught the fat, horned catfish."

120. B   According to the last sentence, Tip's father worked in a "grocery store."

121. B   Since the sentences following the mention of the word *generate* discuss the ways in which the eel uses electricity, the word *generate* must mean something like use or make.

122. A   This author knows a great deal of detail about the electric eel, which is an animal that lives in the sea.

123. B   The word *current* is right next to the word *electric*, so it must have something to do with electricity.

124. C   According to the third paragraph, eels use their electricity "to find fish."

125. **B**   In the sentence prior to the word *buffer*, we see that it is something that "protects its nervous system."

126. **C**   The final sentence of the passage says that it is not certain whether eels use electricity to communicate because "this theory has not yet been proven."

127. **D**   Each of these animals is mentioned somewhere in the passage except the horse.

128. **A**   The fourth paragraph states that the eel has insulation that "protects its nervous system" from the electricity that it generates. Therefore we can infer that electricity harms the nervous system.

129. **B**   The only choice listed that would describe an electric eel is B.

130. **B**   The word *meager* in explained by saying that his salary was so meager that they lived "in an unheated apartment." Evidently he didn't have enough money to afford heat, so the word *meager* must mean small.

131. **B**   The second paragraph says that Pavlov worked on "conditioned reflexes" and showed that they "can be acquired through experience or training."

132. **B**   According to the second paragraph, the knee-jerk response is an example of an "innate" reflex.

133. **B**   Since the word *innate* is used in the second paragraph in contrast to the word *conditioned*, it must refer to something that is not trained and instead had at birth.

134. **C**   The final paragraph says that Skinner was a behaviorist, which was a school of psychology that followed Pavlov's ideas. But we don't know if Skinner was one of Pavlov's students, so C is the best choice.

135. **B**   In the final paragraph, the author says, "Though behaviorism cannot plausibly explain all of human behavior, it has deepened our understanding."

136. **D**   The second paragraph states that Pavlov worked on "conditioned reflexes" and showed that they "can be acquired through experience or training."

137. **B**   The words "bounce up like a ball" are used to describe how Fanny acts when she thinks she sees a mouse.

138. **B**   The word *credulous* in the passage is followed immediately by "would believe anything."

139. **B**   The final paragraph states that she played the piano and sang.

140. **C**   The word *cultivated* is used to describe the "musical gift" of people. A, B, and D are therefore impossible.

141. **C**   According to the first paragraph, "Frank would tell her the most unbelievable and impossible lies" and enjoyed "fooling her."

142. **C**   The final sentence of the first paragraph states that "Caesar's historical influence was so great" that these words "are derived from his name."

143. **A**   The second sentence says that the Roman Empire was "so large and powerful that no other Western government could be considered its equal."

144. **C**   The second paragraph says that Caesar came from a family of politicians, but he "did not simply act in the interests of his family" but rather helped the people.

145. **A** The word *campaign* is used to describe the Gallic Wars.

146. **C** The fourth paragraph states that "Caesar's popularity and strength began to frighten Pompey."

147. **B** This is stated in the first sentence of the third paragraph.

148. **C** The third paragraph says that *Frankenstein* is "a brilliant work of art."

149. **B** In the third paragraph, the author states that "feminist ideas inherited from her mother" influenced her writing.

150. **C** A and B are only details of the passage, and D is not really discussed.

151. **C** According to the second paragraph, she wrote it at the age of 19. Since she was born in 1797, she must have written it around 1816.

152. **B** The word *calamities* is used to describe events that "included several suicides."

Vocabulary

153. **B**

154. **C**

155. **D**

156. **A**

157. **C**

158. **D**

159. **C**

160. **C**

161. **A**

162. **C**

163. **B**

164. **C**

165. **A**

166. **B**

167. **D**

168. **C**

169. **B**

170. **A**

171. **A**

172. **B**

173. **C**

174. **D**

MATHEMATICS

MATHEMATICAL CONCEPTS

175. B First, eliminate choices that have a zero in the tenths place. This leaves A and B. Since B has a 1 in the hundredths place, whereas A has a 0, B is bigger.

176. C The area of a square is length × width. Since this is a square, its length and width are both 5, so the area is $5 \times 5 = 25$.

177. D Plug in each answer choice until you find one that can be divided by 3, 4, and 5. 30 cannot be divided by 4; 40 cannot be divided by 3; 50 cannot be divided by 3.

178. A Remember that the second place to the right of the decimal is called the hundredths place. Therefore $\frac{5}{100} = 0.05$, so the sum = 65.05.

179. C Since $60 + a + b = 180$, $a + b = 120$.

180. D Remember that when you multiply by 100, you move the decimal point two places to the right: $0.28 \times 100 = 28$. The closest choice is D

181. C If we find the factors of 45, they are 1 and 45, 3 and 15, and 5 and 9. Since 9 is not prime, the biggest prime factor is 5.

182. B Percent decrease is calculated by taking $\frac{difference}{original}$. The difference in this case is $40. The original amount of the dress was $160. Therefore we calculate $\frac{40}{160} = \frac{1}{4} = 25\%$.

183. A When in doubt, write exponents out longhand. $10^3 = 10 \times 10 \times 10$. $10^5 = 10 \times 10 \times 10 \times 10 \times 10$. This makes a total of eight 10s, or 10^8.

184. C Try dividing each choice by 8 until you find the one that cannot be divided evenly.

185. C The volume of this box is $6 \times 8 \times \frac{1}{2} = 24$.

186. B We can make this into a proportion: $\frac{3 \ boys}{4 \ girls} = \frac{x}{124 \ girls}$. If we cross multiply and solve for x, we get $x = 93$ boys.

187. B When in doubt, write out the exponents longhand. $(4^2)^3$ is the same thing as $4^2 \times 4^2 \times 4^2 = 4 \times 4 \times 4 \times 4 \times 4 \times 4$. There are a total of six 4s, or 4^6.

188. A The product of the digits is $3 \times 6 \times 5 = 90$. The sum of the digits is $3 + 6 + 5 = 14$. $90 - 14 = 76$.

189. C Remember that the tenths place is the first to the right of the decimal. Since the next digit is 4, we round down to 2.8.

190. B Since the squares have an area of 16, their sides must equal 4. The perimeter of the figure covers 6 sides total, so the perimeter is $6 \times 4 = 24$.

191. B The angles inside a triangle must add up to 180 degrees. If one of the angles measures 85 degrees, then the other two must measure 180 − 85 = 95 degrees. The only choice that adds up to 95 degrees is B.

192. B $\sqrt{2^2}$ is the same as $\sqrt{4} = 2$.

193. B Juan has a total of 17 marbles, and 5 of them are blue. Therefore $\frac{5}{17}$ of his marbles are blue.

194. C You can add only similar roots together, so C is the only true statement.

195. C The first multiples of 4 are 4, 8, 12, 16, 20, and 24. The first multiples of 6 are 6, 12, 18, and 24. The smallest number that is common to each is 12.

196. B Try dividing each choice by 6. 22 ÷ 6 = 3 with a remainder of 4.

197. A Try taking a negative even number such as −2 and a positive odd number such as 3, and multiply them to get −6. This number is negative and even.

198. B Don't forget to memorize your primes! There are four: 2, 3, 5, and 7.

PROBLEM SOLVING

199. B Use the Bowtie to get a common denominator. $\frac{5}{15} + \frac{6}{13} = \frac{65}{195} + \frac{90}{195} = \frac{155}{195}$ which reduces to $\frac{31}{39}$.

200. C To get an average of 48 on 4 tests, her total score would have to be 48 × 4, or 192. Maxine already has 42 + 45 + 46 = 133 points on the first 3 tests, so on her fourth she would need 192 − 133 = 59 points.

201. C Translate this as $\frac{20}{100} \times \frac{40}{100} \times 500 = 40$.

202. C Remember your order of operations! First do parentheses to get 6 − 3(− 2) + 5. Now do multiplication to get 6 + 6 + 5. Now add to get 17.

203. D To make this division easier, let's move the decimal point two places to the right. Now we can divide $\frac{2000}{2} = 1{,}000$.

204. A First we need to find 5% of $25. $\frac{5}{100} \times 25 = \$1.25$. When we take this off the original price, we get $23.75.

205. D Let's set up the proportion: $\frac{8\ miles}{1\ inch} = \frac{x}{3.5\ inches}$. Cross multiply to get $x = 28$.

206. C Remember that the places after the decimal point are the tenths and hundredths. So $0.24 = \frac{24}{100}$, which reduces to $\frac{12}{50}$.

207. **C** Let's plug in our own number to make this easier. Let's say that the shirt begins at $100. When the price is discounted by 20%, it will go down to $80. When it is discounted by another 10%, it will go down to $72. This means that it went from $100 to $72, a discount of 28%.

208. **B** If two numbers have a ratio of 6:9, and the smaller one is actually 18, then we know that we need to multiply the ratio by 3 to get 18:27. The question then asks for the average of these two numbers. The average of 18 and 27 is 22.5.

209. **A** Remember your order of operations! First do parentheses to get $11 + 5 \times 6 + 3 - (-3)$. Now multiply to get $11 + 30 + 3 - (-3)$. Now we can add and subtract to get 47.

210. **D** The volume of this pool is $4 \times 10 \times 12 = 480$. If it gets filled at 8 cubic feet per minute, it will take $\frac{480}{8} = 60$ minutes to fill.

211. **C** If three hamburgers cost $4.05, then each hamburger costs $1.35. This means that two hamburgers cost $2.70. If two hamburgers and an order of french fries costs $3.55, then an order of fries must cost $3.55 - $2.70 = $0.85.

212. **D** If the ratio of boys to girls is 3:5, that means that of every 8 total students, 3 are boys and 5 are girls. If there are 32 total students, then there are 4 groups of 8 students. This means that there are 12 boys and 20 girls.

213. **D** The area of this circle is πr^2, or 64π. The circumference of this circle is $2\pi r$, or 16π. Therefore the difference is 48π.

214. **A** To make this problem easier, let's write out the exponents. $4^4 = 4 \times 4 \times 4 \times 4$. Which one of the choices says the same thing? Let's try them. A says 16×16, which is the same as $4 \times 4 \times 4 \times 4$.

215. **A** First let's find how many do attend. $\frac{2}{3} \times 660 = 440$ students. This means that 220 do not attend.

216. **D** If we multiply these two numbers together we get $6\sqrt{4}$. We can take the 4 out of the root to get $6 \times 2 = 12$.

217. **B** To make this easier, let's add the fractions with common denominators together. This gives us $18 + 1 + \frac{3}{6}$. Since $\frac{3}{6}$ is the same as $\frac{1}{2}$, the sum is $19\frac{1}{2}$.

218. **D** Let's begin by subtracting 5 from each side. This gives us $3x = 18$. When we divide 3 from each side, we get $x = 6$.

219. **A** To divide fractions, flip and multiply: $\frac{1}{2} \times \frac{10}{1} = 5$.

220. **D** Since $x = 2$, we know that $2y + 18 = 36$. Now we can solve for y: $2y = 18$, so $y = 9$.

221. **D** The area of this rectangle is the same as length $\times$ width, or $15 \times 24 = 360$.

222. B There is no need to work out the entire problem. Just one term is probably enough to get the right answer. The first term says $7 \times \dfrac{1}{100}$. Seven-hundredths means a 7 in the hundredths place, or 0.07. Only B has a 7 in the hundredths place.

223. A By Ballparking, you can probably get this one right. Since 5 pounds would be at least $15, B, C, and D are all too big.

224. D To make the division easier, move the decimal point one place to the right. Now divide $\dfrac{55}{2} = 27.5$.

225. D Plug in the answer choices, starting with A. If Alex is 4 years old, then 4 years ago he was 0 years old. Does this make him half as old? No. How about B? If Alex is 5 years old, then 4 years ago he was 1. Does this make him half as old? No. How about C? If Alex is 6 years old, then 4 years ago he was 2. Still not half as old. How about D? If Alex is 8 years old, then 4 years ago he was 4. This is half as old as he is now.

226. B First change these into ordinary fractions, and then multiply: $\dfrac{11}{2} \times \dfrac{7}{3} = \dfrac{77}{6}$ or $11\dfrac{5}{6}$.

227. D A wall 20 feet by 12 feet has a total area of $20 \times 12 = 240$ square feet. One gallon will cover 2.5 square feet, so divide 240 by 2.5 to see how many gallons we will need.

228. B Since $y = 5$, we know that $2x^2 + 5 = 55$. If we subtract 5 from each side, we get $2x^2 = 50$. Now we can divide 2 from each side and get $x^2 = 25$, so x could be 5.

229. A We can multiply these numbers together to get $12\sqrt{36}$. Since $\sqrt{36} = 6$, this becomes $12 \times 6 = 72$.

230. D Since there are 60 seconds in a minute and 60 minutes in an hour, there are $60 \times 60 = 3,600$ seconds in an hour. So in 4 hours there are $4 \times 3,600 = 14,400$ seconds.

231. A This problem is best solved by plugging in the answer choices. Let's start with A. Could there be 62 girls in the group? If there are 62 girls, there are $62 - 24 = 38$ boys. Does this make a total of 100 children? Yes.

232. C Let's solve for x. First, subtract x from each side to get $-5x - 3 < 2$. Now add 3 to each side and get $-5x < 5$. When we divide each side by -5, we have to change the direction of the sign, so $x > -1$.

233. A Multiples of 5 and 6 are multiples of 30. How many multiples of 30 are there between 1 and 100? Three: 30, 60, and 90.

234. B The triangle is formed from two radii, which must be the same length, so the triangle must be isosceles. Since the inside angle is 90, the other two angles must be 45.

235. A We can set up a proportion: $\dfrac{2 \text{ cookies}}{1 \text{ minute}} = \dfrac{150 \text{ cookies}}{x \text{ minutes}}$. Now we solve for x, which becomes 75 minutes, or 1 hour and 15 minutes.

236. **C**   Plug in the answer choices to solve this problem. Start with A. If Jim is 20 years old, then Carl is 40 and Liz is 15. Does this make Carl 15 years older than Liz? No. Let's try B. If Jim is 15 years old, then Carl is 30 and Liz is 10. Does this make Carl 15 years older than Liz? No. Let's try C. If Jim is 10, then Carl is 20 and Liz is 5. Does this make Carl 15 years older than Liz.? Yes.

237. **B**   If the circumference is 8π and circumference $= 2\pi r$, then the radius of the circle must be 4, and the diameter is twice the radius.

238. **A**   To divide \$8.50 among 5 people, we need to calculate $\frac{\$8.50}{5}$. To make it easier to divide, move the decimal points two places to the right: $\frac{850}{500} = \$1.70$.

LANGUAGE

239. **A**   Names of languages such as French should be capitalized.

240. **B**   Since quick describes the way in which Steve ran around the track, it should be the adverb *quickly*.

241. **B**   The correct spelling is father's.

242. **D**

243. **A**   Names of locations such as Lake Michigan should be capitalized.

244. **D**

245. **B**   Names of holidays such as New Year's Eve should be capitalized.

246. **B**   Who's is possessive. The correct word is whose.

247. **C**   A comma should separate city and state in Boston, Massachusetts.

248. **C**   Names of days of the week, such as Monday, should be capitalized.

249. **D**

250. **C**   A comma should follow the word *asked*.

251. **A**   Always use a comma in dates.

252. **A**   Since cat is singular, we need the singular pronoun it.

253. **B**   Since "my friend and I" is the object of a preposition, we need the objective case: "my friend and me."

254. **C**   Since it is a title accompanied by a proper name, Chief Stanley should be capitalized.

255. **A**   "Had already took" is not a valid verb form. It should be took or had already taken.

256. **C**   "Us" is the subject of the sentence, and so should be "We."

257. **B**   This sentence fragment needs a verb.

258. **B**   Rachel's family is singular and requires the singular verb form *is*.

259. **A**   It's = it is. In this case we are showing possession, that the dish belongs to the cat, so we need its.

260. **A**   The word *each* is singular and needs the singular verb form *has*.

261. **B**   "Her" is the subject of the sentence, and so should be the subject pronoun "She."

262. **A**   "Hardly none" is a double negative.

263. **D**

264. **A**   The correct word is *fewer*.

265. **C**   The idiom is "as many as" his brother.

266. **A**   This has a comparison problem, since it compares cookies with a person. It should say, "Peter's cookies are better than Steve's cookies."

267. **C**   Since "my sister and I" are receiving the sandwich, this should be the objective case: "my sister and me."

268. **B**   "More heavier" is an invalid comparative form. It should be simply "heavier."

269. **D**

270. **C**   Since friends is possessive, it should be spelled friend's.

271. **D**

272. **D**

273. **A**   Since the word *close* describes the way in which the teacher looked at the homework, it should be the adverb *closely*.

274. **A**   In this case, the word should be *fewer*.

275. **A**   "Most greatest" is an invalid comparative form. It should be simply "greatest."

276. **D**

277. **B**   This has a problem of parallelism. The second verb should be in the same form as the first: "escaped."

278. **A**   "Our parents" is plural, and requires the plural verb form "help."

SPELLING

279. **B**   The word *admitted* is misspelled.

280. **D**

281. **C**   The word *opportunity* is misspelled.

282. **C**   The word *rehearsal* is misspelled.

283. **D**

284. **B**   The word *preferred* is misspelled.

285. **A**   The word *practices* is misspelled.

286. **B**   The word *surprised* is misspelled.

287. **D**

288. **A**   The word *mathematics* is misspelled.

COMPOSITION

289. **A**   B, C, and D are all in the passive voice.

290. **C**   A and B are awkward; D is wordy.

291. **B**   Some punctuation is required to avoid a run-on sentence.

292. **B**   The sentence to be placed in the paragraph discusses measures that Nightingale proposed. Sentence 4 refers to "These measures," so the sentence should go before sentence 4.

293. **C**   The sentence to be placed further discusses ash. Sentence 4 introduces the ash, so the sentence should follow sentence 4.

294. **B**   The second phrase restricts the first, so an opposite-direction word such as B or D is needed. D doesn't work here.

295. **C**   The second phrase is in contrast to the first, so we need an opposite-direction word such as C.

296. **A**   The second phrase gives more information about the first, so we need a same-direction word such as A.

297. **B**   All of the sentences in this paragraph discuss features of rodents, except sentence 3, which discusses people.

298. **C**   All of the sentences in this paragraph discuss camels except sentence 4.

ABOUT THE AUTHOR

Jeff Rubenstein is the Senior Director of Research and Development for K–12 programs at The Princeton Review. He is the author of several books and articles on test preparation, and believes he was Kermit the Frog in a former life.

The Princeton Review

Completely darken bubbles with a No. 2 pencil. If you make a mistake, be sure to erase mark completely. Erase all stray marks.

YOUR NAME: _____
(Print)   Last   First   M.I.

SIGNATURE: _____ DATE: ___/___/___

HOME ADDRESS: _____
(Print)   Number and Street

_____
        City   State   Zip Code

PHONE NO.: _____
(Print)

COOP Section

PART 1

1. Ⓐ Ⓑ Ⓒ Ⓓ
2. Ⓐ Ⓑ Ⓒ Ⓓ
3. Ⓐ Ⓑ Ⓒ Ⓓ
4. Ⓐ Ⓑ Ⓒ Ⓓ
5. Ⓐ Ⓑ Ⓒ Ⓓ
6. Ⓐ Ⓑ Ⓒ Ⓓ
7. Ⓐ Ⓑ Ⓒ Ⓓ
8. Ⓐ Ⓑ Ⓒ Ⓓ
9. Ⓐ Ⓑ Ⓒ Ⓓ
10. Ⓐ Ⓑ Ⓒ Ⓓ
11. Ⓐ Ⓑ Ⓒ Ⓓ
12. Ⓐ Ⓑ Ⓒ Ⓓ
13. Ⓐ Ⓑ Ⓒ Ⓓ
14. Ⓐ Ⓑ Ⓒ Ⓓ
15. Ⓐ Ⓑ Ⓒ Ⓓ
16. Ⓐ Ⓑ Ⓒ Ⓓ
17. Ⓐ Ⓑ Ⓒ Ⓓ
18. Ⓐ Ⓑ Ⓒ Ⓓ
19. Ⓐ Ⓑ Ⓒ Ⓓ
20. Ⓐ Ⓑ Ⓒ Ⓓ

PART 2

1. Ⓐ Ⓑ Ⓒ Ⓓ
2. Ⓐ Ⓑ Ⓒ Ⓓ
3. Ⓐ Ⓑ Ⓒ Ⓓ
4. Ⓐ Ⓑ Ⓒ Ⓓ
5. Ⓐ Ⓑ Ⓒ Ⓓ
6. Ⓐ Ⓑ Ⓒ Ⓓ
7. Ⓐ Ⓑ Ⓒ Ⓓ
8. Ⓐ Ⓑ Ⓒ Ⓓ
9. Ⓐ Ⓑ Ⓒ Ⓓ
10. Ⓐ Ⓑ Ⓒ Ⓓ
11. Ⓐ Ⓑ Ⓒ Ⓓ
12. Ⓐ Ⓑ Ⓒ Ⓓ
13. Ⓐ Ⓑ Ⓒ Ⓓ
14. Ⓐ Ⓑ Ⓒ Ⓓ
15. Ⓐ Ⓑ Ⓒ Ⓓ
16. Ⓐ Ⓑ Ⓒ Ⓓ
17. Ⓐ Ⓑ Ⓒ Ⓓ
18. Ⓐ Ⓑ Ⓒ Ⓓ
19. Ⓐ Ⓑ Ⓒ Ⓓ
20. Ⓐ Ⓑ Ⓒ Ⓓ

PART 3

1. Ⓐ Ⓑ Ⓒ Ⓓ Ⓔ
2. Ⓐ Ⓑ Ⓒ Ⓓ Ⓔ
3. Ⓐ Ⓑ Ⓒ Ⓓ Ⓔ
4. Ⓐ Ⓑ Ⓒ Ⓓ Ⓔ
5. Ⓐ Ⓑ Ⓒ Ⓓ Ⓔ
6. Ⓐ Ⓑ Ⓒ Ⓓ Ⓔ
7. Ⓐ Ⓑ Ⓒ Ⓓ Ⓔ
8. Ⓐ Ⓑ Ⓒ Ⓓ Ⓔ
9. Ⓐ Ⓑ Ⓒ Ⓓ Ⓔ
10. Ⓐ Ⓑ Ⓒ Ⓓ Ⓔ
11. Ⓐ Ⓑ Ⓒ Ⓓ Ⓔ
12. Ⓐ Ⓑ Ⓒ Ⓓ Ⓔ
13. Ⓐ Ⓑ Ⓒ Ⓓ Ⓔ
14. Ⓐ Ⓑ Ⓒ Ⓓ Ⓔ
15. Ⓐ Ⓑ Ⓒ Ⓓ Ⓔ
16. Ⓐ Ⓑ Ⓒ Ⓓ Ⓔ
17. Ⓐ Ⓑ Ⓒ Ⓓ Ⓔ
18. Ⓐ Ⓑ Ⓒ Ⓓ Ⓔ
19. Ⓐ Ⓑ Ⓒ Ⓓ Ⓔ
20. Ⓐ Ⓑ Ⓒ Ⓓ Ⓔ

PART 4

1. Ⓐ Ⓑ Ⓒ Ⓓ
2. Ⓐ Ⓑ Ⓒ Ⓓ
3. Ⓐ Ⓑ Ⓒ Ⓓ
4. Ⓐ Ⓑ Ⓒ Ⓓ
5. Ⓐ Ⓑ Ⓒ Ⓓ
6. Ⓐ Ⓑ Ⓒ Ⓓ
7. Ⓐ Ⓑ Ⓒ Ⓓ
8. Ⓐ Ⓑ Ⓒ Ⓓ
9. Ⓐ Ⓑ Ⓒ Ⓓ
10. Ⓐ Ⓑ Ⓒ Ⓓ
11. Ⓐ Ⓑ Ⓒ Ⓓ
12. Ⓐ Ⓑ Ⓒ Ⓓ
13. Ⓐ Ⓑ Ⓒ Ⓓ
14. Ⓐ Ⓑ Ⓒ Ⓓ
15. Ⓐ Ⓑ Ⓒ Ⓓ
16. Ⓐ Ⓑ Ⓒ Ⓓ
17. Ⓐ Ⓑ Ⓒ Ⓓ
18. Ⓐ Ⓑ Ⓒ Ⓓ
19. Ⓐ Ⓑ Ⓒ Ⓓ
20. Ⓐ Ⓑ Ⓒ Ⓓ

PART 5

1. Ⓐ Ⓑ Ⓒ Ⓓ
2. Ⓐ Ⓑ Ⓒ Ⓓ
3. Ⓐ Ⓑ Ⓒ Ⓓ
4. Ⓐ Ⓑ Ⓒ Ⓓ
5. Ⓐ Ⓑ Ⓒ Ⓓ
6. Ⓐ Ⓑ Ⓒ Ⓓ
7. Ⓐ Ⓑ Ⓒ Ⓓ
8. Ⓐ Ⓑ Ⓒ Ⓓ
9. Ⓐ Ⓑ Ⓒ Ⓓ
10. Ⓐ Ⓑ Ⓒ Ⓓ
11. Ⓐ Ⓑ Ⓒ Ⓓ
12. Ⓐ Ⓑ Ⓒ Ⓓ
13. Ⓐ Ⓑ Ⓒ Ⓓ
14. Ⓐ Ⓑ Ⓒ Ⓓ
15. Ⓐ Ⓑ Ⓒ Ⓓ
16. Ⓐ Ⓑ Ⓒ Ⓓ
17. Ⓐ Ⓑ Ⓒ Ⓓ
18. Ⓐ Ⓑ Ⓒ Ⓓ
19. Ⓐ Ⓑ Ⓒ Ⓓ
20. Ⓐ Ⓑ Ⓒ Ⓓ

21. Ⓐ Ⓑ Ⓒ Ⓓ
22. Ⓐ Ⓑ Ⓒ Ⓓ
23. Ⓐ Ⓑ Ⓒ Ⓓ
24. Ⓐ Ⓑ Ⓒ Ⓓ
25. Ⓐ Ⓑ Ⓒ Ⓓ
26. Ⓐ Ⓑ Ⓒ Ⓓ
27. Ⓐ Ⓑ Ⓒ Ⓓ
28. Ⓐ Ⓑ Ⓒ Ⓓ
29. Ⓐ Ⓑ Ⓒ Ⓓ
30. Ⓐ Ⓑ Ⓒ Ⓓ
31. Ⓐ Ⓑ Ⓒ Ⓓ
32. Ⓐ Ⓑ Ⓒ Ⓓ
33. Ⓐ Ⓑ Ⓒ Ⓓ
34. Ⓐ Ⓑ Ⓒ Ⓓ
35. Ⓐ Ⓑ Ⓒ Ⓓ
36. Ⓐ Ⓑ Ⓒ Ⓓ
37. Ⓐ Ⓑ Ⓒ Ⓓ
38. Ⓐ Ⓑ Ⓒ Ⓓ
39. Ⓐ Ⓑ Ⓒ Ⓓ
40. Ⓐ Ⓑ Ⓒ Ⓓ

PART 6

1. Ⓐ Ⓑ Ⓒ Ⓓ
2. Ⓐ Ⓑ Ⓒ Ⓓ
3. Ⓐ Ⓑ Ⓒ Ⓓ
4. Ⓐ Ⓑ Ⓒ Ⓓ
5. Ⓐ Ⓑ Ⓒ Ⓓ
6. Ⓐ Ⓑ Ⓒ Ⓓ
7. Ⓐ Ⓑ Ⓒ Ⓓ
8. Ⓐ Ⓑ Ⓒ Ⓓ
9. Ⓐ Ⓑ Ⓒ Ⓓ
10. Ⓐ Ⓑ Ⓒ Ⓓ
11. Ⓐ Ⓑ Ⓒ Ⓓ
12. Ⓐ Ⓑ Ⓒ Ⓓ
13. Ⓐ Ⓑ Ⓒ Ⓓ
14. Ⓐ Ⓑ Ⓒ Ⓓ
15. Ⓐ Ⓑ Ⓒ Ⓓ
16. Ⓐ Ⓑ Ⓒ Ⓓ
17. Ⓐ Ⓑ Ⓒ Ⓓ
18. Ⓐ Ⓑ Ⓒ Ⓓ
19. Ⓐ Ⓑ Ⓒ Ⓓ
20. Ⓐ Ⓑ Ⓒ Ⓓ

21. Ⓐ Ⓑ Ⓒ Ⓓ
22. Ⓐ Ⓑ Ⓒ Ⓓ
23. Ⓐ Ⓑ Ⓒ Ⓓ
24. Ⓐ Ⓑ Ⓒ Ⓓ
25. Ⓐ Ⓑ Ⓒ Ⓓ
26. Ⓐ Ⓑ Ⓒ Ⓓ
27. Ⓐ Ⓑ Ⓒ Ⓓ
28. Ⓐ Ⓑ Ⓒ Ⓓ
29. Ⓐ Ⓑ Ⓒ Ⓓ
30. Ⓐ Ⓑ Ⓒ Ⓓ
31. Ⓐ Ⓑ Ⓒ Ⓓ
32. Ⓐ Ⓑ Ⓒ Ⓓ
33. Ⓐ Ⓑ Ⓒ Ⓓ
34. Ⓐ Ⓑ Ⓒ Ⓓ
35. Ⓐ Ⓑ Ⓒ Ⓓ
36. Ⓐ Ⓑ Ⓒ Ⓓ
37. Ⓐ Ⓑ Ⓒ Ⓓ
38. Ⓐ Ⓑ Ⓒ Ⓓ
39. Ⓐ Ⓑ Ⓒ Ⓓ
40. Ⓐ Ⓑ Ⓒ Ⓓ

The Princeton Review

Completely darken bubbles with a No. 2 pencil. If you make a mistake, be sure to erase mark completely. Erase all stray marks

1

YOUR NAME: _____
(Print)   Last   First   M.I.

SIGNATURE: _____   **DATE:** ___/___/___

HOME ADDRESS: _____
(Print)   Number and Street

_____
City   State   Zip Code

PHONE NO.: _____
(Print)

COOP Section

PART 7

1. Ⓐ Ⓑ Ⓒ Ⓓ Ⓔ   21. Ⓐ Ⓑ Ⓒ Ⓓ Ⓔ
2. Ⓐ Ⓑ Ⓒ Ⓓ Ⓔ   22. Ⓐ Ⓑ Ⓒ Ⓓ Ⓔ
3. Ⓐ Ⓑ Ⓒ Ⓓ Ⓔ   23. Ⓐ Ⓑ Ⓒ Ⓓ Ⓔ
4. Ⓐ Ⓑ Ⓒ Ⓓ Ⓔ   24. Ⓐ Ⓑ Ⓒ Ⓓ Ⓔ
5. Ⓐ Ⓑ Ⓒ Ⓓ Ⓔ   25. Ⓐ Ⓑ Ⓒ Ⓓ Ⓔ
6. Ⓐ Ⓑ Ⓒ Ⓓ Ⓔ   26. Ⓐ Ⓑ Ⓒ Ⓓ Ⓔ
7. Ⓐ Ⓑ Ⓒ Ⓓ Ⓔ   27. Ⓐ Ⓑ Ⓒ Ⓓ Ⓔ
8. Ⓐ Ⓑ Ⓒ Ⓓ Ⓔ   28. Ⓐ Ⓑ Ⓒ Ⓓ Ⓔ
9. Ⓐ Ⓑ Ⓒ Ⓓ Ⓔ   29. Ⓐ Ⓑ Ⓒ Ⓓ Ⓔ
10. Ⓐ Ⓑ Ⓒ Ⓓ Ⓔ   30. Ⓐ Ⓑ Ⓒ Ⓓ Ⓔ
11. Ⓐ Ⓑ Ⓒ Ⓓ Ⓔ   31. Ⓐ Ⓑ Ⓒ Ⓓ Ⓔ
12. Ⓐ Ⓑ Ⓒ Ⓓ Ⓔ   32. Ⓐ Ⓑ Ⓒ Ⓓ Ⓔ
13. Ⓐ Ⓑ Ⓒ Ⓓ Ⓔ   33. Ⓐ Ⓑ Ⓒ Ⓓ Ⓔ
14. Ⓐ Ⓑ Ⓒ Ⓓ Ⓔ   34. Ⓐ Ⓑ Ⓒ Ⓓ Ⓔ
15. Ⓐ Ⓑ Ⓒ Ⓓ Ⓔ   35. Ⓐ Ⓑ Ⓒ Ⓓ Ⓔ
16. Ⓐ Ⓑ Ⓒ Ⓓ Ⓔ   36. Ⓐ Ⓑ Ⓒ Ⓓ Ⓔ
17. Ⓐ Ⓑ Ⓒ Ⓓ Ⓔ   37. Ⓐ Ⓑ Ⓒ Ⓓ Ⓔ
18. Ⓐ Ⓑ Ⓒ Ⓓ Ⓔ   38. Ⓐ Ⓑ Ⓒ Ⓓ Ⓔ
19. Ⓐ Ⓑ Ⓒ Ⓓ Ⓔ   39. Ⓐ Ⓑ Ⓒ Ⓓ Ⓔ
20. Ⓐ Ⓑ Ⓒ Ⓓ Ⓔ   40. Ⓐ Ⓑ Ⓒ Ⓓ Ⓔ

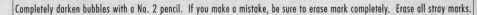

1

YOUR NAME: _____
(Print)   Last   First   M.I.

SIGNATURE: _____   **DATE:** __ / __ / __

HOME ADDRESS: _____
(Print)   Number and Street

_____
City   State   Zip Code

PHONE NO.: _____
(Print)

HSPT Section

1. Ⓐ Ⓑ Ⓒ Ⓓ	21. Ⓐ Ⓑ Ⓒ Ⓓ	51. Ⓐ Ⓑ Ⓒ Ⓓ Ⓔ	71. Ⓐ Ⓑ Ⓒ Ⓓ
2. Ⓐ Ⓑ Ⓒ Ⓓ	22. Ⓐ Ⓑ Ⓒ Ⓓ	52. Ⓐ Ⓑ Ⓒ Ⓓ Ⓔ	72. Ⓐ Ⓑ Ⓒ Ⓓ
3. Ⓐ Ⓑ Ⓒ Ⓓ	23. Ⓐ Ⓑ Ⓒ Ⓓ	53. Ⓐ Ⓑ Ⓒ Ⓓ Ⓔ	73. Ⓐ Ⓑ Ⓒ Ⓓ
4. Ⓐ Ⓑ Ⓒ Ⓓ	24. Ⓐ Ⓑ Ⓒ Ⓓ	54. Ⓐ Ⓑ Ⓒ Ⓓ Ⓔ	74. Ⓐ Ⓑ Ⓒ Ⓓ
5. Ⓐ Ⓑ Ⓒ Ⓓ	25. Ⓐ Ⓑ Ⓒ Ⓓ	55. Ⓐ Ⓑ Ⓒ Ⓓ Ⓔ	75. Ⓐ Ⓑ Ⓒ Ⓓ
6. Ⓐ Ⓑ Ⓒ Ⓓ	26. Ⓐ Ⓑ Ⓒ Ⓓ	56. Ⓐ Ⓑ Ⓒ Ⓓ Ⓔ	76. Ⓐ Ⓑ Ⓒ Ⓓ
7. Ⓐ Ⓑ Ⓒ Ⓓ	27. Ⓐ Ⓑ Ⓒ Ⓓ	57. Ⓐ Ⓑ Ⓒ Ⓓ Ⓔ	77. Ⓐ Ⓑ Ⓒ Ⓓ
8. Ⓐ Ⓑ Ⓒ Ⓓ	28. Ⓐ Ⓑ Ⓒ Ⓓ	58. Ⓐ Ⓑ Ⓒ Ⓓ Ⓔ	78. Ⓐ Ⓑ Ⓒ Ⓓ
9. Ⓐ Ⓑ Ⓒ Ⓓ	29. Ⓐ Ⓑ Ⓒ Ⓓ	59. Ⓐ Ⓑ Ⓒ Ⓓ Ⓔ	79. Ⓐ Ⓑ Ⓒ Ⓓ
10. Ⓐ Ⓑ Ⓒ Ⓓ	30. Ⓐ Ⓑ Ⓒ Ⓓ	60. Ⓐ Ⓑ Ⓒ Ⓓ Ⓔ	80. Ⓐ Ⓑ Ⓒ Ⓓ
11. Ⓐ Ⓑ Ⓒ Ⓓ	31. Ⓐ Ⓑ Ⓒ Ⓓ	61. Ⓐ Ⓑ Ⓒ Ⓓ Ⓔ	81. Ⓐ Ⓑ Ⓒ Ⓓ
12. Ⓐ Ⓑ Ⓒ Ⓓ	32. Ⓐ Ⓑ Ⓒ Ⓓ	62. Ⓐ Ⓑ Ⓒ Ⓓ Ⓔ	82. Ⓐ Ⓑ Ⓒ Ⓓ
13. Ⓐ Ⓑ Ⓒ Ⓓ	33. Ⓐ Ⓑ Ⓒ Ⓓ	63. Ⓐ Ⓑ Ⓒ Ⓓ Ⓔ	83. Ⓐ Ⓑ Ⓒ Ⓓ
14. Ⓐ Ⓑ Ⓒ Ⓓ	34. Ⓐ Ⓑ Ⓒ Ⓓ	64. Ⓐ Ⓑ Ⓒ Ⓓ Ⓔ	84. Ⓐ Ⓑ Ⓒ Ⓓ
15. Ⓐ Ⓑ Ⓒ Ⓓ	35. Ⓐ Ⓑ Ⓒ Ⓓ	65. Ⓐ Ⓑ Ⓒ Ⓓ Ⓔ	85. Ⓐ Ⓑ Ⓒ Ⓓ
16. Ⓐ Ⓑ Ⓒ Ⓓ	36. Ⓐ Ⓑ Ⓒ Ⓓ	66. Ⓐ Ⓑ Ⓒ Ⓓ Ⓔ	86. Ⓐ Ⓑ Ⓒ Ⓓ
17. Ⓐ Ⓑ Ⓒ Ⓓ	37. Ⓐ Ⓑ Ⓒ Ⓓ	67. Ⓐ Ⓑ Ⓒ Ⓓ Ⓔ	87. Ⓐ Ⓑ Ⓒ Ⓓ
18. Ⓐ Ⓑ Ⓒ Ⓓ	38. Ⓐ Ⓑ Ⓒ Ⓓ	68. Ⓐ Ⓑ Ⓒ Ⓓ Ⓔ	88. Ⓐ Ⓑ Ⓒ Ⓓ
19. Ⓐ Ⓑ Ⓒ Ⓓ	39. Ⓐ Ⓑ Ⓒ Ⓓ	69. Ⓐ Ⓑ Ⓒ Ⓓ Ⓔ	89. Ⓐ Ⓑ Ⓒ Ⓓ
20. Ⓐ Ⓑ Ⓒ Ⓓ	40. Ⓐ Ⓑ Ⓒ Ⓓ	70. Ⓐ Ⓑ Ⓒ Ⓓ Ⓔ	90. Ⓐ Ⓑ Ⓒ Ⓓ

91. Ⓐ Ⓑ Ⓒ Ⓓ	121. Ⓐ Ⓑ Ⓒ Ⓓ	151. Ⓐ Ⓑ Ⓒ Ⓓ	191. Ⓐ Ⓑ Ⓒ Ⓓ
92. Ⓐ Ⓑ Ⓒ Ⓓ	122. Ⓐ Ⓑ Ⓒ Ⓓ	152. Ⓐ Ⓑ Ⓒ Ⓓ	192. Ⓐ Ⓑ Ⓒ Ⓓ
93. Ⓐ Ⓑ Ⓒ Ⓓ	123. Ⓐ Ⓑ Ⓒ Ⓓ	153. Ⓐ Ⓑ Ⓒ Ⓓ	193. Ⓐ Ⓑ Ⓒ Ⓓ
94. Ⓐ Ⓑ Ⓒ Ⓓ	124. Ⓐ Ⓑ Ⓒ Ⓓ	154. Ⓐ Ⓑ Ⓒ Ⓓ	194. Ⓐ Ⓑ Ⓒ Ⓓ
95. Ⓐ Ⓑ Ⓒ Ⓓ	125. Ⓐ Ⓑ Ⓒ Ⓓ	155. Ⓐ Ⓑ Ⓒ Ⓓ	195. Ⓐ Ⓑ Ⓒ Ⓓ
96. Ⓐ Ⓑ Ⓒ Ⓓ	126. Ⓐ Ⓑ Ⓒ Ⓓ	156. Ⓐ Ⓑ Ⓒ Ⓓ	196. Ⓐ Ⓑ Ⓒ Ⓓ
97. Ⓐ Ⓑ Ⓒ Ⓓ	127. Ⓐ Ⓑ Ⓒ Ⓓ	157. Ⓐ Ⓑ Ⓒ Ⓓ	197. Ⓐ Ⓑ Ⓒ Ⓓ
98. Ⓐ Ⓑ Ⓒ Ⓓ	128. Ⓐ Ⓑ Ⓒ Ⓓ	158. Ⓐ Ⓑ Ⓒ Ⓓ	198. Ⓐ Ⓑ Ⓒ Ⓓ
99. Ⓐ Ⓑ Ⓒ Ⓓ	129. Ⓐ Ⓑ Ⓒ Ⓓ	169. Ⓐ Ⓑ Ⓒ Ⓓ	199. Ⓐ Ⓑ Ⓒ Ⓓ
100. Ⓐ Ⓑ Ⓒ Ⓓ	130. Ⓐ Ⓑ Ⓒ Ⓓ	170. Ⓐ Ⓑ Ⓒ Ⓓ	200. Ⓐ Ⓑ Ⓒ Ⓓ
101. Ⓐ Ⓑ Ⓒ Ⓓ	131. Ⓐ Ⓑ Ⓒ Ⓓ	171. Ⓐ Ⓑ Ⓒ Ⓓ	201. Ⓐ Ⓑ Ⓒ Ⓓ
102. Ⓐ Ⓑ Ⓒ Ⓓ	132. Ⓐ Ⓑ Ⓒ Ⓓ	172. Ⓐ Ⓑ Ⓒ Ⓓ	202. Ⓐ Ⓑ Ⓒ Ⓓ
103. Ⓐ Ⓑ Ⓒ Ⓓ	133. Ⓐ Ⓑ Ⓒ Ⓓ	173. Ⓐ Ⓑ Ⓒ Ⓓ	203. Ⓐ Ⓑ Ⓒ Ⓓ
104. Ⓐ Ⓑ Ⓒ Ⓓ	134. Ⓐ Ⓑ Ⓒ Ⓓ	174. Ⓐ Ⓑ Ⓒ Ⓓ	204. Ⓐ Ⓑ Ⓒ Ⓓ
105. Ⓐ Ⓑ Ⓒ Ⓓ	135. Ⓐ Ⓑ Ⓒ Ⓓ	175. Ⓐ Ⓑ Ⓒ Ⓓ	205. Ⓐ Ⓑ Ⓒ Ⓓ
106. Ⓐ Ⓑ Ⓒ Ⓓ	136. Ⓐ Ⓑ Ⓒ Ⓓ	176. Ⓐ Ⓑ Ⓒ Ⓓ	206. Ⓐ Ⓑ Ⓒ Ⓓ
107. Ⓐ Ⓑ Ⓒ Ⓓ	137. Ⓐ Ⓑ Ⓒ Ⓓ	177. Ⓐ Ⓑ Ⓒ Ⓓ	207. Ⓐ Ⓑ Ⓒ Ⓓ
108. Ⓐ Ⓑ Ⓒ Ⓓ	138. Ⓐ Ⓑ Ⓒ Ⓓ	178. Ⓐ Ⓑ Ⓒ Ⓓ	208. Ⓐ Ⓑ Ⓒ Ⓓ
109. Ⓐ Ⓑ Ⓒ Ⓓ	139. Ⓐ Ⓑ Ⓒ Ⓓ	179. Ⓐ Ⓑ Ⓒ Ⓓ	209. Ⓐ Ⓑ Ⓒ Ⓓ
110. Ⓐ Ⓑ Ⓒ Ⓓ	140. Ⓐ Ⓑ Ⓒ Ⓓ	180. Ⓐ Ⓑ Ⓒ Ⓓ	210. Ⓐ Ⓑ Ⓒ Ⓓ
111. Ⓐ Ⓑ Ⓒ Ⓓ	141. Ⓐ Ⓑ Ⓒ Ⓓ	181. Ⓐ Ⓑ Ⓒ Ⓓ	221. Ⓐ Ⓑ Ⓒ Ⓓ
112. Ⓐ Ⓑ Ⓒ Ⓓ	142. Ⓐ Ⓑ Ⓒ Ⓓ	182. Ⓐ Ⓑ Ⓒ Ⓓ	222. Ⓐ Ⓑ Ⓒ Ⓓ
113. Ⓐ Ⓑ Ⓒ Ⓓ	143. Ⓐ Ⓑ Ⓒ Ⓓ	183. Ⓐ Ⓑ Ⓒ Ⓓ	223. Ⓐ Ⓑ Ⓒ Ⓓ
114. Ⓐ Ⓑ Ⓒ Ⓓ	144. Ⓐ Ⓑ Ⓒ Ⓓ	184. Ⓐ Ⓑ Ⓒ Ⓓ	224. Ⓐ Ⓑ Ⓒ Ⓓ
115. Ⓐ Ⓑ Ⓒ Ⓓ	145. Ⓐ Ⓑ Ⓒ Ⓓ	185. Ⓐ Ⓑ Ⓒ Ⓓ	225. Ⓐ Ⓑ Ⓒ Ⓓ
116. Ⓐ Ⓑ Ⓒ Ⓓ	146. Ⓐ Ⓑ Ⓒ Ⓓ	186. Ⓐ Ⓑ Ⓒ Ⓓ	226. Ⓐ Ⓑ Ⓒ Ⓓ
117. Ⓐ Ⓑ Ⓒ Ⓓ	147. Ⓐ Ⓑ Ⓒ Ⓓ	187. Ⓐ Ⓑ Ⓒ Ⓓ	227. Ⓐ Ⓑ Ⓒ Ⓓ
118. Ⓐ Ⓑ Ⓒ Ⓓ	148. Ⓐ Ⓑ Ⓒ Ⓓ	188. Ⓐ Ⓑ Ⓒ Ⓓ	228. Ⓐ Ⓑ Ⓒ Ⓓ
119. Ⓐ Ⓑ Ⓒ Ⓓ	149. Ⓐ Ⓑ Ⓒ Ⓓ	189. Ⓐ Ⓑ Ⓒ Ⓓ	229. Ⓐ Ⓑ Ⓒ Ⓓ
120. Ⓐ Ⓑ Ⓒ Ⓓ	150. Ⓐ Ⓑ Ⓒ Ⓓ	190. Ⓐ Ⓑ Ⓒ Ⓓ	230. Ⓐ Ⓑ Ⓒ Ⓓ

1

YOUR NAME: _____
(Print)   Last   First   M.I.

SIGNATURE: _____ DATE: _____ / _____ / _____

HOME ADDRESS: _____
(Print)   Number and Street

_____
              City   State   Zip Code

PHONE NO.: _____
(Print)

HSPT Section

231. (A) (B) (C) (D)
232. (A) (B) (C) (D)
233. (A) (B) (C) (D)
234. (A) (B) (C) (D)
235. (A) (B) (C) (D)
236. (A) (B) (C) (D)
237. (A) (B) (C) (D)
238. (A) (B) (C) (D)
239. (A) (B) (C) (D)
240. (A) (B) (C) (D)
241. (A) (B) (C) (D)
242. (A) (B) (C) (D)
243. (A) (B) (C) (D)
244. (A) (B) (C) (D)
245. (A) (B) (C) (D)
246. (A) (B) (C) (D)
247. (A) (B) (C) (D)
248. (A) (B) (C) (D)
249. (A) (B) (C) (D)
250. (A) (B) (C) (D)

251. (A) (B) (C) (D)
252. (A) (B) (C) (D)
253. (A) (B) (C) (D)
254. (A) (B) (C) (D)
255. (A) (B) (C) (D)
256. (A) (B) (C) (D)
257. (A) (B) (C) (D)
258. (A) (B) (C) (D)
259. (A) (B) (C) (D)
260. (A) (B) (C) (D)
261. (A) (B) (C) (D)
262. (A) (B) (C) (D)
263. (A) (B) (C) (D)
264. (A) (B) (C) (D)
265. (A) (B) (C) (D)
266. (A) (B) (C) (D)
267. (A) (B) (C) (D)
268. (A) (B) (C) (D)
269. (A) (B) (C) (D)
270. (A) (B) (C) (D)

271. (A) (B) (C) (D)
272. (A) (B) (C) (D)
273. (A) (B) (C) (D)
274. (A) (B) (C) (D)
275. (A) (B) (C) (D)
276. (A) (B) (C) (D)
277. (A) (B) (C) (D)
278. (A) (B) (C) (D)
279. (A) (B) (C) (D)
280. (A) (B) (C) (D)
281. (A) (B) (C) (D)
282. (A) (B) (C) (D)
283. (A) (B) (C) (D)
284. (A) (B) (C) (D)
285. (A) (B) (C) (D)
286. (A) (B) (C) (D)
287. (A) (B) (C) (D)
288. (A) (B) (C) (D)
289. (A) (B) (C) (D)
290. (A) (B) (C) (D)

291. (A) (B) (C) (D)
292. (A) (B) (C) (D)
293. (A) (B) (C) (D)
294. (A) (B) (C) (D)
295. (A) (B) (C) (D)
296. (A) (B) (C) (D)
297. (A) (B) (C) (D)
298. (A) (B) (C) (D)

www.review.com

Expert Advice

Talk About It

www.review.com

Pop Surveys

Paying for it

www.review.com

The Princeton Review

Getting in

Word du Jour

www.review.com

Find-O-Rama School & Career Search

www.review.com

Finding it

Best Schools

www.review.com

FIND US...

International

Hong Kong
4/F Sun Hung Kai Centre
30 Harbour Road, Wan Chai,
Hong Kong
Tel: (011)85-2-517-3016

Japan
Fuji Building 40, 15-14
Sakuragaokacho, Shibuya Ku,
Tokyo 150, Japan
Tel: (011)81-3-3463-1343

Korea
Tae Young Bldg, 944-24,
Daechi- Dong, Kangnam-Ku
The Princeton Review—ANC
Seoul, Korea 135-280,
South Korea
Tel: (011)82-2-554-7763

Mexico City
PR Mex S De RL De Cv
Guanajuato 228 Col. Roma
06700 Mexico D.F., Mexico
Tel: 525-564-9468

Montreal
666 Sherbrooke St.
West, Suite 202
Montreal, QC H3A 1E7 Canada
Tel: 514-499-0870

Pakistan
1 Bawa Park - 90 Upper Mall
Lahore, Pakistan
Tel: (011)92-42-571-2315

Spain
Pza. Castilla, 3 - 5º A, 28046
Madrid, Spain
Tel: (011)341-323-4212

Taiwan
155 Chung Hsiao East Road
Section 4 - 4th Floor,
Taipei R.O.C., Taiwan
Tel: (011)886-2-751-1243

Thailand
Building One, 99 Wireless Road
Bangkok, Thailand 10330
Tel: 662-256-7080

Toronto
1240 Bay Street, Suite 300
Toronto M5R 2A7 Canada
Tel: 800-495-7737
Tel: 716-839-4391

Vancouver
4215 University Way NE
Seattle, WA 98105
Tel: 206-548-1100

locations

National (U.S.)

We have more than 60 offices around the U.S. and run courses at over 400 sites. For courses and locations within the U.S. call 1-800-2-Review and you will be routed to the nearest office.